Alta, this chess
book will enhance
your "game" significantly.
Enjoy your victories
one @ a time

CHESS MASTER VS. CHESS AMATEUR

MAX EUWE
AND
WALTER MEIDEN

DOVER PUBLICATIONS, INC.
NEW YORK

Bibliographical Note

This Dover edition, first published in 1994, is an unabridged and unaltered republication of the work first published by the David McKay Company, Inc., New York, in 1963.

Library of Congress Cataloging-in-Publication Data

Euwe, Max, 1901–1981.
    Chess master vs. chess amateur / Max Euwe and Walter Meiden.
       p.   cm.
    Reprint. Previously published: New York : D. McKay, 1963.
    Includes indexes.
    ISBN 0-486-27947-2
    1. Chess problems.   I. Meiden, Walter, 1907–
GV1451.E84   1994
794.1'2—dc20   93-50842
                                             CIP

Manufactured in the United States of America
Dover Publications, Inc., 31 East 2nd Street, Mineola, N.Y. 11501

Preface

When a master plays an amateur, he is normally confronted with a different type and a greater number of inferior moves and errors than he would find in master play. These are precisely the inferior moves and kinds of errors which the amateur meets constantly when playing other amateurs.

What better way could the amateur have of learning how to exploit the weak play of fellow amateurs than to study how a master would handle such positions? If the brilliant games of Paul Morphy against the masters of the nineteenth century seem much more instructive to many amateurs of today than the far subtler victories of twentieth century grandmasters over fellow grandmasters, it is precisely because Morphy's victories over his far weaker opponents provide a more striking example of how to exploit to the maximum the more serious errors of the weaker player.

This work consists of twenty-five games between master and amateur. The amateurs range all the way from weak players who make characteristic amateur moves never found in master games to players just below master strength, amateurs who have studied chess and know a considerable amount of technique, but who fail to grasp all the strategic implications of a position. Since the games themselves have no particular importance, we have not indicated the names of the players. Our criterion for choosing a game was not whether a master was pitted against an amateur, but rather whether one opponent, who was performing as a master, showed in a convincing way how to exploit certain typical errors of another, who was playing like an amateur.

Not only does this work show how to recognize and exploit

weak play; in its running commentary it delves into the very nature of chess and discusses, as they arise in games themselves, the various aspects of chess play.

We are indebted to a number of amateur players who read over various games in manuscript form and raised further questions as to various possibilities. We are especially indebted and very grateful to Mr. Norman Cotter, of Wilmington, Delaware, for his help, comments, and encouragement during the several years in which this work was being written, and for his careful reading of the entire manuscript in its final form.

M. E.
W. M.

Contents

Introduction

A. Chess Players

§ 1. Range of chess players

Chess players range from very strong to very weak. They extend from those whose errors are almost imperceptible to those who frequently lose pieces.

In almost all countries where chess is found, players are classified according to their strength as *grandmaster, master,* or *amateur.* In the United States, amateurs who participate in tournaments are classified as *experts* or A, B, C, or D players. In certain other countries, there are *regional masters, national masters, international masters,* and *grandmasters.*

§ 2. Traits of a master

The master is thoroughly conversant with the technique of handling each phase of the game: opening, middle game, and end game. He treats the game as a whole, each move being part of a certain strategical or tactical concept. He keenly appreciates the possibilities of all positions. He can analyze accurately and foresee rather exactly the consequence of this move or that. He understands the basic principles involved in the various positions. His tactical play is accurate; he makes fewer and less serious mistakes than other players. He knows a great many chess games of the past and is well informed on the lines played in the tournament games of the present.

§ 3. Earmarks of an amateur

The amateur has not yet completely mastered the technique of correct chess play. He is prone to error. He understands the game less profoundly than the master; his general feelings toward chess are less sensitive; he is less accurate; he foresees the consequences of the moves less well; his analytical powers are limited. The amateur is relatively or even totally unacquainted with the great chess games of the past and with the tournament play of the present.

§ 4. Range of amateurs

The range of amateurs is wide, and the types of amateurs are so numerous that they almost defy classification. Some amateurs are so strong that they approach master strength; others, so weak that they lose in a few moves. Some plan their games carefully; others play from move to move, without any concept of the relation between moves. There are amateurs who have a sharp eye for tactical opportunities, but who have no notion whatever of positional play or of strategical planning. There are others who, through study of books on chess and master games, have acquired some feeling for a good position, but whose tendency to play by general rules has completely dulled them to the art of making the most of a position tactically. There are amateurs who know nothing of book openings but have a keen intuitive sense of what constitutes a good chess position. There are others who have learned dozens of book variations but have no idea of why those variations are best nor of what to do with their position in the middle game, once they have reached the end of the book openings.

§ 5. Master vs. master

When master plays master, the opening moves normally follow chess theory, occasionally with some carefully prepared innovation on the part of one of the masters. Masters normally reach the middle game with approximate equality. From there on, although the masters are now on their own, the game is usually free from tactical errors: that is, no pieces or Pawns are lost through carelessness, and the position does not deteriorate through faulty tactical play. Many master games are played along solid strategical lines; sometimes, however, "wild" positions result from the opening, and then the tactical factor dominates.

With both players keenly alert, both quite aware of the possibilities of the game, neither making any glaring errors, the master examines the position of his fellow master very carefully to see whether there is some small weakness which can be exploited. If there is none, the master then tries to play in such a way as to force his opponent into weakening his position in some way or other. But often the play of the White master is countered by equally strong play on the part of the Black master, and the game becomes a real struggle on the part of each player to attain some sort of advantage. In many cases, chances remain equal, and the game ends in a draw. In certain others, where positional considerations dominate, one of the masters succeeds in gaining some small advantage, in gradually increasing it, and finally in winning. But often great complications arise, and there is not such a gradual differential in advantage. Threats and counterthreats have their immediate impact on the course of the game, and chances apparently shift from move to move. Here, the winner will be the one who has the deeper insight into the sharp tactical possibilities of the positions involved, and the one who can calculate farther in advance.

§ 6. Amateur vs. amateur

When amateur plays amateur, the game is usually marred by a certain number of weak moves or by outright errors or both. Such moves may be either strategical or tactical in nature. These weak moves and errors offer to the opponent a marvelous opportunity of gaining some sort of advantage, at times small, at times great. But all too often the amateur does not realize that his opponent has made a weak move and that he himself now stands better, and he therefore fails to make the most of the situation. Instead, he often makes a weak move or error of his own. Thus, it frequently happens that the scale shifts many times during the game, and it often does even from move to move. For example, at a given point Amateur A has an advantage which he fails to press; a move later, through A's inaccurate play, his opponent

Amateur B gets the advantage; and very soon after, through B's inept play, Amateur A again has a theoretical advantage or even a win.

§ 7. Master vs. amateur

When master plays amateur, a player who makes almost no weak moves or errors and understands chess thoroughly is, in effect, pitted against one who makes frequent weak moves and errors and understands chess to a limited extent only. In such games, the technique of the master is to note and take the maximum advantage of all the weak moves and errors made by the amateur.

The winning of the game by the master is so much easier because of the tendency on the part of the amateur to make not just one but many weak moves and errors in the course of a game. Errors are a progressive evil. Three errors in the same game are much more serious and much easier to exploit than three times one error. Each time the amateur makes a weak move, the master replies with a strong move. Each successive weak move of the amateur enables the master to increase his advantage. When the errors are gross and the weak moves numerous, the advantage of the master quickly becomes overwhelming, and the amateur goes down to an early and scathing defeat.

§ 8. The best move

Amateurs playing their fellow amateurs sometimes make an aggressive move which they know (or perhaps do not know) will work only if their opponent fails to discover the proper reply. In other words, in order to gain a big advantage they gamble on the ineptness of their opponent and on his inability to analyze the situation properly.

This is not sound chess. A master does not indulge in this type of chess play even when he *knows* that it is most unlikely that his amateur opponent will ever find a good answer to his aggressive but theoretically inferior move. On the contrary, in every given position he must look for the strongest theoretical reply, regardless of whether his opponent is another master or the weakest of amateurs. Occasionally, a master may make a slightly weaker reply in order to lead his opponent astray, but he normally does not make a definitely unsound or questionable reply simply to win rapidly through the lack of experience of his opponent. Thus, in simultaneous matches, there frequently arise cases where the master is thinking along profound strategical lines to counter plays which the amateur has made after a very superficial tactical analysis or after no analysis of any kind at all.

There are two reasons for which the master makes the best reply possible in a given position. First, if the opponent should discover the best line against the master's questionable move, the latter could find himself at a disadvantage which might even lead to the loss of the game; second, if the score of the game were later examined by analysts, the master's faulty play would be questioned and criticized.

§ 9. Styles of chess play

Not all masters play the same style of chess. Some play aggressive, attacking games; others prefer to build up a strong defensive position. Some show a predilection for rapid combinational chess; others like the slower positional development. The style of play thus depends to a certain extent on the temperament of the player.

There are many positions which can be handled in several ways, depending on the preferences of the player; there are other positions which demand a certain type of play, and any deviation from such play may result in an inferior position.

It might even be said that there is a master style of play and an amateur style of play. For instance, a few years ago a given position was shown to a number of masters and to a number of amateurs. It is significant that the masters all agreed on one certain "best" line, whereas the amateurs almost unanimously recommended another line.

§ 10. Classification of amateurs

Although it is difficult to fit amateurs into hard and fast groups, we may put them into three rough categories for the purpose of study:

(a) The *beginner*, whose play is characterized by almost total lack of purpose, by the careless loss of pieces and Pawns, and by the surrender of all initiative early in the game.

(b) The *coffeehouse player:* that is, the non-book player who deviates from "theory" in the opening and is also more or less ignorant of middle-game and end-game finesses in chess play. Often, however, this coffeehouse player has good tactical ability because of his great experience.

(c) The *book player*, whose opening play is relatively accurate, but whose feeling for strategy and tactical analytic ability are somewhat limited in the middle and end game. Book players may be subdivided into those who, despite their book study, still play rather weak chess and those who not only know "theory" but also play a strong middle and end game: in short, those who are on their way to becoming masters.

§ 11. Master vs. beginner

Since the beginner's play is characterized by lack of purpose, by loss of pieces, by failure to answer pressure with counter-pressure, and by many types of weakening moves, the master can often play for a big advantage early in the game, and the game may end in a few moves. On the other hand, the beginner's play sometimes consists largely of defensive moves, especially of Pawn moves which do not contribute to helping the beginner win his games, but do prevent his opponent from making an early all-out attack. At times, the beginner makes meaningless piece moves which also prevent the master from bringing about a rapid decision even with a favorable position.

§ 12. Master vs. coffeehouse player

The game of the coffeehouse player is often characterized rather by a series of weaker moves than by outright errors. His game is the more interesting because he departs from theory rather early, yet makes plausible replies which, with the proper play, can be exploited in a most profitable manner.

In this type of game, the master usually accumulates a series of small advantages by exploiting the weaknesses of his opponent. Some of the advantages obtained are so slight that they are imperceptible to the untrained eye. But with the successive weaker moves of the coffeehouse player, the master's advantage can become greater and greater and eventually overwhelming. However, the coffeehouse player's specialty, his tactical skill, must be watched very carefully by the master, for in the long run the tactical blow counts more than the strategical.

§ 13. Master vs. book amateur

The play of the book amateur, especially in his correspondence games, is often theoretically correct throughout the entire opening stage. It is in the middle game that such players often begin to go wrong. They frequently fail to find the correct strategy, and all too often they have no strategy at all, simply playing the game from move to move. They also make inaccurate analyses and find themselves in difficulty because of incorrect tactical play.

Against book players, the master gains his first advantage in the middle game. Once he spots a weak move, he focuses his attention on it, and gradually the amateur's position becomes weaker.

Of course, there are a certain number of very strong amateur book players who not only play theoretically correct openings, but also have a rather profound understanding of the middle game, which they play with remarkable correctness. Against such players the master must depend on very slight advantages on his part for a win. It is also against such players that masters most often draw or even lose in a simultaneous match, given the disparity of time for analysis on the part of the master and of the strong amateur. Yet such amateurs differ from masters in that their understanding of chess positions is not as profound, and they are in general weaker in tactical play. However, the master cannot always take advantage of their weaker tactical play, especially if the amateur succeeds in keeping the position quiet.

B. Certain chess terms

§ 14. Chess theory

After chess had been played for a time under its present rules, it was discovered that certain sequences of opening moves were more successful than others. These sequences were played over and over again, and eventually they were given names. As time went on, the opening lines which brought the greatest measure of success were very often used in tournaments. Masters penetrated into the strengths and weaknesses of these openings and endeavored to improve the stronger sequences and find ways of breaking the weaker ones. Part of their analyses were made in actual practice in tournaments; part, by theoretical tries. This process has been going on ever since the beginning of the sixteenth century, but especially since 1850.

Some openings, such as Ruy López, the Queen's Gambit, and the Sicilian Defense, have been analyzed much more than others, because they have been found most effective in tournament play. Certain openings have had a vogue in one period in chess history; others, in another period.

The investigations into opening play have resulted in a vast accumulation of knowledge concerning what could happen in a given opening position, and in an ever-increasing realization of the possibilities on the chessboard. The most successful lines of each opening—that is, the lines recommended by present-day masters for gaining equality or better during the opening—are known as "theory." In discussions on chess, one often hears: "Theory recommends..." or "The theoretical move is..."

Chess theory is not static. Each year, a certain number of new lines are discovered; during each decade, certain older lines are discarded because they seem to be less effective.

§ 15. Book chess

In all countries where chess is currently played, there exist books on openings and end games giving the lines which have been most successful in tournaments: namely, beginnings and endings of games in which "theory" has been created.

Masters follow these lines in general because they understand why they are best and what the disadvantages of alternates are. Amateurs often follow such lines because they are "in the book" and because they feel that by following book they cannot get into difficulty. In fact, beginners often think that successful chess play depends on a rote knowledge of book variations.

Book play does not insure an automatic win. It is convenient for the amateur to know classical openings and endings, but it is unwise to memorize them without studying the reasons behind the moves. Players who learn book lines without understanding their basic ideas risk playing mechanically. Once they have reached the end of the book analysis, they often find themselves completely bewildered, unable to continue successfully, because they do not understand exactly why the position at the termination of the opening analysis is + or ± or because they have not learned to analyze for themselves.

Very interesting is the game between the book player and the non-book player. If the book player knows how to take advantage of the deviations from book, he may soon gain an advantage in the opening phase of the game; if, however, his knowledge of book is superficial, he may gain no advantage whatever from that knowledge.

§ 16. Chess "rules"

During the last century and a half, much study and thought have been given to how to win a chess game. Certain types of moves and certain positions have been found in general to be advantageous; others, disadvantageous. Some pieces have been found to be stronger than others, and it has been discovered that certain pieces are stronger in one position than in another. Through their experience, masters have formulated a number of principles or precepts of good play into generalization known as chess "rules." This has been especially true of certain masters who have written chess manuals, such as Tarrasch and Emanuel Lasker. These are not the rules by which the players must officially abide when playing, but rather general principles embodying what has proved to be successful play.

But chess "rules" are not absolute. They do not work 100 per cent of the time.

Many games have been lost because these chess "rules" were not followed. But many other games have also been lost or needlessly prolonged because these same chess "rules" were followed too blindly. Time and time again, the amateur player has lost the opportunity to make the really best move because he felt bound to follow some chess "rule" he had learned, rather than to make the sharp move which was indicated by the position.

For the amateur, the best general procedure is to follow the chess "rules" unless there is some special circumstance, some compelling reason for doing otherwise. But when that special case arises, then a player who, by analysis, can justify breaking the "rule" must not hesitate to do so.

§ 17. Chess analysis

Analysis is the process of studying a chess position, looking into every reasonable possibility, indicating what the likely continuations of such a position are, and judging their relative values. Analysis, the basis of all good chess play, normally takes place before each new move. In certain positions, where a series of moves is forced, the analysis may lead to an accurate forecast of what will occur over a number of moves.

Chess analysis occurs whether an amateur looks at a position and says, rightly or wrongly, "If I play such and such a move, this is what will happen," or whether a chess columnist writes, "Of course, not 10 NxP, for . . ."

One of the most fascinating aspects of chess is the fact that in many positions, different players (and especially kibitzers) come up with rather diverse ideas embodying varied series of moves.

Because of the greater insight of the master into the nature of the game of chess, the analysis by a master and by an amateur of the same position may be rather different. On the other hand, there are positions in which it might be essentially the same.

For the amateur, it is important first of all not to make moves without analyzing, second to improve his analytical ability.

§ 18. Strategy

Strategy is the process of planning chess play. It consists of defining the objective toward which to work and of conceiving a means of attaining that objective. A strategic plan may encompass an entire game, or it may be limited to securing a specific aim in a phase of the game. Strategic play may consist in trying to obtain a good position for oneself or in forcing one's opponent into a bad position. Strategic moves are positional; they contribute to building up one's position to the point where one can play for an advantage, or to weakening the opponent's position to a point where that weakness can be exploited. Strategy entails plans for attaining various positional advantages: material superiority, strong squares, advantageous Pawn formation, proper use of the Two Bishops, retention of the Good Bishop, elimination of the Bad Bishop, opening lines, controlling lines, attaining a preponderance of control of space, dominating the center, obtaining and using Pawn majorities, gaining a preponderance in time or development, weakening the opponent in various ways, defining the direction in which an attack is to be carried out, etc.

There are games in which strategic concepts are very clear-cut; there are other games or phases of games in which it is difficult to find a definite strategic objective.

It is in strategy especially that the master excels. Whenever the position is quiet, he thinks in strategic terms. He normally conceives a strategic objective and formulates a plan to attain it. Amateurs often play without any strategy whatever: that is, they tend to play aimlessly from move to move, often not even realizing what legitimate objects there are to strive for.

§ 19. Tactics

Tactics is the practical move-to-move play which ensues when the pieces of the opposing sides come into contact with each other or threaten to do so. Tactics entails calculation. Tactical moves are those which take into consideration the immediate replies of the opponent when the pieces of the two players meet or could reasonably meet.

The concept of tactics also includes the detailed moves through which one's strategy is realized. One might differentiate between two forms of tactics, the first being those calculations which aim at realizing some strategical concept. In such cases, one has to calculate only the answers which are related in some way or other to the strategical situation. The other form of tactics we find in the wild combinative positions in which one has to consider almost every acceptable answer and in which tactics play the deciding part.

There are a number of tactical motives or devices which make careful analysis imperative: the threat, the pin, discovered check, double check, double attack, the in-between move, the sacrifice, the overworked piece, indirect attack, the fork, etc. Each of these terms will be explained when it is first exemplified in the games between master and amateur.

As far as tactics is concerned, the master sees more and wider possibilities and calculates farther and more exactly than the amateur. He visualizes the consequences of a position more easily, and his judgment of the relative worth of different lines is sounder.

§ 20. Strategy vs. tactics

A chess situation is strategical as long as the position is quiet and the players are concerned with general objectives to be attained over a certain phase of the game. It becomes tactical as soon as the pieces of the opposing sides come into contact with each other or threaten to come into contact, so that it is necessary to calculate exactly what could happen after one or more moves and to evaluate the consequences of those moves.

Whenever a situation becomes tactical, tactics *must by force* take precedence over strategy. A tactical situation must be resolved whenever it exists. In other words, when the situation is tactical, a player cannot wisely ignore the tactical side and continue thinking only in strategical terms.

The result of an error of strategy is likely to be a slow and gradual loss of terrain, of mobility, or of some other chess potentiality or advantage; the result of a tactical error is often the immediate loss of a Pawn or a piece or even the game.

Strategical and tactical thinking are rather different; their domains are at the same time closely related and somewhat separate. A player who has a good strategic sense may be working toward a given goal, while his tactical opponent may have no idea of what he is doing. A player with tactical skill may be able, through his ability to analyze consequences of moves, attain a favorable position without a perfect understanding of strategy. It is the tactical player who makes the so-called "sharp" moves which threaten to annihilate the opponent.

The player whose chief concern is strategy plays the so-called positional game; the player who is mainly concerned with tactics tends to play combinative chess.

§ 21. The combination

Allied both to strategy and tactics, but especially to the latter, is the combination. "By a combination we mean a short part of the game within which a certain purpose is attained by force. Its sequence of moves forms a logical chain and cannot be divided. When looked at one by one, these moves may seem to be purposeless or even mistakes, yet together they form an exceedingly beautiful unit. After a series of moves incomprehensible by themselves, the solution suddenly follows and their real purpose comes clearly to light. From this it follows that the aim must already have been conceived from the first move of the combination . . .

"Every combination, carefully examined, consists of three parts: (a) tracing the *idea* of the combination; (b) calculation of the *moves* of the combination; (c) evaluation of the *results* of the combination." [1]

Combinations are not accidental. They normally arise because of some weakness in the opponent's position. The combination almost always involves a sacrifice of some sort.

During most of the nineteenth century, the combination was considered the ultimate in chess, and players frequently made the search for combinations the chief basis of their play. But combinative play requires imagination and calculative skill, and

[1] Dr. Max Euwe, *Strategy and Tactics in Chess* (1937), pp. 58-59.

it entails risks. Therefore, today many players prefer the quieter positional play.

The master naturally sees more combinative possibilities than the amateur and analyzes these situations more profoundly. Because of weaknesses in the amateur position, there are frequent opportunities for combinative play. Sometimes these combinations suddenly evolve out of an apparently quiet position.

C. Elements of chess applied to master vs. amateur games

§ 22. The nature of the chess struggle

A chess game is essentially a struggle for supremacy on the board between two opponents: White and Black. At the outset, White holds a very slight advantage over Black by virtue of having the first move. In the initial phase of the game, the opening, White attempts to retain and, if possible, to increase this slight advantage; Black tries to overcome his slight disadvantage and to obtain at least equality.

When the master plays the amateur, if the master plays White, the amateur often never attains equality; if the master plays Black, he often overcomes his initial handicap as Black rapidly and soon converts it to a sizable advantage.

§ 23. Equality

By equality is meant equal material, about equal development of pieces, about equal control of squares (especially of center squares), about equal initiative or chances to attack. In a game between two players of approximately the same strength, this state of equality is sometimes maintained through the entire game. The game then ends in a draw. In master vs. amateur, equality is usually not maintained.

§ 24. Pressure

The game of chess is developed by bringing pieces into the open field. Each piece exerts a certain force, called pressure, on the squares to which it could move or on which it could take a piece. For instance, the Rook exerts pressure along the rank and along the file, the Bishop along the diagonals, the Knight to the points to which it can move (eight points if the Knight is in the center of the board). As contrasted to the pieces, the Pawn exercises pressure only diagonally on the squares on which it can take.

The concept of pressure is very important in chess, for the sum total of all pressure exerted constitutes the force of a player at a given moment.

Pressure has a special significance in master vs. amateur games, inasmuch as a master frequently exerts far more pressure than the amateur and thereby maintains initiative, obtains an attack, and sometimes paralyzes his opponent.

§ 25. Neutralization

Pressure can be met by counterpressure: that is, when one side exercises pressure on an important square, the other side may apply pressure there, too. Meeting pressure with counterpressure may be called "neutralization." This may be accomplished by bringing a piece to bear on a square already commanded by an opponent or by pinning or exchanging the opponent's piece which is exerting pressure on a square. Neutralization prevents the opponent from gaining the upper hand and makes for the maintenance of an equality of force.

In master vs. amateur games, the beginner often fails to neutralize at all. He thus loses all initiative and goes on the defensive early in the game. The coffeehouse player neutralizes sporadically; the book player, regularly, at least during the opening.

§ 26. Accumulation of power or force

In cases where a player fails to neutralize, the opposing player is often able to build up a considerable accumulation of power and exert tremendous pressure on his opponent's position. In such cases, the player exerting the pressure is often able to sacrifice one piece or even more, in order to open up the position and bring all his forces to bear on the position of the opponent. This may result in an all-out attack against the hostile King, in which the player with the superior pressure is able to overwhelm his opponent because of the greater activity of his own pieces.

§ 27. Space control

Space control is attained by bringing one's pieces and Pawns into effective places, as, for instance: Pawns in the center of the board, Bishops along effective diagonals unhampered by one's own Pawns, Knights on strong squares in the center of the board, etc. Of special importance in space control is the domination of squares of a given color when the opponent has exchanged the Bishop controlling such squares.

The master often gains such a superiority of control of space that he virtually paralyzes his amateur opponent. An examination of positions where this near-paralysis exists will show that the master has gained overwhelming space control because of the failure of the amateur to neutralize.

§ 28. Center control

By the center is meant the four squares in the very middle of the board: K4, Q4, K5, Q5. It has long been recognized by good players that he who controls these squares has a far better grip on the position than he who does not. Control of the center may be obtained through actual occupation of the squares by pieces or Pawns, or it may come through pressure exerted on the squares from afar.

We have already mentioned neutralization as a means of lessening the pressure of the opponent on certain squares. Neutralization of the center may be carried out by various means, but especially by exchange of Pawns. Various games will show how Black neutralizes White's center control by diminishing or even annihilating White's Pawn structure in the center.

§ 29. Initiative and counterchances

One of the most valuable intangible temporary advantages in a chess game is the initiative, which carries with it the power to harass the opponent and to make him play to one's tune.

The skilful player who has the initiative tries to retain it and uses it to tie up his opponent in such a way that he cannot strike back.

When the player with the initiative relinquishes that initiative to the extent of also giving his opponent a certain measure of initiative, this is called *giving counterchances to the opponent*.

The player with the initiative normally looks for the line which will give his opponent the least possible number of counterchances.

§ 30. The attack

Closely related to the initiative is the attack, which consists in bringing one's pieces against the opponent in such a way that the latter is forced to defend himself. The attack is advantageous in that it forces the opponent to play on the defensive, rather than make moves constructive to his own plan.

Playing for an attack is justified only if it can be shown that the position has certain characteristics, such as, for instance, an accumulation of power on the King's side, a weakening of the hostile King's position, the opportunity to bring many pieces to the front. But if none of these characteristics exists, then one should try to attain them rather than attacking immediately.

The player with the attack must calculate carefully, to be sure that his attack either will be overwhelming enough to mate his opponent or to insure material advantage. Often, the opponent attempts to reduce the attack through exchange; and the attacking player, if he has not planned carefully, may find that the attack has vanished and that he is at a material or positional disadvantage, or at least that so many pieces have disappeared from the board that he can hope for no better than a draw.

When a player has a sufficient advantage to play for attack, he is bound to play for attack. Should he fail to attack under such circumstances, he may never again get the opportunity to use his advantage. This Dr. Emanuel Lasker has pointed out in his *Manual of Chess*.

§ 31. Open and half-open lines

Open lines are files or diagonals completely unobstructed by Pawns. They are of prime importance to the player who has the advantage, for they allow him to bring his pieces into play very rapidly. The opponent will try to neutralize the play along the files or diagonals by placing pieces of his own along the same lines. Rooks are normally used along files; Bishops, along diagonals.

Half-open lines are those unobstructed by one's own Pawns but blocked by an opponent's Pawns. Play on the half-open file is of strategical nature quite different from play on the open file.

§ 32. The rank

Apart from the vertical and diagonal lines, there are also horizontal lines known as ranks. Especially for the Rooks, it is important to have ranks along which to play from one front to the other. A free rank improves mobility, gives greater flexibility to the strategic project.

There are two special horizontal lines, the 7th and 8th ranks. The 8th rank comes into play if the hostile King, after having castled, has no flight square and the 8th rank is not at all or scarcely protected by the opponent's own pieces. In such cases, a mate on the 8th rank is among the possibilities. Sometimes beautiful combinations are based on this concept.

The 7th rank can also have both tactical and strategical implications: tactical in the sense that two heavy pieces maneuvering along the 7th rank might easily build up a mating position; strategic in that the Rook can attack the hostile Pawns on the side or from behind. The Pawns are, in those cases, more vulnerable than against frontal attack. That is why, especially in endings, penetrating to the 7th rank may play such an important part.

§ 33. Pawn majorities

The division of Pawns on either side of the board can be different, and the consequence may be that one side has a majority on the Queen's wing and the other on the King's wing. Characteristics of this sort not only can influence the strategy but can even dictate the strategy of both sides.

A King-side majority can often be used as a very strong attacking weapon. A Queen-side majority can be productive of a passed Pawn.

Not infrequently, one side has a center majority. This center majority means a certain preponderance of space and more possibilities of shifting the pieces from one side to the other, for the center is a bridge of communication between the two wings. Advancing the center Pawns can be very strong, because the advance may increase the preponderance in space and its resulting possibilities. On the other hand, the advance sometimes enables one's opponent to seize a strong square between the advanced Pawns.

§ 34. Advantages

Certain situations on the chessboard are more favorable than average—these are advantages.

There are many kinds of advantages: material (more Pawns or pieces), superior development, great mobility, more command of space, solid Pawn formation, a secure King position, the initiative, the attack, etc.

Certain of these advantages, such as the possession of more material, are relatively permanent; others, such as that of development and mobility, are relatively temporary.

It is often wise to convert a temporary advantage into a permanent one. For instance, an advantage in development might be used to win a piece; the advantage of the Two Bishops might be exchanged for giving the opponent a double isolated Pawn.

§ 35. Small and big advantages

Some advantages are so minute that they are considered as *small* advantages; others are so important that they are known as *big* advantages. It is possible to arrive at a rough scale of advantages, but this scale can be only approximate, because the weight of an advantage is, for the most part, dependent on special circumstances.

Considered as small advantages are the win of a tempo, pressure against an opponent's weak Pawn, the possession of an open file or of a Good Bishop, etc. Among the bigger advantages are the advanced passed Pawn, the weakening of the hostile King position, an overwhelming majority of attacking pieces, and a material advantage.

In the course of a game, a player tries to accumulate small advantages and to increase them in order to be able to play for bigger advantages. This must be done with caution. As has already been noted in § 30, one must not play for a big advantage without having reason to do so, and this reason must stem from the favorable characteristics of the position. If one plays for a big advantage without good reason, he risks both not attaining his goal and also ending up with a disadvantage. On the other hand, if play for a big advantage is indicated, then the player must play for the big advantage or risk losing his small advantages.

§ 36. The role of advantages and weaknesses in chess play

A chess game is normally won through obtaining and increasing one's advantages and through creating and exploiting the weaknesses of one's opponent. This is true of all types of chess play, but it is particularly the case in master vs. amateur games, in which the master, who makes almost no weak moves, exploits the play of the amateur, whose game is riddled with weak moves and errors.

D. Learning chess from the study of master vs. amateur games

§ 37. Advantages of studying master vs. amateur games

Most of the chess players in the world are amateurs, and amateurs normally play against other amateurs. They are therefore confronted with the kinds of weak moves and errors which amateurs normally make. We have seen that games are won through the exploitation of weak moves and errors. Thus, the basic problems are to know: (a) What types of moves are weak? (b) What is the best way to exploit a given type of weak move or error?

Obviously, it is the player with the knowledge, the skill, and the experience of a master who can best point the way to the exploitation of errors and weaknesses.

For that reason, a thoroughly annotated game of master vs. amateur—teaching (a) how to recognize typical amateur weak moves and errors and (b) how to exploit such weak moves and errors to one's advantage—must be a very effective medium for showing an amateur the way to improve his play against fellow amateurs.

§ 38. The organization of *Chess Master vs. Chess Amateur*

This book consists of a series of twenty-five games played between master and amateur. The early games of the book were played against beginners; later games, against coffeehouse players of various types; the last games, against amateur book players.

Each game has been chosen to study certain aspects of chess. The introduction of the game lists the important points illustrated in the course of the game and discusses in detail one or two aspects of chess which are exemplified in the game. The running commentary after the moves discusses various chess terms and concepts, usually at the point at which they first occur. Since the book is designed for all types of players, it is assumed that some of the readers will not understand current chess terminology. Therefore, such terms are defined and explained where they first occur.

As far as possible, the games are presented in order of their degree of amateurishness, but this order has occasionally been varied so as to present openings as a group or in some advantageous sequence.

The majority of the games have King Pawn openings, since the weaker amateur normally prefers this type of opening to others. Games in which the amateur loses Pawns or pieces through carelessness or oversight have been avoided for the most part, but such tactical possibilities are occasionally indicated as variations.

§ 39. Variations

Any variation from the text which constitutes a reasonable and interesting tactical possibility is analyzed and discussed in the commentary, so that the reader can appraise its merits as compared with the text move and can have some idea of what would have happened if the alternate move had been played.

Throughout the book, but especially in the earlier games, we have taken the opportunity to present analyses of variations which are favorites of amateur players, especially of weaker amateurs, but which are never seen in tournament play. Such variations have been included in order to show the reader how a master would exploit certain types of amateur play. These variations may prove the more valuable inasmuch as they are not included in books of openings based on master play nor in other instructional manuals.

Occasionally a long and complete analysis of all possible variations of a given position is presented. This is in order to provide the student of chess with a complete picture of what could have happened at a critical point in the game and to afford him the opportunity of improving his own analytical skill by giving him a model with which to compare his own analysis.

For players who have not had much chess experience, such variations can be confusing and sometimes more of a hindrance than a help. It is therefore recommended that only those players who feel the need of exploring variations use these analyses. On his first time over a given game, a reader could well confine himself to the study of the actual moves played in the game and to the comments on those moves; on subsequent perusals of the game, he can study as many of the variations as seem to fit his needs. Using a pocket set in addition to the regular board is a good way of studying complicated variations without disturbing the position of the game itself.

How to Use the Book

Improvement in chess comes partly from gaining a better understanding of what makes for a strong chess position, partly from getting more experience in chess analysis. Both are acquired more effectively through books when you participate actively in the game you are studying. When going over these games in *Chess Master vs. Chess Amateur*, therefore, you may find it interesting and profitable to try to anticipate the moves of the master and to work out your own continuation of some of the variations before you read the analysis given.

The commentary on each game consists of: a discussion of the reasons for each significant move of the actual game; general ideas on the opening used; explanations of important concepts from all areas of chess as they arise in the positions of the game; and, often, detailed analysis of tactical variations which could have been played at various points in the game.

On the first reading, we suggest that you study only the actual moves of the game along with the reasons for those moves. On later readings, you can go through those of the variations which interest you.

The Chess Notation

If you play chess but have had no experience in reading chess books or columns, a few words concerning the descriptive notation currently used in English-speaking countries may prove helpful.

The following symbols are used in this notation:

K — King		O-O — castles K-side
Q — Queen		O-O-O — castles Q-side
R — Rook		ch — check
B — Bishop		dis ch — discovered check
N — Knight		db ch — double check
P — Pawn		. . . — a Black move follows
— — moves to		! — a very good move
x — takes		!! — excellent move
x e. p. — takes en passant		(?) — questionable move
/ — on		? — bad move
( ) — becomes		?? — very bad move

The chessboard is divided into ranks (horizontal rows) and files (vertical rows). In the descriptive notation, each file is indicated by the name of the piece which stands on that file at the beginning of the game. There are eight files: the Queen-Rook file, the Queen-Knight file, etc. There are also eight ranks. The rank is indicated by the number of squares a piece is distant from the lowest rank. For White, number starts from the White side; for Black, from the Black side.

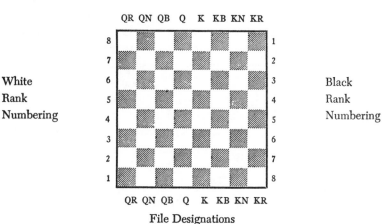

White
Rank
Numbering

Black
Rank
Numbering

File Designations

Let us illustrate how this system works with some typical moves.

1 P-KB4

The White Pawn moves to the 4th square of the KB-file. Since only the KBP can move there, this means that the Pawn originally on the KB2-square goes to the KB4-square.

1 ...   N-KB3

The Black Knight goes to the 3rd square of the KB-file.

5 BxQ

The White Bishop takes the Black Queen.

9 PxP e. p.

Pawn takes Pawn *en passant*. In order to take *en passant*, the White Pawn must have been standing on its 5th square, and the Black Pawn in the adjacent file must have just moved from its 2nd to its 4th square. In such a case, the White Pawn can take the Black Pawn as if the Black Pawn had moved to its 3rd rank. After 9 PxP e. p., the White Pawn will stand on its 6th rank.

27 ...   R/3-K4

The Black Rook on the 3rd rank goes to Black's K4-square. Such a designation as R/3 will be used only when both Black Rooks can go to the same square and when it is no longer obvious which is the KR and which the QR.

31 P-N8 (Q)

The Pawn goes to the 8th square of the N-file and becomes a Queen.

With a little practice, it becomes very easy to read the descriptive notation.

CHESS MASTER
VS.
CHESS AMATEUR

Game 1

Amateurs frequently have the idea that a master can overwhelm them with a few swift blows. How often one hears at a simultaneous exhibition: "Oh, he'll *mate* me in five or six moves."

Such is not usually the case. As a matter of fact, the master sometimes requires more moves to down an amateur than to win from another master, even though the amateur's position may be clearly inferior or even lost early in the game. This is partly because a master resigns when his position becomes untenable, whereas many amateurs play on until they are mated.

There are, however, types of games in which the master does mate the amateur very rapidly. In many such instances, the master is able to open lines and to develop a preponderance of pieces early in the game because of the faulty play of the amateur. The mating pattern also plays its part in these rapid mates.

There exist in chess dozens of standard mating positions, and with these the master is well acquainted. Once the game goes in the direction of a given mating pattern, the master, who recognizes the outlines of the approaching pattern, keeps this pattern well in mind. He does not neglect, however, to look into all reasonable alternate lines.

In the following game, which is a fine example of the tremendous difference between master and amateur chess thinking, because the amateur has weakened his position by opening diagonals unfavorable to him, there suddenly appears in the position a pattern based on the Fool's Mate (1 P-KB3 P-K4 2 P-KN4 Q-R5 mate). The master explores the possibilities not only of giving mate but also of reasonable alternatives, should his opponent be able to ward off the threat of mate. Confident through his analysis that he will come out ahead in any variation, he plays for the mating pattern. Thanks to the presence of this pattern and to the full cooperation of his amateur opponent, he is able to deliver mate on his 8th move.

Bird Opening

Beginner	Master
1 P-KB4	

The beginner probably plays this move without any idea of its real strategic significance, but let us consider what the move means to the master.

To the master, the opening phase of the game is a struggle for control of the center: that is, for control of squares K4, Q4, K5, and Q5. (Read Introduction § 28—Center Control.) By playing 1 P-KB4, White exerts pressure on his K5-square, for Black cannot now put a Pawn or a piece there without its being taken. (Read Introduction § 24—Pressure.)

1 P-KB4 also opens the K1-R4 diagonal for White, but this open line does not aid White to develop any of his pieces, and under certain circumstances Black could use the diagonal for attack, as he will later in this game.

The move 1 P-KB4 is perhaps not the strongest opening move, but it is an acceptable one.

1 ...	P-Q4

Black, in turn, works toward center control in two ways. He takes possession of his center square Q4 by occupying it, and his QP now exerts pressure on White's K4-square, so that White cannot put pieces on this square without their being taken. The move also opens a diagonal for the development of Black's QB.

The move 1 ... P-Q4 has one disadvantage—as many good moves do. Black no longer has the possibility of playing 1 ... P-Q3, and thus he has relinquished the possibility of controlling his K4-square with his QP. This square therefore becomes more important to White.

2 P-QR4?

A typical beginner's move, made without any valid purpose. It does nothing to occupy or to control the center and little to help the development of White's pieces. For the moment, it does offer White the possibility of developing his QR via R3, but even if White should succeed in playing R-R3, it would not have much effect. A Rook on the third rank in the early part of the game hems in its own Pawns.

2 ...   P-K3

The best move in this position, because it contributes most to the fundamental idea of the position, namely, the struggle for the possession of Black's K4-square. Let us see why.

It is not yet clear whether Black's KN will be more useful in the center struggle on its KB3 or on its K2. Therefore, it is better to defer the development of the Knight. But 2 ... P-K3 opens up the possibility of ... B-Q3, where the Bishop can play its part in vying for control of Black's K4-square.

Incidentally, in playing 2 ... P-K3, Black opens two diagonals and closes one. The result of the open diagonals is that Black's KB is now guarding its QR6-square, so that White will not wish to move his Rook there. If he did, it could be exchanged, and a Rook is normally worth more than a Bishop. Likewise, the Black Queen can now go to its KR5 and give check. For the moment, this is of no importance, but it might become significant later on. On the other hand, the diagonal for the Black QB is now closed; but, since this QB does not have much future along the diagonal, the shutting-in of the QB is of minor importance.

3 P-QN3

Very likely the beginner made this move because he was fascinated by the Pawn configuration PQR4-PQN3-PQB2, rather than because he understood its basic significance in relation to the requirements of the position.

Actually, the move is good in that it allows White to play B-N2, from which square the Bishop will play its part in the struggle for control of Black's K4-square by exerting pressure on that square.

This move also permits White to play B-R3, from which point it could threaten to exchange the Black KB. Under certain circumstances, this exchange could favor White.

3 ...   P-QB4

This move serves several purposes:

(a) In general, it plays its part in controlling the center by exerting pressure on White's Q4-square.

(b) It opens up Black's game for future development in a way that is always to be considered in the ... P-Q4 openings.

(c) It allows Black to bring further pressure on his K4-square by playing ... N-QB3, which he would not normally play before moving ... P-QB4, because then his Q-side would remain cramped.

(d) It anticipates and stops White's possible attempt to exchange Bishops by 4 B-R3.

4 P-N3

Another Pawn move. The beginner probably likes the looks of the two chains of Pawns, and he possibly has no deeper motive for this move. The real importance of 4 P-N3 is that it allows the development of White's KB to N2. This move is, however, less effective, because Black's QP, solidly protected by his KP, blocks White's Bishop at KN2 for the moment.

The move 4 P-N3 is not bad, but more in harmony with the basic idea of gaining control of Black's K4-square would be one of the following:

(a) 4 B-N2, exerting pressure on Black's K4-square.

(b) 4 P-K3, opening the long diagonal for White's KB, so

that White could answer 4 . . . N-QB3 by 5 B-N5, neutralizing Black's pressure on his K4-square.

(c) 4 N-KB3, bringing this Knight both to its natural square and to a square where it would participate in the struggle for Black's K4-square.

Notice that all these suggested moves are in harmony with the strategy indicated by the nature of the opening. (Read Introduction § 18—Strategy.)

4 ...   B-Q3

Here the master sees this move theoretically and strategically as an adjunct to the center struggle, inasmuch as the Bishop now exerts pressure on Black's K4-square, thus participating in the struggle for center control.

However, the move also brings the game into the realm of tactics. (Read Introduction § 19—Tactics; § 20—Strategy and Tactics.) Black is now threatening to win a Pawn by 5 . . . BxP, and White cannot reply 6 PxB because of 6 . . . Q-R5 mate. Black's open diagonal (Q1-KR5) is already beginning to play a part in the game.

Ordinarily, a move which attacks an enemy piece or Pawn and forces the opponent to take protective measures is sharper than one which merely develops a piece. A move which obliges the opponent to take action is called a *threat*. A threat is a very important weapon in a chess game. It has the effect of limiting the opponent's reply to a few moves. We shall see the threat used again and again in the games that follow. On the other hand, the

5

threat has one advantage to the opponent. It makes his choice of a reply easier, since he has fewer moves to choose from. By a threat, one may "force" one's opponent to make a good move.

The threat 5 ... BxP is made possible because of the consequences of the opening of White's diagonal K1-R4.

5 B-QN2

Does White fail to see Black's threat, or does he merely realize that by 5 B-QN2 he is making the counterthreats of 6 BxP and 7 BxR?

With White's last move, the game takes on an entirely different aspect. The strategic importance of controlling Black's K4-square gives way to the tactical possibilities afforded by the position. Strategy must give way to tactics. (Reread Introduction § 20—Strategy vs. Tactics.)

Black, looking ahead to what can happen and fully cognizant of what can happen, plays

5 ...   BxP

If now 6 PxB? Q-R5 mate, and Black uses the open diagonals to administer this variation of the Fool's Mate.

But White does not even look into this possibility. Delighted at the prospect of winning first Black's KNP and then his KR, he plays

6 BxP

Black, who has analyzed the position thoroughly, replies

6 ...   Q-N4

Analysis is the basis of all good chess play, especially when the position becomes tactical. (Read Introduction § 17—Chess Analysis.) Let us see what an analysis of the position shows.

Black now threatens mate either by 7 ... BxPch 8 PxB (forced) QxP mate, or by 7 ... QxPch 8 PxQ (forced) BxP mate. At the same time, he threatens 7 ... QxB, followed by 8 ... QxR, so that White cannot save himself by moves such as 7 N-KR3 on account of 7 ... QxB 8 NxB QxR.

But the beginner, not seeing even the threats, much less possible defenses, seizes what he thinks is an opportunity to win a piece, and plays

7 BxR?

The correct move here, one which would limit White's loss to two Pawns, is one which would probably never be found by a beginner. White must play 7 B-Q4, and after 7 ... PxB 8 N-KR3 BxPch 9 PxB QxPch 10 N-B2, and while White comes out of the scuffle with two Pawns down and a bad position, he at least has escaped an early mate.

This variation shows what we shall also find in several later games, namely, that even when the loss of a piece or mate threatens, there is often a way out if one investigates all possibilities.

7 ...   BxNPch

Equally well and with the same result could have been played 7 ... QxNPch, etc.

8 PxB   QxNP mate.

Notice the role played by the mating pattern: that is, mate by the Black Queen along with the White diagonal K1-R4. As soon as the possibility of such a mate came into view, Black kept it constantly in mind. But note also that he explored alternate possibilities which would have left him with material superiority, had White succeeded in defending himself against mate itself.

Game 2

The discarded line

Playing for the big advantage

Chess rules

The open line

King and Queen of the same color on an open file

The present chess rules have been in force since about 1500, and the development of chess technique is due in great measure to the lessons learned from the games played since that time.

Some lines have always proved strong; others have been considered strong until a refutation was found; others failed from the very outset. The last two categories of play may be called "discarded lines," since they never appear in tournament play today.

But the amateur, especially the beginner, not realizing that these lines have been discarded, often plays them, for they look plausible. And his amateur opponent, who may even know that the line in question is no longer played, frequently neither sees the fundamental weakness of the discarded line, nor knows how to meet the line so as to derive an advantage from it.

The analysis of these discarded lines may be found in Bilguer, *Handbuch des Schachspiels,* the exhaustive German work on chess openings, which dominated the last decades of the nineteenth and the early decades of the twentieth century; but they are not usually included in present-day manuals on openings, because there are no recent tournament games to exemplify them.

In the game that follows, the beginner adopts a discarded line. The master replies with a sacrifice justified by the weakness in the amateur's position. Before making the sacrifice, the master could have analyzed the continuation move by move; but, knowing the theoretical analysis of the discarded line, he can confidently sacrifice and then play the theoretical analysis until his opponent deviates from it—being sure that the deviation would be even worse than the main line.

Because of Black's second move, a strategical error which White can refute by a sacrifice which requires calculation, the play immediately becomes tactical. From then on, tactics reign in Game 2. No important strategical ideas come into play, as they did in Game 1.

It is not always easy for the beginning player to find the refutation of discarded lines, either through his own analysis or in books. As a matter of fact, often he does not even recognize these discarded lines as questionable. In this work, therefore, several games are based on discarded lines often played by amateurs. But more frequently such lines are analyzed as variations of games given. The student of chess may find the analysis of some of these variations as instructive and as helpful as the games themselves.

Irregular KN Opening—Damiano Defense

Master	Beginner
1 P-K4	

As we have pointed out in the previous game, the object of the opening moves is to gain control of territory on the chessboard, particularly of the center.

To accomplish that purpose, 1 P-K4 is a good move. White's KP now controls one of the center squares; in addition, it exercises a measure of control over White's Q5- and KB5-squares by making it impossible for Black pieces to move there without the risk of being taken. This move also opens two diagonals, one for White's Queen, one for his KB. These open lines permit pieces to develop and thus to control territory on the chessboard.

1 ...	P-K4

Black's first move is good for the same reason as was White's.

2 N-KB3

Of the many possible moves, there is none more effective at this point than 2 N-KB3. White develops an important piece to a square where it will be of most use. In this position, the Knight has the greatest possible radius of control. It exercises pressure on the White center squares K5 and Q4. It also attacks and threatens to take the Black KP, obliging Black to do something about this attack.

In general, in the opening it is preferable to play the KN before the Bishop, partly because in moving to KB3 the Knight is developed to its natural square (the one from which it exercises a measure of control over the greatest number of squares), whereas White does not yet know whether he will want to develop his Bishop to QB4 or QN5, partly because, in this particular opening, the Knight can be developed so as to attack a Black Pawn, whereas the Bishop, if developed at this point, would not threaten anything. Ordinarily, a move which attacks an enemy piece or Pawn and forces the opponent to take protective measures is sharper than one which merely develops a piece.

There are several ways in which Black can meet the threat:

(a) He can play 2 ... N-QB3, which is excellent, for at the same time that it protects the attacked Pawn, it develops an important piece to its natural square (see Game 3).

(b) He can play 2 ... P-Q3, the Philidor Defense, which is less active, because it shuts in the Black KB, but nonetheless satisfactory (see Game 11).

(c) He can reply by the counterattack 2 ... N-KB3, leading to the Petroff Defense.

(d) Beginners often play 2 ... B-Q3?, which is very bad. It protects the Black KP, but it blocks all center development and thus prevents Black from playing his QP and opening his center, which is indispensable if Black is to develop his game actively. If Black should play 2 ... B-Q3, the game might continue: 3 B-B4 N-KB3 4 N-B3 N-B3 5 0-0 0-0 6 P-Q3, and Black would have to lose a move or a tempo by either 6 ... B-K2 or 6 ... B-B4 in order to get into a position where

he could develop his QP. Or if 6 ... P-QN3 7 B-KN5 B-N2
(7 ... B-K2 is more natural) 8 N-Q5 B-K2 (practically
forced) 9 NxBch QxN 10 N-R4 N-Q5 (10 ... P-KR3?
11 N-N6!) 11 P-B4 with a strong attack. This is just an example, which shows that a bad move such as 2 ... B-Q3 does
not necessarily lead to an immediate loss but does give Black
an inferior position in the long run.

Instead, Black meets the threat by another plausible but incorrect move. He plays

2 ...   P-KB3?

The discarded line. Let us see why it is no longer used.
This move is incorrect on several counts:

(a) It is a Pawn move rather than a piece move, and, as a
general rule, although not always, Pawn moves afford a
player less influence in the center than piece moves.

(b) By occupying Black's KB3 it takes the natural square
from the KN.

(c) Most important, it opens up the Black K-side, especially
the diagonals radiating from Black's KB2-square.

2 ... P-KB3 is a serious weakening move. The move is so er-
roneous that White can already afford to play for a big advantage.
(Read Introduction § 34—Advantages; § 35—Small and big advantages.) But how?

He must open the diagonals even wider. This he does by a sacrifice: that is, by temporarily giving up something to gain something else. He plays

3 NxP

The sacrifice. A piece is sacrificed only in order to gain some counteradvantage. Here the sacrifice gives White a strong attack which leads either to mate or to the win of sufficient material counterweight. Otherwise, the sacrifice would not be justified.

3 ...   **PxN?**

Before accepting a sacrifice, one should always look into the motive for the sacrifice and the various possibilities arising after the sacrifice. The continuation of the game will show why 3 ... PxN was bad.

A better move is 3 ... Q-K2 4 N-KB3 (not 4 Q-R5ch P-N3 5 NxNP QxPch, followed by 6 ... QxN) 4 ... QxPch, winning back his Pawn; but in that case White still has the better of it, for the Black Queen is developed too early in the game, is vulnerable, and will be driven back with tempo: e.g., 5 B-K2 N-B3 6 0-0 P-Q4 7 R-K1.

4 Q-R5ch

As we have pointed out above, it is a rule that the Queen should not be played early in the game, but, like all chess rules, this is a generality which does not apply in special cases. (Read Introduction § 16—Chess "rules.") Here, the unprotected state of the Black King justifies White's immediate attack with the Queen both strategically and tactically. In fact, White *must* attack with the Queen in order to justify his Knight sacrifice. He *must* play for a big advantage. (Read Introduction § 30—The attack.)

4 ...   **P-N3**

The only alternative was 4 ... K-K2, after which 5 QxPch K-B2 6 B-B4ch K-N3 (better 6 ... P-Q4) 7 Q-B5ch K-R3 8 P-Q4 dis ch P-N4 9 P-KR4, etc., and White not only has certain material com-

pensation for his Knight (two Pawns), but he has an attack which
must lead to a decisive advantage.

5 QxPch   Q-K2

The alternative 5 ... K-B2?? 6 B-B4ch P-Q4 7 BxPch leads to a
quick win for White.

6 QxR

White now has a Rook and two Pawns plus an attack on Black's
KN in return for the sacrificed Knight. However, his Queen is
temporarily relatively out of play, and Black has the initiative.
Moreover, under certain circumstances, White's Queen position
might easily become a liability.

6 ...   QxPch

The beginner sees an opportunity to give check and win a Pawn
at the same time. But, in so doing, Black has opened a line—the
K-file. Open lines favor the player with the advantage. Especially
dangerous to the player who has such a position is the open file
with the King and Queen of the same color, for the opponent can
often bring his Rook on the open line and thus win the opposing
Queen in exchange for the Rook.

Less ambitious and probably better would have been 6 ...
N-KB3 7 P-Q3 K-B2, and Black can work toward trapping the
White Queen. White's best answer is then 8 B-N5.

7 K-Q1

In order to protect his QBP and to clear the K1-square for the White Rook. Moreover, the alternate 7 B-K2 could lead to 7 ... QxNP with a loss of time for White.

7 ...   Q-K3

To protect his KN. Better might have been 7 ... N-K2 8 QxP.

8 B-Q3

There is a chess rule which states that a Bishop should never be developed to its Q3 before the QP has been moved to Q4 in order not to impede the development of the center Pawns. This rule is almost absolute. Yet here the master flagrantly violates it and puts his Bishop in a seemingly bad position. Why? Because after the White Queen has captured the Black KRP, White's KB threatens the Black KNP and because, in this position, White threatens to win the Queen by 9 R-K1. This threat will gain him an important tempo. In other words, the Black position is now so bad that ordinary rules of development give way to the forming of a rough mating pattern.

Black sees the threat to his Queen and covers by

8 ...   B-K2

Perhaps slightly better would have been 8 ... Q-B2 in order to protect the KRP. Then the game might continue 9 R-K1ch N-K2 (or 9 ... B-K2) 10 P-QN3.

9 QxP

White now takes the RP, which he might not be able to get later. He also threatens to win the KNP by 10 BxPch.

9 ...   Q-N5ch

Another check! Beginners enjoy checking.
Certainly every check should be investigated, since a check often leads to an advantage by forcing the opponent to take immediate action to end the check. But a check should not be given without due reason.

10 P-B3   QxP

Having won another Pawn, Black is now threatening to win a Rook also. But White has the initiative, and Black loses quickly.

There was no satisfactory alternative to 10 ... QxP. If Black tries to protect his Knight by 10 ... Q-K3 11 R-K1 Q-Q4 12 N-B3, and Black must give up protecting his Knight, for if 12 ... Q-B2 13 BxP.

11 QxNch	B-B1
12 R-K1ch	K-Q1
13 QxB mate.	

Game 3

The hole and how to exploit it

Playing with a sound purpose

The sacrifice to improve one's position

Combinational motifs: pin, discovered check,

　　Pawn fork, Knight fork, Bishop and Queen

　　on the same file, the in-between move

A beginner differs from other amateurs in his degree of unfamiliarity with the chessboard and in the seriousness of his errors. He has little or no notion of chess technique. He has no concept of positional strengths and weaknesses. He is completely lacking in a knowledge of strategy. He is unable to analyze accurately tactically. He cannot find his way through the busy traffic on the chessboard. His method of handling the critical situations which arise on the board are often naïve and inadequate.

The outstanding characteristic of the beginner's move is its total lack of purpose. Completely unaware of what needs to be done or of what might be done to improve the situation, he frequently makes a move simply in order to be moving, a move which in no way corresponds to the requirements of the position. Yet the characteristically aimless moves of the beginner sometimes serve quite by chance to set up a protective barrier around his King, which results in requiring more moves, rather than fewer, to bring about the eventual mate, even though the master's theoretical superiority is evident from the very earliest stages of the game.

The technique of winning from a beginner consists in exploiting his weaknesses in the most accurate manner. The master notes the weaknesses as soon as they appear, chooses the proper method of exploiting them, increases his own advantage move by move until the inevitable victory.

In the game that follows, the outstanding weakness is the hole created by an incompleted fianchetto. We shall see how many of the master's moves stem from the theme of exploiting the weak square in the amateur's position.

The Four Knights Opening

Beginner	Master
1 P-K4	P-K4
2 N-KB3	

As was pointed out in Game 2, this move threatens 3 NxP.

2 ...	N-QB3

This move meets the White threat by developing a piece to its natural square.

3 N-B3

A sound move which develops a new piece to a central position. True, this move threatens nothing for the moment, but the mere development of a piece to a central position is the beginning of a concentration of power which, in the long run, may be as potent or more potent than the direct threat. With such a move, the initiative is a bit slower in coming but not less powerful in the long run, and the advantage is that White does not risk very much.

3 ...	N-B3

Bringing out the four Knights gives each side a solid, if somewhat unimaginative, set-up. The theory of this set-up will be discussed in Game 8.

4 P-KN3?

In this position a typical beginner's move.

Moving the NP one square, then bringing the Bishop to its N2 is known as a *fianchetto* (flank development). On its N2, the Bishop dominates the long diagonal and exercises a strong pressure diagonally across the entire board. Under certain circumstances, the fianchetto is a powerful weapon. It is widely used by present-day masters.

In our game, the beginner, having heard of the fianchetto, thinks: "Why not try it myself?" He makes the initial NP move, but, not undertsanding the purpose behind the move, he fails to complete the fianchetto with B-N2 and, as a matter of fact, soon forgets completely about the fianchetto.

By moving his Pawn to N3, White has created at his KR3 and KB3 squares which can no longer be protected by Pawns. In chess terminology, such squares are known as *holes*. When the fianchetto is completed by B-N2, the Bishop guards these weakened squares, but, when the Bishop does not go to N2, these holes constitute serious weaknesses on the wing where they exist, as will be shown later in the game.

Here, the fianchetto would be inefficient even if the Bishop were developed to N2, because the diagonal extending from White's KN2-K4 is blocked by White's own KP, which limits the power of a Bishop on N2.

4 ...   B-N5

Black now threatens to win a Pawn, not on the very next move, but by 5 ... BxN followed by 6 ... NxP. This type of threat is more subtle than the direct threat. By this threat, the Black Bishop exerts a certain pressure on the White center.

Black could also have taken immediate possession of the center by 4 ... P-Q4. But this would have helped White to control the diagonal after B-N2. After 4 ... P-Q4, the game might have continued 5 PxP NxP, followed by either (a) 6 B-N2 or (b) 6 NxN QxN 7 B-N2, and in either case White is not badly off. This variation illustrates how a player who has gotten behind in an opening may re-establish equality because of unskilful play on the part of his opponent.

Possible also at this point is 4 ... B-B4, which would place Black's KB in a position to attack White's KBP. In analogous positions, White usually tries the *Fork Trick* (see Game 8, Black's 4th move), but in this position, because of White's ill-advised and incompleted fianchetto and the hole at his KB3, the Fork Trick would result in the loss of a piece for White: 5 NxP? NxN 6 P-Q4 BxP 7 QxB?? N-B6ch, winning the Queen.

5 P-QR3?

A second typical beginner's move. White attacks Black's Bishop with a Pawn. He fails to see that Black threatens by 5 ... BxN to win his KP and that he must do something to meet the threat.

It is not difficult to see that White could have protected his indirectly threatened KP by 5 P-Q3. But there is another way which is much more subtle and which furthers White's development, namely, 5 B-N2. This second way is based on the power of the Bishop along the diagonal. If then 5 ... BxN 6 QPxB NxP 7 NxP! NxN 8 BxN (or 8 Q-Q5).

5 ...   BxN

Black exchanges his Bishop for White's Knight in order to win White's centrally placed KP one move later.

White is now faced with the problem of which way to retake. Each method has its advantages. If he plays 6 QPxB, he attains better development and creates open lines for his Queen and his QB and better chances to win back his Pawn. If he plays 6 NPxB, he ends up with a more solid center.

White prefers open lines and plays

6 QPxB   **NxP**

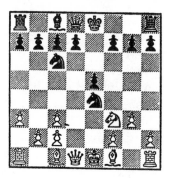

Black now captures White's KP. But, before so doing, he calculated what might happen next. We learned in Game 1 that this is called *analysis*. The analysis here is more extensive than it was in Game 1, in that there are several lines to investigate. Black's analysis went as follows: If

(a) 7 Q-Q5 N-B3, and the White Queen has to retreat.

(b) 7 Q-K2 P-Q4.

(c) 7 B-N2 (threatening 8 NxP) 7 ... N-B3.

(d) 7 NxP (temporarily sacrificing a piece in the hope of getting it back with a Pawn) 7 ... NxN 8 Q-Q5 Q-K2 9 QxKN N-B6ch, winning the Queen. The weakness created by 4 P-KN3 is already making itself felt.

(e) 7 B-Q3 (see continuation of game).

In no way could White regain his lost Pawn.

7 B-Q3

The natural square for this Bishop was N2, because of the incompleted fianchetto P-KN3. At that square, it guards the holes created by P-N3.

7 ...   **N-B3**

Black withdraws his Knight in order to threaten to fork White's Knight and Bishop by ... P-K5.

Supposing that here Black should instead make the very plausible developing move 7 ... P-Q4, protecting his Knight, opening the game, and controlling the center. White by a series of forced moves could then win back his Pawn and come out with at least equality. Strategically, 7 ... P-Q4 is a fine move, but here is what could happen tactically: 8 BxN PxB 9 QxQch KxQ 10 N-N5 (attacking Black's KP and his KBP simultaneously). Black must reply 10 ... K-K2 in order to avoid losing his KR, and White wins back his lost Pawn by 11 NxP.

8 0-0

White does not see the fork ... P-K5. Or does he?

8 ...   P-K5

Attacking two pieces at the same time by a Pawn or a Knight is known as a *fork*. Fortunately for White, he has a way out.

9 R-K1

Black cannot now take with his Pawn, because in so doing he would expose his King to check, which is illegal. In the bargain, White is now attacking Black's KP twice, threatening to win it by 10 BxP.

An incorrect execution of the same idea would be 9 Q-K2?, for then Black could win the White Bishop after 9 ... 0-0 10 BxP R-K1 11 N-Q2 P-Q4.

Note that 9 BxP NxB 10 R-K1 P-Q4 would not be sufficient for White.

9 ...   P-Q4

Black must protect his twice attacked Pawn, but now he is threatening to win either the Knight or the Bishop after 10 ... 0-0.

10 B-QN5

White wishes to escape the consequences of the fork. Preferable, however, would have been 10 N-Q4, in order to avoid the Knight pin which follows.

10 ...   B-N5

Attack on an enemy piece which then cannot move without exposing a more valuable piece (usually the Knight, Queen, or Rook) is called a *pin*. The pin is one of the common weapons used in chess, especially in the middle game.

Black can make such a serious pin only because of White's bad move 4 P-KN3. He again threatens to win a piece after 11 ... 0-0. An immediate 11 ... PxN is impossible, and 11 ... BxN does not accomplish anything because of 12 QxB.

White looks over the situation. He sees that if he moves his Queen away from the diagonal in order to unpin the Knight, Black can immediately win the Knight by 11 ... BxN. Or if he tries to support the Knight a second time by 11 K-N2, then 11 ... 0-0, and there is no way to stop Black from winning the Knight by 12 ... PxNch. For that reason, White decides to unpin his Knight by

11 B-K2?

White apparently overlooks the fact that with this move he closes the K-file, which now enables Black to grab the Knight.

The only way to save the White Knight is by 11 P-R3, a standard method of handling a situation where a pinned piece is attacked twice. This, however, would lose White a second Pawn, as follows: 11 ... BxP, which puts Black's Bishop on an excellent square for a mating attack. If, instead, Black should play 11 ... BxN, 12 QxB, and Black does not win the extra Pawn.

11 ...   PxN

Black avails himself of the opportunity to win a piece, since White has made possible the taking of the Knight by blocking the action of the White Rook along the K-file. White, however, now has the possibility of giving a discovered check, one of the strongest weapons in chess.

12 BxP dis ch

If Black should now answer 12 ... K-B1, White would then win back the piece and a Pawn. But, unfortunately for White, Black can cover the discovered check with the threatened Bishop and thus save it.

A discovered check is so potent that all possibilities must be examined. If, instead of 12 BxP dis ch, White had played 12 B-QR6 dis ch, Black would have to play carefully: (a) 12 ... B-K3? 13 BxP (attacking the Black Rook and Knight) 13 ... N-K2 (to save the Knight) 14 BxR, winning the exchange; (b) 12 ... N-K2 (removing the Knight from QB3) 13 BxP R-QN1, and White wins only a Pawn for his piece.

12 ...   **B-K3**

With one move, Black covers White's check and saves his Bishop.

13 B-N5

White makes a pin of his own. But there are pins and pins, and the White pin does not entail the threats that the Black pin did.

13 ...   **0-0**
14 BxN

White reasons: "If Black plays 14 ... PxN, I will have opened up his K-side and given him a double isolated Pawn; if he plays 14 ... QxB, I can win a Pawn by 15 BxP BxB 16 QxP." White has looked two moves ahead, which is commendable, but he should have looked ahead still farther, as we shall soon see.

14 ...   **QxB**
15 BxP?

This is as far as White had analyzed when he played 13 B-N5. He either failed to analyze farther, or he did not realize that it is dangerous to place one's Queen and Bishop on the same file, especially when one's opponent can post his Rook on that file.

15 ...   **QR-Q1**

White's Bishop is now pinned, and Black threatens ... RxB or ... BxB.

16 P-QB4

His only possibility—to protect his Bishop a second time.

16 ...   **N-K4**

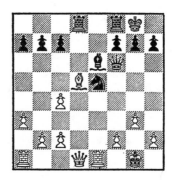

This move has two purposes:

(a) Black threatens to win the Bishop by attacking it by ... P-B3, which demonstrates a general situation in which one can win a pinned piece by attacking it with a Pawn.

(b) He places his Knight on a central square from which it radiates pressure and in particular threatens at a suitable time to occupy his KB6-square and harass the White King.

17 Q-K2

This move looks very good to White, for he gets his Queen out of the range of the Black Rook, he unpins his Bishop, and attacks the Black Knight twice. But Black has a superior position because of White's weak squares at his KB3 and KR3. A little better would have been 17 Q-R5, which accomplishes just as much and also protects White's KR3-square from invasion by the Black Bishop. We shall soon see what this means.

17 ...   **RxB!**

Black sacrifices the *"exchange"* (a Rook for a minor piece) in order to bring his Bishop to the long central diagonal which White should be controlling by a fianchettoed Bishop at his KN2.

A Rook is normally stronger than a Bishop, but when it is clearly desirable to have a Bishop perform a certain piece of work, then one must not hesitate to sacrifice the exchange.

17 ... BxB would have netted only a Pawn: (a) 18 PxB RxP; (b) 18 QxN QxQ 19 RxQ BxP. So Black would have regained the Pawn he lost on the 15th move and would again be a clear piece ahead.

With 17 ... RxB, Black takes the maximum advantage of the holes on the K-side. Moreover, the Black Knight is now protected by the Black Rook, so that White is forced to retake the Rook.

18 PxR   **N-B6ch**

If Black had continued in the sequence and played 18 ... BxP?, White would have won back his piece by 19 QxN. But Black first plays what is known as an *in-between move:* that is, a forcing move between the moves of a sequence, in order to force the King to go to a less favorable square and also to get his Knight out of danger. Because of the priority of check, White must move his King immediately, and if 19 K-B1?? B-R6 mate.

19 K-N2   **BxP**

By putting his Bishop in a straight line with the White King, Black has two deadly threats based on discovered check: (a) to win the Queen by 20 ... N-Q5 dis ch; (b) to win the Rook by 20 ... NxR db ch.

20 K-B1

Anything to get the King out of range of the terrible discovered check. But by this move, which is doubtless the least bad of the few moves at his disposal, White has created the possibility of another type of combination. He has moved his King onto a straight line with the Queen. When the King and Queen are in a straight line, whether diagonal, horizontal, or vertical, look for a combination!

20 ...   **B-B5!**

Black is apparently sacrificing his Bishop. Why?

He could have first won an extra Pawn by 20 ... NxPch 21 K-N1 N-B6ch, and the White King would have to return to his KB1. But why make this extra effort? Black's advantage is already overwhelming.

21 QxB

If the Queen does not take the Bishop, the Bishop will take the Queen. But now the King and Queen have two diagonal squares between them—just the right number for a Knight fork.

21 ...   **N-Q7ch**

22 Resigns

For the King is compelled to move, and with 22 ... NxQ, White loses his Queen.

With a Black Queen, Rook, and Knight against White's two Rooks, Black has an overwhelming advantage. Even against such odds, beginners often play on, and perhaps against other beginners they have some chance of recovering. But against a stronger player White has no chance whatever, and there is no point in prolonging the agony. When the odds are overwhelmingly against you, resign and get on with the next game.

Game 4

Center control in the opening

Not playing the same piece twice during the opening

Opening lines to attack the unprotected King

The power of open lines

Combinational motifs: discovered check, double check,
  the loose piece

When a master or a strong amateur plays a beginner, it is not winning that counts—for it is almost certain that, during the course of the game, the beginner will make a sufficient number of errors to lose, no matter how his more experienced opponent plays. The real challenge to the stronger player is how to handle in a theoretically correct manner the successive positions which arise from the unconventional play of the beginner, and how to win the game in the shortest and most direct manner.

Uneconomical and incorrect as the beginner's play may be, he is by no means irretrievably lost at every point in a game, and at times he stumbles by mere chance into positions which, if properly continued from his side by a master, could lead his opponent into considerable difficulty.

Positions from beginners' games are especially fascinating in that they often pose in the most elementary form some of the basic problems of chess technique. To see how a master handles a given position in his game against the beginner is the more interesting because the punishment of an error is likely to be more overwhelming as a result of the beginner's complete inability to find his way out.

In Game 4, the beginner compromises his position increasingly by a succession of inferior moves, and the master steadily increases his superiority until he can announce mate.

Irregular Opening

Beginner	Master
1 P-K3	

Almost no one but a beginner ever opens with the neutral 1 P-K3, because White also has at his disposal the positive 1 P-K4, which takes a firmer command of the center and begins a process of opening more lines.

Yet 1 P-K3 cannot be considered a bad move. With the White pieces one can permit oneself this neutral move, for White can afford to take more liberties than Black. In short, since 1 ... P-K3 is one of the standard replies to 1 P-K4 (French Defense—see Games 6 and 21-23), the text cannot be bad.

1 ...	P-Q4

Black, who is striving to overcome the slight disadvantage he had from being the second player (read Introduction § 22—The nature of the chess struggle), makes this normal and efficient move in which he occupies the center and now exercises some measure of control over his QB5 and K5 squares, since no White piece could now go to these squares without running the risk of being taken.

2 N-KB3	N-KB3

Both players move their KN to what is, in general, the natural square for the KN, namely, the square at which the Knight brings the greatest pressure on the center and commands the largest number of squares on the board.

3 N-B3

A beginner's move.

It is true that the White QN is now developed to its natural square, but, made at this point, it blocks the development of the

QBP, which could also aid very effectively in the control of the center.

The same criticism could not as effectively be made of 2 N-KB3. It is true that 2 P-KB4 would also help to control the center, but this move has its negative aspects:

(a) The K-wing is weakened thereby (compare with the remarks concerning 1 P-KB4 in Game 1).

(b) White's important K4-square might then become a weak square for White and a strong square for Black (after White had played P-Q4), because, if Black should then post a piece on it, that piece could no longer be driven back by a White KBP.

There are cases, however, in which it is preferable to play P-KB4 before N-KB3.

Best here is 3 P-QB4, to be followed later by N-B3.

3 ...   P-K3

Black continues to build up a strong center and to open a diagonal for his KB. In so doing, it is true that he shuts in his QB, but, in the position at hand, he cannot be criticized for doing this.

Whether to bring the QB outside the chain of Pawns is a problem in itself. It has advantages and disadvantages. If White can exchange the Black QB for a Knight, the disadvantage to Black prevails. In this position, for instance, White could answer 3 ... B-B4 by 4 N-KR4, and if Black wants to avoid the exchange of Bishop for Knight, he has to retreat to Q2 or B1. Black will have lost a tempo, but White's Knight will also have lost a tempo.

4 N-QR4?

A typical beginner's move, wrong on several counts:

(a) The same piece is moved twice in the opening, whereas in general it is more efficient to develop different pieces once each during the opening.

(b) A Knight is moved from the center of the board, where it brings to bear the greatest amount of pressure, to the side

of the board, where its radius of influence is much decreased.

(c) The Knight is moved to a square on which it is unprotected; therefore, it becomes a *loose piece,* and loose pieces are always more subject to attack than protected pieces.

(d) The move is made completely without purpose, either strategical or tactical.

It must be kept in mind that such a move would not be entirely bad if White had played it there with a purpose. But in this game it was moved without any purpose. The continuation of the game will show how vulnerable the Knight is.

4 ...   **P-B4!**

Strong. First of all, this is a center move which increases Black's command over the center squares; second, it opens a diagonal which permits Black's Queen to go to its QR4, and this is especially significant because it can now do so in connection with White's poorly posted QN at QR4. At certain points in the game, the Black Queen may not derive any advantage from going to QR4, but the important thing is that it always has the possibility of going there.

5 P-Q4

A good move. It occupies a center square and increases the pressure against Black's QB4, apparently threatening to win

Black's QBP. Thus, the move means a kind of rehabilitation of White's last move. White's decision to occupy the center was a strategic one: that is, it had to do with general positional planning. In making this move, White had to look into Black's possible replies: that is, he had to look into the tactical implications of his move or the immediate consequences of such a position on the board. He had to take account of the continuation 5 . . . Q-R4ch, attacking both King and Knight. If White replies

> (a) 6 P-B3, parrying the double threat in one move, he renders Black's attack ineffective for the moment, since after 6 . . . P-QN4 7 NxP loses a Pawn for Black; yet White's QN is far from ideally placed—Black first plays 6 . . . P-B5 and then threatens 7 . . . B-Q2 or 7 . . . P-QN4; if White replies
>
> (b) 6 N-B3, then Black is able to increase his pressure by moves such as 6 . . . N-K5 or 6 . . . PxP followed by 7 . . . B-N5.

Actually, White does not threaten to win the QBP, since 6 PxP can be answered by 6 . . . BxP 7 NxB Q-R4ch. But Black would have to exchange his Bishop for the White Knight, which he does not wish to do. Therefore, he replies:

5 . . .   **QN-Q2**

Black protects his QBP by developing his QN.

What should White do now? His QN is badly placed; therefore, he should try to get out of his compromised position with the least possible disadvantage. Relatively best, therefore, is 6 NxP, after which 6 . . . NxN 7 PxN BxP. Black will have won one tempo and will have gained superiority in the center, the relatively minor consequences of White's faulty 4 N-QR4. But White, who does not realize what constitutes good and bad positions, plays another typical beginner's move:

6 N-K5?

White again makes the elementary error of moving a developed piece a second time in the opening. This can be done when a player has a special purpose, such as completing a double attack against a vulnerable spot in the opponent's position; but here there was no special reason for such a move. 6 N-K5 is so much the worse because it gives Black the possibility of ... NxN and after PxN, White's QN is again very badly situated (because he lacks the possibility of QNxP), and whatever benefit White had obtained from his 5 P-Q4 (pressure against Black's QBP) has been nullified.

White has already made two errors, thus compounding his weaknesses. Black now has the right to expect more than equality. So he follows the line suggested above and plays:

6 ...   NxN

Black makes the exchange simply because, after White retakes, the Black position will be vastly superior: a strong center, developed pieces to contrast with White's lack of center control and no pieces developed except one badly placed Knight.

7 PxN

Black could now continue 7 ... N-Q2, after which he could win a Pawn in an enterprising way if White should try to protect his advanced KP by 8 P-KB4? The win of the Pawn is based on the fact that White's K-side is now open and his QN is a loose piece: 8 ... NxP 9 PxN Q-R5ch, followed by 10 ... QxN. Here is another example of the disadvantage White has incurred by having his Knight displaced and loose at QR4. But 7 ... N-Q2 will not win a Pawn by force, for White could play 8 B-N5 and if 8 ... Q-R4ch 9 N-B3. Nonetheless, with 7 ... N-Q2, certainly Black has the best of it because of his control of the center and his better development.

But Black is out for bigger game, so he plays

7 ...   N-K5

This move prevents the White Knight from effectively returning to its B3. Because the Knight is loose, it also threatens to win a Pawn by 8 ... NxP 9 KxN Q-R5ch, followed by 10 QxN.

How can White meet this threat? A simple developing move like 8 B-K2 will not do, since Black simply carries out his threat. Note the force of a threat.

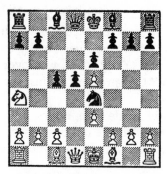

(a) 8 N-B3 would keep Black from carrying out his threat, but would give White a bad Pawn position after 8 ... NxN 9 PxN.

(b) 8 P-QB3 B-Q2! threatens to win the Knight by 9 ... P-QN4.

(c) 8 P-KB3? Q-R5ch (a well-known type position) 9 P-N3 NxP and Black wins the exchange, as he would also after 9 K-K2 N-N6ch.

(d) Best is 8 B-N5ch B-Q2 9 BxBch QxB; and now both sides threaten to win a piece, Black directly by 10 ... QxN, White by 10 P-KB3 N-N4 11 P-R4, and the Black Knight has no place to which to retreat.

Does White see the threat 8 ... NxP? It is not certain. He plays another beginner's move, probably just to be playing something.

8 P-KN3?

Does the beginner see that he is now threatening to win the Black Knight by 9 P-KB3 N-N4 10 P-R4? Probably not. In any case, the move is bad because Black now wins a Pawn, which would not have been possible had White played 8 B-N5ch.

8 ...   Q-R4ch

Taking advantage of the bad position of the White Knight.

9 P-B3

The obvious, but not the best. The White Knight is now protected, but it has no square to which to retreat if attacked.

Preferable was 9 N-B3 NxN 10 PxN (10 B-Q2? NxQ 11 BxQ NxNP loses a piece and a Pawn for White and 10 Q-Q2 loses at least a Pawn after 10 ... P-Q5) 10 ... QxPch 11 B-Q2 QxP/K4, which loses two Pawns for White but leaves him with the possibility of ruining castling for Black by 12 B-N5ch B-Q2 13 BxBch KxB. To prevent Black from castling might be worth one Pawn, but certainly not two Pawns.

| 9 ... | B-Q2 |

The obvious 9 ... P-QN4 wins the White Knight for Black, but then 10 P-B3 wins the Black Knight for White. With the text, 10 P-B3 is refuted by 10 ... BxN 11 Q-K2 NxQBP, etc. If instead, after 10 ... BxN White plays 11 P-N3, then 11 ... QxPch clearly maintains the piece for Black. This last variation leads with exchange of moves to the actual game.

10 P-N3

Forced.

| 10 ... | BxN |

Black removes the Knight in order to strip White's QBP of its defense. Moreover, the text move ruins the White Q-side Pawn structure.

| 11 PxB | QxPch |

Notice that Black must take with the Queen in order to force the issue.

Consider 11 ... NxQBP, which would be answered by 12 Q-Q2, pinning the Knight, and

(a) 12 ... P-Q5 13 B-N5ch! K moves 14 B-N2, winning back material.

(b) 12 ... 0-0-0 13 B-QN2 P-Q5 still gives Black some advantage, but not as much as in the actual game.

| 12 B-Q2 | NxB |

And Black has won a piece, for 13 QxN? QxRch.

White is now a piece and a Pawn down. He must therefore find the line which will cause Black the most trouble, one in which Black could easily go wrong.

13 R-QB1?

White misses the opportunity to spoil Black's castling by 13 B-N5ch, which would have created complications, making it more difficult for Black to find the right way, as appears from 13 ... K-Q1 14 R-QB1 Q-N5! (14 ... N-B6 db ch? 15 K-K2 winning the Knight) 15 QxN P-B5! and Black threatens to win White's QB by 16 ... P-QR3:

(a) 16 BxP QxQch 17 KxQ PxB.

(b) 16 RxP QxQch 17 KxQ PxR.

13 ...   **N-B6 db ch**

Double checks are always more forcing than others, for the King must meet two checks at the same time and therefore has to move.

14 K-K2

Black has forced White to move his King to a square where it blocks his Bishop, thus preventing it from giving check on QN5 and also depriving Black of his right to castle.

14 ...   **QxKP/4**

As will become evident after Black's next move, 14 ... QxKP indirectly protects the Black Knight. But White does not see this, and in his eagerness to win a piece, he loses the exchange.

15 KxN?

White does not see the continuation, which leaves him with a Rook down. A better move would be 15 B-N2 N-Q5ch, after which White is a minor piece down.

15 ...	**Q-K5ch**
16 K-K2	**QxR**
17 K-Q2!	

White becomes sly and threatens to win the Queen by 18 B-N5ch.

| **17 ...** | **P-B5** |

Black parries the threat and mobilizes his Bishop.

17 ... QxP would have won Black a Pawn but cost him his castling privilege after 18 B-N5ch. All in all, Black is further ahead by mobilizing his Bishop.

| **18 R-N1** | **0-0-0** |

In one move, Black defends the threatened QNP and brings the Rook into the game on a file where it is ready to support the attack against the White King.

19 Q-R5

A useless attack against Black's KBP, made with no coordination of pieces. Preferable was 19 Q-B2, keeping the pieces together.

| **19 ...** | **Q-K5** |

Black brings his Queen back into the center with tempo: that is, he now threatens White's Rook, which will have to move before White can undertake anything else. Since a move with tempo forces the opponent to protect something, it gives the side that makes it a free move.

20 R-N5

Now Black has gained sufficient material, and he starts thinking how to force a quick decision.

20 ...   **P-Q5!**

The right strategy! When the hostile King is out in the open, open the position. Black brings his Rook into the direct offensive.

21 BxP (?)

Equally bad is 21 PxP. Relatively best would have been 21 QxBP, which could have been followed by 21 ... PxP db ch 22 K-K1 PxP db ch 23 KxP R-Q7ch 24 K-N1 and Black has to make good moves in order to break all resistance: e.g., 24 ... B-Q3 or 24 ... B-R6, threatening ... R-B1. The White Queen and Bishop control White's KB2 and KN2 squares sufficiently so that Black is rather limited in his possibilities.

21 ...   **PxP db ch**

Attacking the King and the Bishop simultaneously.

22 K-B3   **PxP**

To free Black's K6-square.

23 QxBP

Catch as catch can. White would do better to look to his defenses, but there is actually very little to be done in the light of Black's overwhelming control of open lines. White could offer to exchange Queens by 23 Q-K2 and get into a hopeless ending.

23 ...   **Q-K6ch**
24 K-N2

If 24 K-B2 R-Q7ch and mate in two.

24 ...   **B-R6ch**

All lines are at Black's disposal.

25 K-R1

If 25 K-N1 Q-B8 mate; if 25 K-B2 Q-B8ch, followed by 26 ... Q-N7 mate.

| **25 ...** | **Q-B8ch** |
| **26 R-N1** | **B-N7 mate.** |

Game 5

When experienced chess players meet each other over the board, they follow familiar theoretical lines known as *openings* for a certain number of moves at the outset of the game. The beginner, unaware of these lines, often accidentally starts out his game with some known opening, but after a few moves he deviates from the theoretically correct continuation. His opponent is therefore obliged to think early in the game but gets the opportunity to apply the basic chess principles which will improve his position. Once he obtains an advantage in the opening, he can cast about for the continuation which will increase this advantage and lead to eventual victory.

An advantage at a given point in the opening by no means assures a player of an automatic win nor even of a continuing superiority. Each move offers its strategical and tactical problems. At each move, the player must take stock of the situation and look for the correct continuation. If he fails to find it, his opponent frequently has ways at his disposal to regain at least equality.

Beginners often think that successful chess play depends on a rote knowledge of book variations. For them, it would be quite impossible to learn the hundreds of variations of book openings. It is desirable rather to learn the general principles of opening play, to study the basic strategical ideas behind the most common openings, and to learn how to handle the tactical problems which arise during the opening.

The Ponziani Opening

Beginner	Master
1 P-K4	P-K4
2 N-KB3	N-QB3

These moves, which we have already studied in Games 2 and 3, are excellent. No better have been found. The question before White now is how to continue.

At this point, he has a number of possibilities, most of which will be discussed in this book. Among these are:

(a) 3 N-B3, leading to the Four Knights Openings (see Games 3 and 8).

(b) 3 P-B3, the Ponziani Opening (see the continuation of this game).

(c) 3 P-Q4, the Scotch Game (see Game 18).

(d) 3 B-N5, Ruy López (see Game 12).

(e) 3 B-B4, leading to the Giuoco Piano (see Game 25), or to the Two Knights Defense.

Of these, White chooses a continuation which is sufficient, not bad, but neither is it the strongest move possible at this point. He plays

3 P-B3

White, the beginner, has fallen by chance into the Ponziani Opening. He hopes to continue with 4 P-Q4 and to build a strong Pawn center for himself. This is his strategic aim. Strategy deals with general planning. It does not deal with the problems which arise one by one in carrying out the moves as the pieces come in contact with the opponent's pieces. Those problems are in the realm of tactics, as we shall soon see.

The general idea behind 3 P-B3 is good, but the move has three disadvantages:

(a) It develops a Pawn, rather than a piece, leaving White behind in development.

(b) It places a Pawn on White's QB3, the natural square to which to develop the QN.

(c) It temporarily creates a hole on his Q3. On the other hand, the move is advantageous in that it opens a second diagonal for the Queen, and, as we shall see in the comments after White's 4th move, the use of this diagonal can be tricky in the hands of experienced players.

3 ...   P-Q4

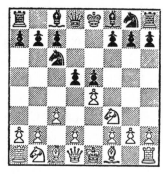

Since White, in playing 3 P-B3, has relinquished the initiative, Black now seizes it and at the same time opens up his game.

Usually Black cannot attain ... P-Q4 successfully early in the KP openings, because, after PxP QxP, White can drive the Black Queen away with a gain in tempo by playing N-QB3. In this game, on the contrary, Black can play 3 ... P-Q4 successfully, for, after 4 PxP QxP, White does not have at his disposal the continuation 5 N-B3. Contrast this with the situation in the Center Counter Gambit: 1 P-K4 P-Q4 2 PxP QxP 3 N-QB3, where the Black Queen must move with a loss of tempo (compare Game 15, moves 2 and 3).

By bringing his QP in contact with White's KP, thus threatening to win it, Black has created a tactical situation which White will have to handle in some way if he hopes to retain equality.

What should one do with this opening? It is no opening for beginners, because tactics predominate in the play. There are no simple strategic principles to govern the general lines in this opening. If, after 3 P-B3 P-Q4, White does not make use of his tactical chances by 4 Q-R4 or 4 B-N5—as our beginner does not—he may get into trouble. Then the opening is very bad indeed.

The advanced player will be interested in looking into the tactical opportunities:

(a) 4 Q-R4

(a1) 4 ... PxP (obvious but not best) 5 NxP Q-Q4 6 NxN PxN (6 ... QxN?? 7 B-N5) 7 B-B4 Q-Q2 8 0-0 N-B3 (8 ... B-Q3? 9 B-N5 PxB 10 QxPch followed by 11 QxR) 9 P-Q3 PxP 10 BxP (tricky again—White threatens B-B5 and Black's Queen is tied down to the defense of the QBP) 10 ... B-N2 11 Q-B2 and White is better off.

(a2) 4 ... B-Q2 (a gambit—Black sacrifices a Pawn for a quick development) 5 PxP N-Q5 6 Q-Q1 NxNch 7 QxN P-KB4 8 P-Q4 P-K5 9 Q-Q1 B-Q3 (not so convincing especially for a beginner, and this applies to the whole variation).

(a3) 4 ... N-B3 (again a Pawn sacrifice) 5 NxP B-Q3 6 NxN PxN 7 P-Q3 (or 7 QxPch, taking a second Pawn, after which Black enlarges his advance in development by 7 ... B-Q2) 7 ... 0-0 8 B-N5 P-KR3 9 BxN QxB (theory states: Black has sufficient compensation—difficult to explain).

(a4) 4 ... P-B3 (solid and best, but against all principles because it takes the natural square from the Black KN) 5 B-N5 N-K2 6 PxP QxP 7 P-Q4 B-Q2 8 0-0 PxP 9 PxP N-K4! 10 BxBch QxB (with an even game).

(b) 4 B-N5

(b1) 4 ... P-B3 (see a4).

(b2) 4 ... PxP 5 NxP Q-Q4 6 Q-R4 N-K2 7 P-KB4 PxP e.p. 8 NxP/B3 P-QR3 9 B-K2 N-N3 10 0-0 with about an even game.

In the game at hand, the beginner, seeing the threat to his KP, makes a move calculated to take care of the immediate situation, but the move fails to take into account the long-range strategy indicated for White.

4 B-Q3?

A typical beginner's move. It is bad because it prevents White from later playing the natural P-Q3 or P-Q4.

4 ...   N-B3

This is an important move from several points of view: (a) Black develops his KN to its KB3, where it is the most effective because it brings pressure on the largest number of center squares; (b) an additional piece is brought to bear on White's PK4, which was already attacked by Black's QP. Thus, Black's threat to win White's KP has been renewed.

Black will not help White by playing instead 4 ... PxP, for then White improves his position by 5 BxP, and after 5 ... B-Q2 (to prevent BxNch PxB and its double isolated Pawn) 6 P-Q4, and White has retrieved his mistake of 4 B-Q3? (blocking the advance of the QP) and taken full advantage of his 3 P-B3, which prepares P-Q4.

The questionable Black move 4 ... PxP illustrates how players sometimes make moves which improve their opponent's position, and how a player who has gotten into an unfavorable opening variation can sometimes retrieve an unfavorable position and turn it into a favorable one.

The position at hand after 4 ... N-B3 calls for analysis. It is necessary to consider each reasonable move, how one's opponent will answer that move, and, if possible, what the continuation will be. Then it is necessary to evaluate the positions arising from the various possibilities and to choose the one which is best or, if there are several which seem equally good, the one which is most suited to one's temperament.

Let us consider the possibilities one by one. This will show how many facets the position may offer.

(a) 5 Q-B2. Black can now exchange his Knight for White's Bishop, a slight advantage, and put White's Queen in an unfavorable position as follows: 5 ... PxP 6 BxP NxB 7 QxN P-B4 8 Q-K2 B-Q3, and Black has greater control of the center and better development. Or Black need not even liquidate in the center. He can also play 5 ... B-Q3. This line, however, can become complicated: 6 PxP NxP 7 BxP P-N3 8 BxP PxB 9 QxPch—three Pawns and attacking chances for White against a piece for Black.

(b) 5 Q-R4. The result can be the same as in the preceding variation: 5 ... PxP 6 BxP NxB 7 QxN, etc., as in (a). Again 5 ... B-Q3 is possible, maintaining the tension, which, in general, is favorable for the normal developer.

(c) 5 PxP QxP. Black has a powerful center and threatens (in addition to 6 ... QxB) 6 ... P-K5, winning a piece by a fork.

(d) 5 Q-K2. Black can either play 5 ... PxP with the same continuation as in (a) or 5 ... B-Q3 as in (a).

(e) 5 B-N5, counterattacking instead of protecting his Pawn. The game might continue 5 ... PxP 6 NxP Q-Q4 and (1) 7 BxNch PxB followed by either (a) 8 P-Q4 PxP e.p. (losing the KNP) or (b) 8 Q-R4 B-N2 and Black is a little better off; (2) 7 NxN QxB 8 N-Q4 Q-KN4 with superior development and initiative; (3) 7 Q-R4 QxN 8 BxNch B-Q2 9 BxBch NxB with superior development and initiative. Here as well, 5 . . . B-Q3 is to be considered.

For White, the least bad of these variations is 5 Q-B2 or 5 B-N5.

But White, a beginner, not being capable of analyzing, thinks only of the necessity of supporting his KP once more. He plays

5 N-N5?

A naïve way of protecting his KP. The move is insufficient and temporary, since the defender, the KN, can be driven back immediately.

5 . . .   **P-KR3**

Black follows the rule which states: "Attack the defender with a Pawn if possible—other kinds of attack might also be useful— thus forcing the defender to move and abandon the square from which it protects."

If White should now return to his KB3-square where his Knight is most powerful, Black would win a piece by 6 . . . PxP. Therefore, he is compelled to withdraw his Knight to a side square and plays

6 N-KR3

From this side square, the Knight controls little territory. But that is not the worse. Black replies

6 . . .   **BxN**

Why does Black capture here and thus not only exchange a Bishop for a Knight but also reduce his attacking force? For one thing, his QB has not yet moved, and by playing 6 . . . BxN, he exchanges an undeveloped Black piece for a developed White piece. More important still, by this exchange he mutilates the White Pawn position.

7 PxB

White now has a serious weakness—a set of doubled isolated Pawns. Such Pawns are especially weak since they cannot be defended by other Pawns and can be advanced only by slow steps. Here, the situation is even worse because White was compelled to take toward the side instead of toward the center. Also, the Pawn protection for the King is demolished on the K-side.

7 ...   PxP

Black not only wins a Pawn—he improves his position, for his extra Pawn is in the center of the board, where it acts as a restraining force on White's development and from which point it can be pushed to advantage when the time comes.

8 B-N5

White, who is forced to move his Bishop, pins the Black QN, a positive action. But on QN5, the Bishop is loose. We shall see how Black gains in time and therefore in development because of this. He makes a double threat.

8 ...   Q-Q4

Black threatens both to win the White Bishop by 9 ... QxB and to break up White's K-side position by 9 ... P-K6, since White will then be forced to protect his KR.

9 Q-R4

White protects his Bishop. Perhaps he would have done better to simplify by 9 BxNch and then try to attack along the KN-file by R-N1. Yet that line does not offer many prospects either, for after

9 BxNch QxB 10 R-N1 0-0-0, White is completely tied up. No action is possible along the KN-file; the center is blocked because of the presence of the Black Rook on Q1; the QN cannot develop to its natural square because of the QBP on QB3. One piece alone cannot do very much. What counts is the cooperation of several pieces.

9 ...	**P-K6!**

By his 9th move, White was able to protect the loose Bishop and thus eliminate one threat, but Black now uses his double center Pawn to the best advantage. He threatens simultaneously to capture White's KR and to break up the K-position further by . . . PxPch.

10 BxNch

Black must now take care of the check before continuing his own attack. He has the choice of taking the Bishop with the QNP or with his Queen. He would not think of playing 10 . . . QxB, for then White could reply 11 QxQch, and, after 11 . . . PxQ 12 QPxP, White would win back his Pawn, and much of Black's attacking power would be gone. Black himself would have a double isolated Pawn and an isolated RP so that the position would be even.

This line illustrates how important it is, even when one has a clearly superior position, to choose the move with which one can press one's advantage, and how dangerous it is to play mechanically or indifferently.

The side that has the attack must avoid the exchange of pieces as far as possible, for exchanges cut down attacking power. As a corollary, the side that is being attacked should force exchanges as far as possible in order to cut down the power of the attack.

10 ...	**PxB**
11 0-0	

11 R-B1 was perhaps a little better; it is not usually wise to castle when the side on which one castles is wide open.

11 ...	**PxPch**

Black strips the White King of its Pawn support.

12 RxP

No better would be 12 KxP, which would be followed by
12 . . . B-B4ch.

| 12 . . . | B-B4 |

Pinning the Rook.

Black takes possession of the open lines at his disposal. Notice
Black's superior development, his greater command of territory.
His pieces are either developed or can be developed quickly
along the open lines. White's position is cramped; his King is
virtually out in the open undefended.

13 P-Q4

The only way to save the exchange.

| 13 . . . | PxP |

White now takes advantage of the temporary lull in the Black
attack to initiate a little attack himself. He plays

14 R-K2ch

Thus White saves his Rook. Checks often force the opponent
to play to his detriment, but this check results only in causing
Black to make a move which he would have made anyway. The
loss of the castling privilege to Black does not mean anything in
this case.

| 14 . . . | K-Q2 |

In this way Black brings his King to a square where it is completely safe, and the opportunity is made to win the exchange by
15 . . . P-Q6 dis ch 16 R-B2. 15 K-B1 will not help, for Black only
replies 15 . . . Q-R8ch 16 K-B2 P-Q6 dis ch, winning the exchange.
Therefore,

| 15 PxP | BxPch |

Black is now in full control of two adjacent diagonals. If 16 K-B1 Q-R8 mate. Therefore, White gets out of check by a *self-pin*, that is, he interposes his own Bishop so that it is pinned.

16 B-K3

Black now has at his disposal a number of good replies, such as 16 ... R-K1 and 16 ... Q-B6. But he takes full advantage of the pin and the open lines to draw White into a mating net, a situation where the pieces of the attacking side control an overwhelming number of squares and by checks force the opposing King to advance into these squares, where it is then mated. Black plays

16 ...   **Q-N4ch**

White cannot reply 17 BxQ, because his Bishop is self-pinned.

17 K-B2

To protect his twice-attacked Bishop, for 17 K-B1, BxB loses a piece. After the text Black could win a piece by 17 ... Q-B5ch 18 K moves BxB. But when it is a question of a mating net, it is much more important to bring additional pieces into the game, especially if one can do so with tempo. Black therefore plays

17 ...   **N-K5ch**

A third piece comes into the fray.

18 K-B3

If 18 K-B1 BxB 19 RxB (19 QxN? Q-N8 mate) 19 ... QxR and an early mate.

18 ...   Q-B4ch

19 B-B4?

Better but insufficient as well is 19 K-N2 BxB and (a) 20 RxB? Q-B7ch 21 K-R1 Q-B8 mate; (b) 20 N-B3 NxN 21 PxN Q-Q4ch 22 K-N3 (22 K-B1? Q-R8 mate) 22 ... Q-N4ch 23 K-B3 Q-R4ch, etc. (24 KxB? R-K1ch). If on either the 23rd or 24th move, White plays Q-N4ch, ... QxQ simplifies, the point being that, although Black has a piece to the good, he must be very careful, since his King is out in the open and in some danger. But as soon as the Queens disappear, whether on the 23rd or 24th move, this danger is eliminated.

Notice how the White King is confined by Black's control of squares. If White had time to make a move or two, he could eliminate some of the attacking pieces. But the checks continue relentlessly.

19 ...   N-N4ch
20 K-N3   QxP mate

Or if 20 K-N2 QxPch 21 K-R1 Q-B8 mate.

Once White played 11 0-0, he did not have a chance. Each Black blow entailed some sort of threat or the equivalent, which prevented White from developing and brought his King into an ever more compromising position. All this was the result of the fact that Black took advantage of White's inferior moves and errors.

Game 6

General ideas behind the opening moves 1 P-K4 P-K3

Theory behind and possible continuations after 3 P-K5 P-QB4

Disadvantages of the move B-QN5, followed by BxNch in the
   French Defense

Play along diagonals

Sacrifice of Pawn to create flight square

Maneuvering opponent into untenable position

Behind every chess opening is some fundamental idea for gaining control of the chessboard. Every theoretical opening consists
of a series of moves by White designed to retain and increase the
slight superiority White has by virtue of playing first and of a
series of countermoves by Black designed to neutralize White's
efforts. In all sound openings, equality results after a given
number of moves. In certain openings, equality is much more
difficult to attain than in others.

Of prime importance in playing an opening is an understanding
of the basic ideas behind that opening. A rote knowledge of a
number of variations of an opening is superficial, if helpful, but
the player who knows only variations does not get along when
his opponent deviates from the variations with which he is
familiar. On the other hand, a player who understands the basic
ideas behind an opening realizes where the real strength of the
opening lies, and plays accordingly.

When one player understands the ideas behind the opening and
the opponent has no inkling of these ideas and therefore does not
meet thrusts with counterthrusts, the better informed player often

attains the maximum advantage which can be derived from the opening he is using.

But chess is so complex that, once players leave a book line, the game may proceed in channels rather different from the conventional ones. In such cases, more important even than an understanding of the opening is a knowledge of the fundamental strengths of a chess position and an ability to apply them in the position at hand.

Once a side has superiority, open lines are very useful in allowing players to make the most of the developed pieces. In the game that follows, White's typical amateur errors give Black wide-open lines and the maximum opportunity to capitalize on his advantages. We shall see how he uses them.

The French Defense

Amateur	Master
1 P-K4	P-K3

Compared with 1 ... P-K4, this looks like a timid move; but, in the hands of a player who knows the ideas behind it, it is the beginning of an excellent system of strategy called the French Defense, in which the Black player plans (a) to build up a solid Pawn wall of defense by ... P-Q4; (b) to attack the White center by means of ... P-QB4 at a propitious moment, supposing that White has played P-Q4, as he usually does. This type of game gives chances to both sides, but the opening may lead to a debacle for White if he fails to understand Black's over-all aims and the import of his individual moves. The theory of the French Defense will be explained in detail in Game 21 and further in Games 22 and 23.

2 P-Q4

White quite properly takes immediate command of the center. Non-book players often reply 2 N-KB3, after which Black still continues by 2 ... P-Q4, which may lead to the same variations as we get in the book lines: e.g., (a) 3 PxP PxP 4 P-Q4 (exchange variation of the French); (b) 3 P-K5 P-QB4, which may lead to positions analogous to those in the game. If White neither takes nor pushes but plays 3 N-B3, then Black has the choice between several good moves: 3 . . . N-KB3, 3 . . . P-QB4, and 3 . . . P-Q5.

2 . . .	**P-Q4**

Black completes his defensive Pawn-formation and threatens 3 . . . PxP, thus compelling White to do something to meet his threat.

White must now either protect his threatened Pawn by 3 N-QB3 (the commonest continuation) or by 3 N-Q2 (the Tarrasch variation) or exchange center Pawns by 3 PxP (the exchange variation), which tends to lead to symmetrical positions with an eventual draw, or continue by pushing the KP, a variation often played by amateurs and occasionally by masters.

3 P-K5

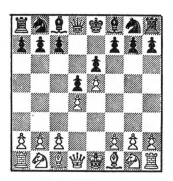

At first glance, this push appears strong, for it brings the White KP to the fifth rank and into enemy territory. However, the move also entails serious disadvantages: (a) White loses a tempo by moving his KP a second time; (b) he relieves the tension which existed in the center when either side could exchange and instead substitutes a set position by fixing the Pawns—in general, it is best to maintain tension in the center as long as possible; (c) as soon as the White KP is on K5, White's QP must take over the task of defending it and therefore becomes more vulnerable to attack; thus, by 3 P-K5, White creates in his QP a target for Black's attack.

As to the value of 3 P-K5, chess theory has varied considerably during the past century. Played all through the nineteenth century, this variation was discredited in the early twentieth century, only to be revived by Nimzovich, who gave it a new lease on life with his theories. At present, 3 P-K5 is considered satisfactory, although not leading to advantage.

3 ...   P-QB4

Black immediately threatens to break up White's center. The problem of what White should do about it is very fascinating from a theoretical point of view.

According to many chess theoreticians, White must try to maintain his center as long as possible. To this end, he supports his PQ4 by 4 P-QB3, and a long struggle for the possession of the center usually ensues. The game might continue: 4 ... N-QB3 5 N-B3 Q-N3 6 B-K2 (White cannot bring his QB to the support of the center by means of 6 B-K3 because the Black Queen is pressing down on White's QN2) 6 ... PxP (Black exchanges at this point to prevent White from getting command of his Q4-square, for if 6 ... B-Q2 7 PxP! BxP 8 0-0, followed by 9 P-QN4, 10 QN-Q2, 11 N-N3 and mastery of the Q4-square. See the comment to White's 4th move in the game. Notice that when White exchanges QP for QBP earlier, he gets into trouble on his KB2) 7 PxP KN-K2, after which several continuations are possible: ·

(a) 8 0-0? N-B4, losing a Pawn for White.

(b) 8 N-B3 N-B4 9 N-QR4 Q-R4ch 10 B-Q2 B-N5 11 B-B3.

(c) 8 N-R3 N-B4 9 N-B2 B-N5ch 10 K-B1 (10 NxB leads to the eventual loss of White's QP), since it does not do White much harm to lose his castling privilege in this case.

(d) 8 P-QN3 N-B4 9 B-N2 B-N5ch 10 K-B1 and Black should then play 10 ... B-K2! in order to be ready for ... N-R5 after P-KN4.

In b, c and d, White keeps his QP but has some difficulties. In compensation, White has a free game.

But other chess theoreticians think otherwise about the maintaining of the center.

4 PxP

The beginner, not understanding the importance of maintaining control of the four center squares (Q4, K4, Q5, K5), exchanges and thus gives up the center. The move has several disadvantages: (a) it gives up, in a sense, the all-important center, thus co-operating with Black in his purpose of destroying White's center; (b) it permits Black to gain a tempo by taking the Pawn with his Bishop; (c) it leaves White with no development at all except that of a lone and rather advanced KP; (d) it weakens the KP.

But, ironically, the beginner, doubtless without the slightest inkling of the chess principles which come into play here, has fallen into a very playable variation also used by masters. By taking Black's QBP, he creates for himself on his Q4 a strong square: that is, a square on which he can post a piece which cannot easily be dislodged by his opponent. The force of this strong square will be shown in Game 21, also a French Defense.

4 ...   **N-QB3**

Before taking on his QB4, Black first attacks White's KP. He can do this safely, for he will win one of the two Pawns in any case.

The obvious 4 ... BxP entails a slight disadvantage in that it leaves Black's KNP vulnerable to attack. After 5 Q-N4, Black must either play 5 ... K-B1, forfeiting his castling privilege, or weaken his K-side by 5 ... P-KN3, or play a gambit: 5 ... N-K2 6 QxNP N-N3, and Black will win back his Pawn.

5 P-KB4 (?)

A positional blunder which not only gives Black an opportunity to increase his margin of development but also opens up the White K-side for an eventual attack.

White should protect his KP by 5 N-KB3 and after 5 ... BxP 6 B-Q3, White is not too badly off. As soon as Black castles, White could start a K-side attack, and his Pawn on K5 would hinder Black from defending. Such an attack is one of White's strategic weapons in the French Defense. For instance: 6 ... KN-K2 7 0-0 0-0? 8 BxPch! KxB 9 N-N5ch K-N1 (9 ... K-N3 is another variant, also favorable to White—compare Game 19) 10 Q-R5 R-K1 11 Q-R7ch (better than first 11 QxPch, which gives the Black King more room) 11 ... K-B1 12 Q-R8ch N-N1 13 N-R7ch K-K2 14 B-N5ch N-B3 (14 ... P-B3? 15 QxP mate) 15 PxNch K-Q3 16 QxP and White has two Pawns to the good and an excellent position. But if Black does not castle K-side, there is a good chance of preserving equality on either side: 7 ... N-N3! (instead of 7 ... 0-0?) 8 R-K1 B-Q2 9 P-B3 Q-K2 10 QN-Q2 0-0-0 11 N-N3 B-N3 and White now has his Q4-square at his disposal but is a little handicapped by the weakness of his KP. Chances are about equal.

5 ...	BxP

Black continues to develop pieces toward the center. He now has a solid formation with two pieces and two Pawns in play, in contrast to White's two Pawns and a weakened K-side.

White could, of course, still take advantage of the absence of Black's Bishop from the K-side and continue 6 Q-N4—and he should have done so—but now after 6 ... K-B1 7 N-KB3 N-R3 8 Q-R3 N-B4, the Black pieces obtain excellent posts, and the lost castling does not do much harm. White has no attacking power on the K-side, and Black could continue by ... P-KR4, ... P-KN3, ... K-N2. Notice that the White QB is hampered by its own KBP.

6 B-N5?

A favorite beginner's move in the 3 P-K5 variation of the French Defense. White pins Black's QN. At this point, the move is bad partly because it is imperative that White first develop his KN, partly because the White KB can now be attacked sooner or later with tempo by ... Q-N3. White then faces the choice of withdrawing his Bishop with loss of time, of supporting it with

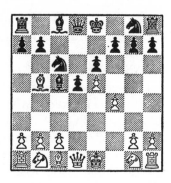

moves such as N-QB3 or P-QR4, after which Black can again attack it by ... P-QR3, or of exchanging the Bishop for the Black QN, opening lines for Black.

The main drawback of this move is strategical. By strategical, we mean that there is no immediate threat to White's position, that Black will do nothing on the next move to give White a material disadvantage, but that, in terms of long-range planning, it *is* disadvantageous. Although beginners often do so, White can never properly think of taking Black's Knight, because: (a) it leaves Black with the Two Bishops; (b) it strengthens Black's center; (c) it opens the QN-file for the Black Rook; (d) it opens a diagonal for Black's QB. In general, one makes such a move only if it is forced: for instance, in order to avoid the loss of a Pawn.

6 ...   **Q-N3**

By threatening both 7 ... BxN and 7 ... QxB, Black compels White to play 7 BxNch in order to avoid the loss of a piece.

By now, White has committed several errors, and these errors have put him into such a compromised position that he is obliged to further Black's play and allow him to increase his advantage.

7 BxNch   **PxB**

By retaking with his QNP, Black opens diagonals for his otherwise inactive QB. Both for this reason and in order to keep the Queen and KB on the same diagonal, where they exercise strong pressure and threaten White's KN, Black would not think of capturing the White Bishop with his Queen.

8 N-KB3??

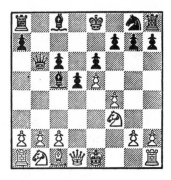

Correct although unsatisfactory—since White can no longer castle—was 8 N-K2 or 8 N-KR3.

In general, it is better to develop a KN to B3 than to K2 or R3, but amateurs frequently make the mistake of playing chess moves on general principles instead of by the specific tactical requirements of a position, and thus come into difficulties. (Read Introduction § 16—Chess "rules.") In this specific position, 8 N-KB3 is a mistake because it does not attempt to close the diagonal which has just been opened to Black's QB by 7 ... PxB. 8 N-K2 would have developed the Knight and at the same time closed that diagonal. 8 N-KR3 would have protected White's KB2-square and prevented a direct catastrophe.

With his overwhelming superior development and the open lines at his disposal, Black now has a right—and a duty—to attack. If he does not do so now, White may catch up in development, and Black's advantage could disappear. Black therefore continues:

8 ...   B-B7ch

9 K-K2!

Better than 9 K-B1?, which would lose at once after 9 ... B-R3ch, and much better than 9 K-Q2?? Q-K6 mate. Although the text does not seem to be much different, there is a hidden defense after 9 ... B-R3ch, as the continuation will show.

9 ...	B-R3ch
10 P-B4!	

This is the point of the White defense. By giving up his QBP, White creates a flight square, QB2, for his King.

10 ...	BxPch
11 K-Q2	

The White King is still very exposed, and there is no compensation whatever for his lost Pawn or for his compromised King position, not to speak of the fact that Black has the initiative. But—there is no mate in sight, and as long as there is life there is hope.

11 ...	Q-K6ch
12 K-B2	

White escapes to his flight square.

But in such a position, with three of Black's pieces free to move at will in enemy territory, White's King in the open, and all White's pieces inactive, Black must either find a mate or attain a big material advantage.

12 ...	Q-K5ch!

This check drives the King to the open field.

13 K-B3

If 13 K-Q2 Q-Q6 mate.

13 ...   **B-K7!**

Again a hard blow. White's Queen must now move to a square which will block the movement of the White King.

14 Q-B2

If 14 Q-Q2 Q-B5 mate. 14 Q-N3 loses on account of 14 ... Q-Q6ch 15 K-N4 R-N1ch, and Black has the agreeable choice of winning the hostile Queen or mating.

14 ...   **P-Q5ch**

15 K-N3   **R-N1ch**

16 Resigns

White is forced to give up his Queen. There is no point in continuing. In general, there is nothing to be gained by continuing with two pieces down (except two Knights in the end game), nor with a Bishop, Knight, or Rook down, unless your position has positive counterchances; but with a Pawn or even two Pawns down, never resign unless your position is very bad.

Game 7

Meeting the premature attack with developing moves

The neutralizing move

Moving with tempo

Sacrifice to open lines and bring pieces into active play

Attack against weakened and castled K-side

The discovered-check shuttle attack

One of the most spectacular activities in a chess game is the attack. An attack can be overwhelming and devastating—it can, in fact, lead to sudden death for the hapless opponent who is unable to meet it. So satisfying is the attack that for some amateurs it is the essence of chess play. "Attack, always keep on attacking," said one of them in advising a less sophisticated player.

But chess is not that easy. Attacks are not always successful. An attack may even boomerang to the disadvantage of the attacker if it is poorly conceived. The solid chess player does not launch an attack until conditions are ripe for it, although he may use attacking moves throughout the game in order to oblige his opponent to play to his tune.

An all-out attack should be begun only when the attacker has superiority in some respect and when his opponent, therefore, has some weakness or inferiority in some direction. When such a situation exists, the player who has superiority has almost the duty to look for his opponent's weakness. Once he finds it, he must study means of taking advantage of it. No weakness is more exploitable than that of a K-side which harbors the monarch himself. If the opponent's K-side is unprotected or if one or more of its Pawns has left its original square, and if the attacker has greater mobility, more open lines, more control of space, the latter can often penetrate his opponent's K-side Pawn structure and overwhelm him before he has the time to bring forces to his defense.

On the other hand, there are players who try from the very outset of the game to overwhelm their opponents in a few quick moves by an all-out attack, often made with a combination of Queen and Bishop. Generally, such blitz attacks are based on some variation of the *Scholar's Mate*: 1 P-K4 P-K4 2 B-B4 N-QB3 (for instance) 3 Q-R5 (or 3 Q-B3) 3 . . . P-Q3?? 4 QxP mate. Such attacks can be deadly if not properly met, but result only in the loss of time for the violently attacking player if the defender protects himself adequately with developing moves.

When in a well-conceived attack the position seems desperate, the defender should, even so, always look for a way out. Perhaps he can find one small variation which does not lead to direct mate; perhaps the defender can create complications for his opponent by an unexpected sacrifice which may upset some well-laid plans based on the supposition that the defender will follow an obvious line; perhaps the attacker has overextended himself and sacrificed too much material for an attack which he cannot quite maintain.

In this game we shall see an ill-conceived and premature attack, a well-conceived and well-executed attack, and a possible although inadequate defense in a desperate position.

Irregular King's Pawn Opening

Beginner	Master
1 P-K4	P-K4
2 Q-R5	

A favorite attacking move of a beginner.

This is one of the bluntest and most direct ways of launching an attack against the Black King: by bringing pressure against his relatively unprotected KB2-square and threatening at the same time to win Black's KP. Over and above the fact that White does not yet have superiority and Black does not yet have any real weaknesses, the move is questionable on at least two counts:

(a) In general, it is wise to complete one's development before attempting to start an attack. There are instances where an early attack is not premature and is quite justified, but this is not one of them.

(b) As a rule, it is bad to bring the Queen out early in the game, for the Queen is very vulnerable to attack, and when it is attacked by lesser pieces it must move, thus losing tempi and retarding development.

2 ...   N-QB3

Black protects the attacked KP by a simple developing move. Black could also have protected his KP by 2 ... P-Q3, which is slightly inferior to the text because the Pawn on Q3 would shut in Black's KB.

3 B-B4

Continuing his blitz attack, White now threatens 4 QxP mate. It is not difficult for an experienced player to refute this vigorous attack, but to do so Black must not play indifferently.

Black has at least four ways of meeting the threat. Let us consider the merits of each:

(a) 3 ... N-R3? The Knight does protect the KBP, but it is now posted at the side of the board where its radius of influence is very limited; moreover, after 4 P-Q3, White threatens 5 BxN PxB 6 QxP mate.

(b) 3 ... Q-K2. The Queen protects the KBP, but it blocks the development of the Black KB and no longer helps control the Q4-square, which might be desirable if Black later wished to play ... P-Q4.

(c) 3 ... Q-B3. From this square, the Queen protects the KBP and is itself on a square from which it can bring pressure to bear on the White position. It has the disadvantages of taking from the KN the KB3-square, at which that Knight is most effective, and it no longer brings pressure to bear on the Q-file. In addition, White might soon be able to play B-KN5 and drive the Queen away from this square.

(d) 3 ... P-KN3. This forces the White Queen to lose time by moving and keeps the Black KB3-square free for the Knight. It has the disadvantage of slightly weakening the Black K-side.

Black can equally well choose 3 ... Q-B3 or 3 ... P-KN3. So he plays

3 ...   **P-KN3**

4 Q-B3

White again threatens 5 QxP mate. But he has lost time by moving his already developed Queen a second time.

4 ...   **N-B3**

In one move Black covers the attacked square and develops his important KN to its most effective square.

5 Q-QN3

By moving his Queen a third time and losing another tempo, White now threatens 6 BxPch.

5 ...   **Q-K2**

Black protects his KB2 with his Queen. The fact that he blocks the diagonal on which the KB stands is no longer significant, since it is now almost certain that the KB will develop to N2 in order to guard the KB3- and KR3-squares, which would otherwise become weak, as they were in Game 3.

Black now threatens to end the White attack by 6 ... N-QR4, forcing the exchange of the White Bishop. He also threatens 6 ... NxP.

6 N-KB3

Desirous of continuing his attack against Black's KB2 by 7 N-N5, White does not see or ignores Black's threats. Although it is doubtful that White realized that he was giving a Pawn in order to accelerate his development, inasmuch as his moves up to this point were just the contrary, under the circumstances this is the best line to pursue.

| 6 ... | N-QR4 |

In violation of the general rule which says that pieces should be moved only once during the opening, Black plays his already developed QN a second time. But general rules may be ignored when there are special circumstances, and Black has a double purpose in playing 6 ... N-QR4: (a) he exchanges a Knight for a Bishop, a slight advantage; (b) he puts an end to White's attack, which is somewhat annoying because it must always be taken into account and might become dangerous. A move which blunts or puts an end to an attack is known as a *neutralizing move*. (Read Introduction § 25—Neutralization.)

6 ... NxP would disturb Black's harmonious development but should certainly be investigated. It is playable, but after 6 ... NxP 7 0-0, White could annoy Black along the K-file. To win White's KP costs Black *two* tempi, because the Knight will soon be driven back by the White Rook. Is it worth that much? The game might have continued (a) 7 ... B-N2 8 R-K1 N-B4 9 Q-R3 0-0 10 P-Q4! with advantage to White; (b) 7 ... N-QR4 8 Q-K3 NxB 9 QxN, regaining the Pawn (9 ... N plays 10 QxKP or 9 ... Q-K3 10 P-Q3 or even 10 N-N5). In the light of such lines, Black is wise first to consolidate by removing the KB and to develop, then later to try to obtain material advantage.

| 7 Q-B3 | NxB |
| 8 QxN | P-Q3 |

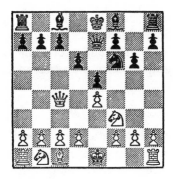

Black protects his QBP by a developing move which opens a useful diagonal for his QB.

At this point, White has developed two pieces and one Pawn, but there is no cooperation between his pieces, and his Q-side pieces are woefully undeveloped. It is obvious that he did not attain anything by his violent attack. Black has developed two pieces and three Pawns and has opened two important diagonals. He is considerably ahead of White.

9 P-KR3?

White now makes a defensive Pawn move in order to prevent Black from playing ... B-N5. This is unwise for several reasons. First of all, the move weakens the K-side, as will be seen later. Whenever the K-side Pawns move, the King position tends to become weaker if the King should castle on that side. Second, ... B-N5 is not a particularly annoying threat, since it would not result in a pin. Third, White, already behind in development, should be thinking of bringing out pieces and should make a move such as 9 N-B3 or 9 P-Q3.

9 ...   B-K3

Black develops with tempo: that is, he forces White to move his Queen, thus to lose one more move.

10 Q-N4

Since White feels obliged to protect his KP, this move, which threatens Black's QNP, is as good as any.

Beginners, who take special delight in giving check, might prefer to play 10 Q-N5ch, which Black would answer by 10 ... P-B3, putting an end to the check and protecting his QNP and at the same time building up his center and compelling White to move his Queen still again.

10 ...   0-0-0

Black, who has a fine sense of economy of movement, protects his attacked QNP and brings his Rook to the center in a single stroke. If White's pieces were developed, it might be dangerous for Black to castle Q-side, for Black's own pieces are concentrated on the K-side and the Black King would then be vulnerable to attack. But with only White's Queen on the Q-side of the board, it will be some time before White will be able to launch an attack. Nonetheless, the latent possibilities of a White attack against the Black King are there, and it is important that Black keep White occupied, so that he will have no time to bring his undeveloped pieces into play.

11 Q-R4

White now moves the Queen once more in order to attack Black's QRP, thus losing another tempo, since in general K-N1 should be played after 0-0-0 in order to shorten the castling line. It would have been somewhat preferable for White to play 11 N-B3 or even 11 P-Q3. Black can easily protect his QRP. He plays

11 ...   K-N1

A move such as 11 ... P-QR3 has no merit. It simply serves to weaken Black's Q-side and to supply a target for an attack.

12 0-0 (?)

White brings his King to a weakened wing. A better move might have been 12 N-B3 or 12 P-Q3.

We now have a classical middle-game chess position: White has castled on the K-side; Black, on the Q-side. In such a situation, it is normal for White to look for a Q-side attack; Black, for a

K-side attack. In this position, it is Black who is the more inclined to look for an attack because (a) his pieces are concentrated on the K-side; (b) White's pieces are relatively undeveloped; (c) White's K-side is weakened by P-KR3. Black realizes that, if he does not take positive action, White will develop his pieces and start his own attack rolling.

Attacks are often made against weaknesses in the opponent's position. Here, White's general weaknesses are his K-side and lack of development; his specific weakness is the PKR3, which makes White's position much more vulnerable than it would have been if the KRP were still on its KR2. We'll soon have the opportunity to see the role which White's KRP plays in Black's attack.

The technique of executing a K-side attack against a castled King consists in opening lines and placing pieces on squares near and in the enemy territory. Black therefore begins his attack by

12 ...   N-R4

This move will enable Black to open files by means of . . . P-KB4 and possibly to post his Knight on his KB5, where it would constitute a constant nuisance and threat to White.

13 N-B3

White finally develops this important piece. If Black gives him time, he can now initiate action such as N-N5 at a later stage of the game.

13 ...   P-KB4

Consistent with Black's plan of opening files for attack. He need not fear White's N-QN5, which can easily be repulsed by ... P-QR3.

14 PxP?

Opening the KN-file for the opponent. White would have done better to answer 14 P-Q3 so as to bring pressure along the diagonal commanded by his QB. In that case, Black might have continued by ... P-B5, ... P-KN4, ... P-KN5, taking advantage of White's weakness on his KR3. Notice that Black would not have opened the KB-file by ... PxP, since that file is not so important.

14 ...   PxP

Since he has the choice of an open KN-file or KB-file, Black naturally opens the KN-file. The attack along the KN-file is strong (a) because Black can double heavy pieces (Q and R) along this file, (b) because the White KNP is protected only by the White King, and (c) because, with the text, Black's KP and KBP exert tremendous pressure on the enemy territory and prevent White's pieces from moving in.

If Black had the open KB-file at his disposal, he would find the White KBP protected by both King and KR. There is not much possibility of attack along that file, but if Black were compelled to make the attack along the KB-file, he would probably play ... R-KB1, ... N-B5, followed by ... NxNP or ... NxRPch.

15 N-QN5?

A beginner's move which threatens to win a Pawn by 16 QxPch or 16 NxRP. The threat can easily be parried with a gain of tempo, but it is true that by 15 ... P-QR3 Black would somewhat weaken his Pawn position.

White could have played 15 Q-R4, attempting to neutralize the Black K-side attack by an exchange of Queens (in general an excellent means), but Black would have then continued 15 ... Q-K1, protecting his KN, maintaining the protection of his QR, and preparing ... B-K2.

15 ...	P-QR3

16 N-R3?

Another typical beginner's move. The White Knight had to re-treat with a loss of time. White does not want to admit that his last move was wrong, so he places his Knight on a less useful square, the QR3, where its radius of influence is very limited. From QB3, the Knight controls its Q5-square, which is very important in what follows.

If White had played 16 N-B3 and thus returned the Knight to QB3, the position would have been approximately as it was before 15 N-QN5, but now with Black to move. Black would then have continued by 16 ... R-N1, threatening 17 ... N-B5 with double attack. After 17 P-Q3, controlling Black's B5-square, things would not have been as easy as in the game. Black would gradually in-crease the pressure by moves such as 17 ... Q-N2, 18 N-K1 B-K2; e.g., 19 K-R2 P-B5 20 N-K4 B-R5. A fierce struggle, about the outcome of which there is not the slightest doubt.

After the bad text move (16 N-R3?), things go smoothly for Black. The big difference is that Black has the Q4-square for his Bishop, and this constitutes a considerable plus.

16 ...	N-B5

One should not be surprised that Black has *two* winning lines in this position. 16 ... R-N1 wins just as convincingly. For in-stance:

(a) 17 P-Q3 (to prevent 17 ... N-B5) 17 ... B-Q4!

(a1) 18 N-K1 (or 18 N-R4) 18 ... BxNP 19 NxB Q-N2 wins

(a2) 18 K-R2 BxN 19 PxB Q-N2 wins

(a3) 18 any other move BxN

(b) 17 Q-R4 Q-K1

(b1) 18 N-K1 B-K2 19 Q-QN4 N-B5 20 K-R2 Q-R5 with the threat 21 ... RxPch, etc.

(b2) 18 P-Q3 B-K2 19 B-N5 (19 Q-QN4 B-Q4) 19 ... BxB 20 NxB Q-N3 and wins.

(c) 17 N-K1 N-B5 18 K-R2 Q-R5 (threatening 19 ...
RxPch) 19 R-KN1 QxBP, etc.

Likewise, by transposition of moves 16 ... N-B5 17 N-K1 R-N1
18 K-R2 Q-R5 wins.

17 P-Q3

White finally opens the diagonal in order to exert pressure on
his KB4-square and to threaten to remove Black's Knight, which
would seriously reduce his attack.

But Black has so many pieces within attacking radius and so
many open lines at his disposal that he can now afford to begin his
all-out attack with a sacrifice. Such an all-out attack is possible
only when pieces and open lines are present and when the opponent cannot bring up forces which might oblige the attacker
to exchange pieces.

However, even when open lines and pieces are available, it is
not sensible to sacrifice on general principles. One should calculate in advance the variations and their consequences.

17 ...	NxPch
18 PxN	

In return for his sacrificed Knight, Black has completely opened
the KN-file. He must now be able either to mate or to retain sufficient material; otherwise he will be lost.

18 ...   R-N1ch

Also possible here is 18 ... B-Q4.

19 K-R2

After 19 K-R1 B-Q4 is overwhelming, and after 19 B-N5 or
19 N-N5, 19 ... P-R3 regains the piece with a Pawn up and an
overwhelming position.

Black now controls the KN-file, but White can easily neutralize
this control by 20 R-KN1. Black must therefore find a move which
forces White to play something other than R-KN1.

19 ...   B-Q4

White's KN cannot be protected, therefore must move. (a) After 20 N-N1 or N-Q2, 20 ... R-N7ch is killing; (b) after 20 N-N5, there is the simple 20 ... P-R3; (c) after 20 N-R4, the simple 20 ... P-B5 or the beautiful sacrifice 20 ... QxN (see later) or finally 20 ... B-B3 21 Q-QB4 P-Q4; (d) after 20 B-N5 BxN! 21 BxQ R-N7ch 22 K-R1 BxB and wins; this discovered-check situation is the theme of the finish of the actual game; (e) after 20 R-KN1 RxR 21 NxR Q-N2 22 P-B3 B-K2 followed by 23 ... R-N1 is killing. White does have one temporary defense. He plays

20 N-K1

Guarding the vulnerable KN2-square.

20 ...   **Q-N2**

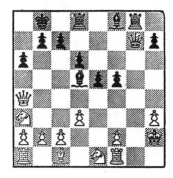

To prevent White from playing 21 R-KN1 and from closing the diagonal by 21 P-B3, for then 21 ... Q-N6ch 22 K-R1 QxRP mate.

21 B-K3

To protect the KBP and clear the first rank.
If instead White plays 21 Q-R4, Black has two lines:

(a) 21 ... Q-N7ch immediately (see continuation of game) wins back the piece and leaves Black with a Pawn to the good. This is only a mediocre reward for Black's tremendous attack. Far better is

(b) 21 ... B-K2 22 Q-N3 Q-B2 23 Q-K3 Q-N3 24 Q-N3 Q-R4 25 Q-K3 P-B5 26 Q-Q2 Q-N3, etc.

| 21 ... | B-K2 |

A preparatory move which prevents the White Queen from coming to its KR4 and clears the first rank for the movement of the Black Rooks.

The Queen sacrifice 21 ... Q-N7ch would also work, but not as effectively as later: 22 NxQ RxNch 23 K-R1 R-N5 dis ch (or first takes all Pawns from 7th rank) 24 Q-K4!

22 P-QB4

White, not knowing what else to do, makes a move which simply drives Black's QB to a square from which it attacks the White Queen and shuts his Queen entirely from the K-side. However, there was nothing better, and the Black attack is in no way altered. One advantage of the text is that after an eventual ... Q-N7ch; NxQ RxNch; K-R1, Black has no discovered check to win the White Queen.

| 22 ... | B-QB3 |
| 23 Q-N3 | |

With overwhelming control of the KN-file and the long diagonal, Black is ready for the second and still more costly sacrifice:

23 ...	Q-N7ch
24 NxQ	RxNch
25 K-R1	RxP dis ch

Any other reasonable move would allow White to close the diagonal by P-B3. Now comes a series of discovered checks in which the Rook shuttles back and forth, known in German as the *Zwickmühle*.

| 26 K-N1 | R-N7ch |
| 27 K-R1 | |

At this point, 27 ... RxP dis ch (or any other Rook move along the 7th rank) looks good, but there are some finesses. Sometimes a seemingly hopeless position offers at least a fighting chance and even a way out, as we have seen in Games 1 and 6. There exists

the possibility of interposing a piece to give the King an escape square. White, who is for the moment a whole Queen up, must offer his Rook, thus making available to him his KB1-square. Thus, after 27 ... RxP dis ch, 28 R-B3! postpones mate. We continue 28 ... BxRch 29 K-N1 R-N1ch and if

(a) 30 K-B1 B-K7ch and (1) 31 K-B2 B-R5 mate !! (2) 31 K-K1 B-R5ch 32 B-B2 R-KN8 mate; but

(b) 30 B-N5! RxBch 31 K-B1 and Black no longer has a direct mate. However, after 31 ... RxQ 32 PxR, Black has sufficient material to win.

This shows that:

(a) In this special case 27 ... R-K7 dis ch or 27 ... R-Q7 dis ch or 27 ... R-QB7 dis ch would not be good; e.g., 27 ... R-K7 dis ch 28 R-B3! BxRch 29 K-N1 R-N1ch 30 K-B1 and the result is doubtful. At the price of "only" one Rook, the White King has retained his freedom of movement, while Black has sacrificed a Queen to bring the White King into this situation.

(b) In general, one should not despair too soon. By sacrificing a Rook and a Bishop, White prevented mate, and, except for the fact that Black was able to regain sufficient material, these sacrifices might have been a refutation of the combination.

Therefore, Black replies

27 ...   QR-N1

Now there is no longer any escape. Black threatens 28 ...
R-KB7 mate, and White can only postpone the mate by giving up
his Bishop on KN5 and his Rook on B3.

28 B-N5	RxB dis ch
29 K-R2	R-N7ch
30 K-R1	R-KB7 mate.

Game 8

The Four Knights Opening

Loss of initiative through passive moves

The Fork Trick

Premature pinning of opponent's KN

Loss of tempo by playing same piece several times in opening

Attack against uncastled King: opening the position

Transforming advantage in space into advantage in material

Restricting movement of opponent's pieces

As the beginning player becomes more experienced, he gradually loses the characteristic traits of a "beginner." He no longer blocks his center development; he hesitates to bring his Queen out early in the game; he becomes more aware of the tactical requirements of the position; and his moves take on an increasing semblance of purpose.

However, there are still large areas of chess with which he is unfamiliar, and often it is not until much later in his career as a chess player that he fully understands the importance of time and the value of piece development in chess.

There is a principle which states that the more pieces you have developed to key positions, the greater your chess power will become. It follows that if your opponent does not bring out a sufficient number of pieces to neutralize your growing power, you will soon get an attack which could become overwhelming.

Making the best use of superiority in time and development is a sensitive matter. The problem of launching and executing an attack is not always simple. There are times when the player with superiority in development must settle for converting it into superiority of material rather than trying to maintain a superiority of force. It must be noted that superiority in force is a temporary state, which can disappear if the opponent is given time to catch up, whereas a superiority in material can remain permanently.

In this game, Black attains a considerable advantage in development, due to White's continuing loss of tempi. At a given point, Black can do nothing more than exchange his superiority in development for a Pawn and the initiative, but the last part of the game shows how this advantage is quite sufficient for a win.

The Four Knights Opening

Amateur	Master
1 P-K4	P-K4
2 N-KB3	N-QB3
3 N-B3	N-B3

The Four Knights Opening, the beginning of which we have already seen in Game 3.

Black is almost compelled to follow in the same passive style as White. For him, this is not serious, since Black's habitual role is one of meeting White's moves and not seizing the initiative until the position warrants it.

In the Four Knights Opening, one of the problems of the second player is how to get the initiative in an almost symmetrical position. This is especially important if Black is a considerably stronger player than White. To this end, there are at each point in the opening ways of avoiding absolute symmetry. Here, there is 3 . . . B-N5, but it does not afford Black many possibilities.

White now has the choice between three kinds of Four Knights games:

(a) The Spanish version, 4 B-N5, exerting pressure on Black's QN and indirectly on the center, since White threatens under circumstances 5 BxN followed by 6 NxP; e.g., 4 . . . P-QR3 5 BxN QPxB 6 NxP (doubtful is the continuation 6 . . . NxP 7 NxN Q-Q5 8 0-0). Nowadays, the Spanish version is considered as the strongest continuation of the Four Knights, because it maintains the tension, which is the right procedure for White, and because it does not simplify, as does the Scotch continuation, nor permit the sham sacrifices, as does the Italian.

(b) The Scotch version, 4 P-Q4, which gives Black equality after 4 . . . PxP 5 NxP B-N5 6 NxN NPxN 7 B-Q3 P-Q4 8 PxP PxP 9 0-0 0-0.

(c) The Italian version, 4 B-B4, often preferred by amateurs, who do not realize that it leads to the Fork Trick, which involves a sham sacrifice: 4 . . . NxP! The game can continue:

(c1) 5 BxPch KxB 6 NxN, and at the moment it looks as though White has the advantage, with two well-placed Knights against a Black King whose position is compromised, but then 6 . . . P-Q4 7 QN-N5ch K-N1 8 P-Q4 P-KR3 9 N-R3 BxN 10 PxB PxP, with advantage to Black notwithstanding the loss of the right to castle, because of his greater mobility and possibilities of direct action against the White King.

(c2) 5 NxN P-Q4
  (1) 6 B-Q3 PxN 7 BxP B-Q3 8 P-Q4 PxP 9 BxNch PxB 10 QxP, recommended by theory, which gives Black possibilities because of the Two Bishops and the greater

freedom of movement, and this is all one needs when playing the Black pieces in the Four Knights Opening. True, Black is left with a double isolated Pawn, but the greater mobility of the Black pieces entails sufficient compensation. As a rule, this will lead to an attack against the King with all chances involved. On the other hand, if White succeeds in defending his position, the double isolated Pawns may count against Black in the end game, just as in Game 15. But chances in this variation have to be considered as equal.

(2) 6 B-N5 PxN 7 NxP Q-Q4 8 BxNch PxB 9 P-Q4 P-QB4, and Black again has the advantage of the Two Bishops.

(3) 6 BxP QxB 7 P-Q3 B-KN5, and Black has a fine free game.

The White player in the game, however, has had no contact with theory and does not understand the importance of getting out his pieces. He plays a typical beginner's move.

4 P-Q3

Tactically, there is nothing wrong with this move, but it leaves much to be desired strategically, since it surrenders all the initiative. White shuts in his KB, thereby giving up the advantage he had in playing the first move. In other words, White now plays Black's role with the White pieces.

4 ...   **B-B4?!**

Strategically good. On this square, the Black Bishop aims at the White KB2. If the Black KN should come to its KN5, the combined action of the Knight and the Bishop could prove embarrassing to White.

However, by placing the Bishop on B4, Black invites White to play the very Fork Trick described in (c) above: namely, 5 NxP NxN 6 P-Q4 B-Q3 7 PxN BxP 8 B-Q3, giving White the characteristic position in the Fork Trick. The game might continue 8 ... P-Q4 9 PxP BxNch 10 PxB QxP, with difficult problems for both sides, already mentioned in the variation (c2-1) above.

Instead, Black might have continued 4 ... P-Q4 5 PxP NxP, which gives him the center and the initiative, or 4 ... B-N5, which pins White's QN and prepares ... P-Q4 with even greater force.

5 B-N5

A relatively aggressive move, which turns out to be premature. As a rule, one should not pin the hostile KN before the hostile King has castled, because then the unpinning by P-KR3 and P-KN4 is so easy.

5 ...   P-KR3

If Black had already castled, such a move would have been weakening and perhaps a waste of time. Since he has not castled, it may be considered as the beginning of an attack, for Black will probably not castle on the K-side.

6 B-R4 (?)

Here, the Bishop comes to a dead end and soon becomes the object of the hostile Pawn storm. In other words, after ... P-Q3 and ... P-KN4, White's Bishop will find itself on its KN3, facing the wall of granite of Black's chain of Pawns QB2-Q3-K4. In such cases, it is preferable to exchange the Bishop for the Knight. Therefore, not bad here would have been 6 BxN QxB 7 N-Q5 Q-Q1 8 P-QB3, followed by 9 P-Q4. In this way, White seizes the center and frees his Bishop. This continuation would have justified White's 5 B-N5, which was played contrary to the rule not to pin the hostile Knight before the opponent has castled but with the special purpose of obtaining the center.

As we have hinted previously, general rules may often be ignored when there are special circumstances which justify ignoring them. It is important to be aware of general rules, but one must not follow them blindly nor 100 per cent.

6 ...   P-KN4

This would have been the logical and ideal continuation if White had already castled, but even in the text position the move has many advantages. For instance, the White Bishop is shut in by Black Pawns; Black has at his disposal many possibilities such as P-KR4-R5 and N-KR4-B5. Of course, under special circumstances, such a Pawn advance might prove to have weakened Black's position because it creates a hole at Black's KB4. But White cannot occupy that hole for a long time.

7 B-N3   **P-Q3**

Protecting his KP, setting up a wall of granite for the White QB, and opening a line for his QB.

8 P-KR3

It would be interesting to know exactly what White had in mind when he played this move. Amateurs often make such moves in analogous positions in order to prevent the pinning of their KN by ... B-KN5. If White made the move with this intention, he did not understand the requirements of the position. He need not play the move in order to prevent the pin as long as the pin can be answered by B-K2. But there are other considerations which make 8 P-KR3 a reasonable move: (a) it discourages ... P-N5, which might be a nuisance; (b) it makes room for the retreat of White's QB, which is shut in by its own Pawns and by Black Pawns. As soon as Black can play ... P-KR4, White *must* play either P-KR3 or P-KR4. The move also prevents N-KN5, but for the moment that is not so important.

8 ...   **B-K3**

When a Bishop cannot be developed to N5 where it would pin the opponent's Knight, K3 is often the best for it. From there, it commands two diagonals.

Both players have now made sound developing moves, with the exception of White's 4 P-Q3, which was passive, and his 5 B-N5, which gave Black the opportunity to make the aggressive 5 . . . P-KR3 and 6 . . . P-KN4.

9 N-K2?

Another typical amateur move. Instead of developing the as yet undeveloped pieces, he plays a developed piece a second time. This is contrary to the principle that pieces should normally be moved only once during the opening, which is logical. If you violate it, you end up with a reduction in development. Yet one cannot be too dogmatic. See the comment on ignoring rules after White's 6th move.

White wants to bring his Knight to his QN3 (via QB1)—which will take time. He has a solid position, and in such cases it is not too risky to lose time. Still, the move is to be condemned.

Best here was 9 B-K2.

9 . . .   Q-Q2

Black continues his development and prepares for castling on the Q-side.

White might now consider playing 10 P-B3, apparently threatening to win a piece by 11 P-Q4 and 12 P-Q5. Actually, there is no such threat, for 10 P-B3 0-0-0 11 P-Q4 PxP 12 PxP B-N5ch 13 N-B3 NxKP 14 P-Q5 NxN and wins, for if 15 PxQN (or PxB) 15 . . . NxQ dis ch.

10 N-QB1

Following his plan to bring the Knight to QN3, he plays it a third time, thus giving Black another tempo.

Many of White's first nine moves are truly amateur; still, after *eight more moves*, the total advantage to Black will be only one Pawn. This may seem a paltry result, but it is sufficient for a win. One must often work hard to get a small advantage in chess, and a player can often play the second-best move without incurring any serious disadvantage.

10 ...	0-0-0

Now White has developed two pieces and three Pawns; Black, six pieces and four Pawns. Black has completed his development and must now try to take advantage of his superior development.

If Black, in order to bring his Knight to KB5, had tried instead the typical maneuver 10 ... N-KR4, making the Knight a loose piece, White would win a Pawn by discovery as follows: 11 NxKP PxN 12 QxN.

11 N-N3

The Knight has finally reached a square from which it can annoy Black slightly. This does not seem worth three tempi.

11 ...	B-N3
12 KN-Q2 (?)	

Perhaps White plans to play his Knight to B4 later, or perhaps he plans P-KB3, followed by B-B2, or he may fear ... P-N5, or, finally, he is preparing the development of his KB via K2 to B3 or another square on the diagonal line K2-R5. In any case, this latest violation of the principle of developing new pieces instead of old ones cries for revenge!

12 ...	KR-K1

The player with superior development must try to open his game and then overwhelm his opponent. The text is one of the preparations, inasmuch as he has placed his KR on a direct line with White's uncastled King.

13 B-K2

This move permits the White Bishop to play to KR5, KN4, or KB3. It also prevents the move ... P-KR4.

13 ...	P-Q4

Black now opens his game. He does so because (a) his development is now complete; (b) he could not play ... P-Q4 earlier, since both the N/KB3 and the B/KN3 were directed against his KP.

Black attacks in the center in order to force the White King to decide on which side to castle. He does not attack White's K-wing, partly because White has not castled K-side, partly because he cannot play ... N-KR4, partly because ... P-N5 might be answered by B-R4.

14 PxP

White is not compelled to take in the center. 14 B-B3 might have opposed Black's plans more effectively. But then Black would have been able to lay open White's center also: e.g., 14 ... PxP 15 NxP NxN, followed by either (a) 16 BxN P-B4 or (b) 16 PxN Q-K2 17 Q-K2? BxN 18 RPxB N-Q5.

14 ...	BxP

Strongest because the Bishop attacks White's KNP and thus forces the opponent's game in a special way.

Note that 14 ... NxP was also possible. Then 15 N-B4 N-B5 16 NxBch RPxN 17 B-B3 or BxN, and Black now stands well, but nothing decisive has been obtained.

15 B-B3?

White should have castled, but that would have been a success for Black in that he would have forced his opponent to castle on the vulnerable side. Black in that case would have first played 15 ... B-K3 in order to parry the threat 16 P-QB4 and 17 P-B5, and after some preparation he could have realized ... P-N5, which would have led to a powerful K-side attack.

The continuation in the actual game will give an idea of how to carry an attack against an uncastled King.

| 15 ... | BxB |

To open the game further.

15 ... P-K5 looks very tempting, and it could have been played, but it gives Black a much smaller advantage: e.g., 16 PxP NxP 17 NxN and (a) 17 ... BxN 18 0-0, which leads to a small advantage; (b) 17 ... P-B4 18 0-0 PxN 19 B-N4 B-K3 20 BxB with equal chances.

16 QxB

After 16 NxB, there follows 16 ... P-K5! 17 PxP RxPch, which loses at once.

| 16 ... | N-Q5 |

Forcing the Queen back, since

(a) 17 QxN NxPch
  (a1) 18 K-Q1 NxR 19 NxN QxQP 20 N-N3 B-R4 21 Q-B3 Q-N8ch or 21 ... BxN costs material
  (a2) 18 K-B1 NxR 19 NxN QxPch, followed by 20 ... QxN

(b) 17 NxN PxNch forces White to give up castling (18 N-K4? NxN 19 PxN P-KB4 costs a Pawn)

But White should have answered 17 NxN in any case, since it is the lesser evil.

17 Q-Q1   P-K5

This is the breakthrough Black was playing for while White was still uncastled. He follows the principle of opening the game if you have the greater development. White's uncastled King is now in great danger because of the threat of a discovered check. By threatening to win a Pawn, the master again tries to prevent White from castling.

18 0-0

White finally castles despite the fact that it loses him a Pawn, since it seems to be the lesser of two evils. For 18 PxP NxKP and (a) 19 0-0? NxB 20 PxN NxN dis ch or (b) 19 NxKN? RxNch 20 K-B1 would have cost him more.

18 ...   NxN

This simplifying move weakens Black's attack but enables him to win White's QP.

Black no longer plays for the attack, because his QB, which is an important support for the attack, is no longer on the board, and this is an important consideration. Apart from that, if one has the choice between a sound Pawn and a promising but not absolutely certain attack, one will do well to take the Pawn. Better a bird in the hand than two in the bush!

19 NxN   PxP

One does not hesitate to win a Pawn if one can do so without compensation to the opponent. In this position, it also entails the exchange of Queens, but Black's attack is largely dissipated by exchanges, and his win will now depend not on superior mobility, but on his plus Pawn. He has transformed an advantage in space into an advantage in material. The former was temporary; the latter will be permanent.

20 PxP   QxP

Black has finally won a Pawn, and there was probably no way for him to win more with the given position, despite his advance in tempi. But, in addition to the Pawn, he maintains the initiative by threatening White's Bishop. This is all the logical consequence of his accumulation of power.

21 QxQ

If White had wished to avoid the exchange of Queens, he could not have, as 21 Q-B1? is refuted by 21 ... QxB. He could, however, have allowed Black to exchange Queens by playing 21 K-R2. In that case, Black would probably have avoided the exchange by 21 ... Q-B4, since his Queen is more active than White's.

21 ...   **RxQ**

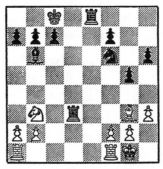

Threatening 22 ... RxB. That Black has continuing threats proves that his attack has not suffered from winning the Pawn and making exchanges.

22 K-R2

Perhaps a better move would have been 22 K-R1, so as to leave a square of retreat for the Bishop.

22 ...   **P-KR4**

Threatening to win the Bishop by 23 ... P-R5. Observe how the White pieces are hindered in their movements. The Bishop can move nowhere along its diagonal; the White Knight is limited in its movement because of the Black Bishop.

23 QR-K1

In order to secure the K5-square for his Bishop.

23 ...   **RxR**

In order to win a second Pawn.

24 RxR   **P-R5**

In order to deprive White's KBP of its last protection.

25 B-K5   **BxP**

Winning a second Pawn.

26 R-KB1

If 26 R-K2? B-N6ch 27 BxB PxBch 28 K-N1 R-Q8ch, followed by mate.

26 ...   **N-K5**

Black could also play 26 ... B-N6ch 27 BxB PxBch 28 K-N1, but then 28 ... N-K5 would cost a Pawn: 29 RxP R-Q8ch 30 R-B1.

27 N-B1   **R-Q4**
28 B-B3

In addition to his material disadvantage, White is in the embarrassing situation of having no really good place to move his Bishop.

28 ...   **B-N6ch**
29 K-N1   **NxB**

To reduce the number of pieces on the board.

30 PxN   **P-KB4**

Protecting the KBP and preparing ... P-KB5.

31 P-B4

A last try—an attack against the Rook, which is protecting the KBP. If White should succeed in taking Black's KBP, he could have some hope of eliminating Black's Bishop (in that case deprived of the additional support of his KBP), which seriously restricts the White King.

31 ...   R-R4
32 N-N3

Consistent. White, who does not want to be completely shut in after ... P-B5, gives up his RP in order to win Black's KBP.

32 ...   RxP
33 RxP   P-N3

To limit the mobility of the White Knight and to give the Black King a flight square, which is not needed at the moment, but which could be very much needed after an eventual N-B5, threatening R-B8 mate. After 33 ... R-N7 34 N-B5, Black can force the exchange of Rooks by 34 ... R-N8ch 35 R-B1 RxRch 36 KxR, and this would certainly win, but not very easily.

34 P-B5

Not 34 RxP? on account of 34 ... R-N7!, threatening both 35 ... RxN and 35 R-N8ch, followed by mate.

34 ...   R-N7
35 P-B6?

A false hope. True, Black cannot take the Knight, as White is threatening 35 R-B8 mate. Black, however, has a neat continuation.

| 35 ... | R-N8ch! |
| 36 R-B1 | |

Forced.

| 36 ... | B-R7ch! |

This check has two implications: (a) White cannot take the Bishop without losing the Rook; (b) the White King cannot play 37 K-B2 without losing the Knight.

| 37 K-B2 | RxN |

Black takes advantage of the fact that the KB-file is now closed to the Rook, thus eliminating the possibility of mate for at least one move.

38 K-K2

Again threatening mate.

| 38 ... | B-B5 |
| Resigns | |

White is a piece and two Pawns down.

Game 9

In certain well-known openings there are lines which are almost never encountered in master play but look logical and strong to amateurs and are not infrequently played by them. More often than not, the inexperienced opponent against whom such a line is used does not understand the inherent disadvantage of the unconventional move, and, failing to meet it with best play, allows his adversary to realize much more from the line than he could against someone who understood the position and knew how to counter it.

One of the most common non-book lines often played by amateurs of a certain level in the Queen's Gambit Declined is 1 P-Q4 P-Q4 2 P-QB4 P-K3 3 P-QB5. Despite the fact that 3 P-QB5 appears superficially strong to the amateur, it is strategically bad for a number of reasons. The problem is how to answer 3 P-QB5 so as to exploit White's error of strategy to the maximum degree.

The game that follows is an excellent illustration of three points: first, how White's mistaken strategy can give Black a mighty center; then, how White's attempts to maintain his badly placed Pawn outpost by supporting Pawn moves result in his loss of two Pawns; finally, how the player with the center and a material plus should press his various advantages so as to win the game quickly.

The Queen's Gambit Declined—3 P-B5?

Amateur	Master
1 P-Q4	P-Q4
2 P-QB4	

The Queen's Gambit, a system of play which is very popular in tournament play. Other variations occur in Games 16, 19, and 20.

2 ...	P-K3

There exists in the center at present a state of *tension*. Tension in the center is a fundamental chess concept, which we shall try to clarify here.

In the opening of the game, both sides will aim to develop pieces and to obtain influence in the center. They can obtain this influence by directing pieces and Pawns toward the center, a process called centralization, and by placing Pawns on the center squares K4 and Q4. As a consequence of this center strategy, there will be created a situation analogous to a tug of war and known as tension. For instance, at this point we see that Black's Q4-square is a contested square. White attacks; Black defends. It is normal, now, that White should try to strengthen the tension by 3 N-QB3 and that Black, on his part, should defend the point by 3 ... N-KB3. In the classical line, White then continues by 4 B-N5, indirectly attacking the pivotal point, Black's Q4-square. The tension or struggle for possession of the center which has been built up will be eased at some point in the game. For instance, if Black plays ... PxP or if White plays P-QB5, as actually happens in this game, the tension will be broken. It may be stated in general that easing the tension facilitates the opponent's play and should be done only if it is necessary or if the player has some special purpose in mind. If you can force your opponent to ease the tension, it may be considered as a small measure of success.

3 P-B5?

A typical beginner's move, which amateurs often play with the mistaken idea that by pushing into enemy territory they impede their opponent's development. The move is bad for several reasons:

(a) White has eased the tension in the center, which makes things easier for Black.

(b) It strengthens Black's influence in the center, since he can now play ... P-K4 without giving up a Pawn as he must in the Albin Countergambit (1 P-Q4 P-Q4 2 P-QB4 P-K4 3 PxP ...). Our game can now continue 3 ... P-K4 4 PxP BxP. It is a general disadvantage of 3 P-B5 that it facilitates Black's carrying out the counterpush ... P-K4.

(c) White cannot maintain any pressure by his advanced Pawn, because he will be forced to exchange the QBP as soon as Black plays ... P-QN3.

(d) White has lost time by moving the same piece twice in the opening, which, in general, is bad unless some special purpose is served by it. It is difficult to count tempi in such a case, but after 3 ... P-QN3 4 PxP RPxP: (1) Black is a tempo ahead, because his KB is already free; (2) he is another tempo ahead because his QR has an open file (but this is an unusual way of counting).

One of the means of taking advantage of White's 3 P-B5? would be to occupy the center by 3 ... P-K4. True, Black loses a tempo with it; but, on the other hand, he threatens 4 ... PxP and if 5 QxP N-QB3, White will have difficulty in defending his advanced QBP. Taking Black's KP by 4 PxP is answered advantageously by 4 ... BxP. White, therefore, has no better move than 4 P-K3, whereupon Black plays 4 ... N-Q2, etc. In this position, Black is a little better off, as he is now attacking White's Q4. Black has created tension, and White is playing a more or less defensive role. Moreover, Black has more terrain on the K-wing than White. One of the immediate consequences of this situation is that White's possible N-KB3 can be answered by ... P-K5, increasing Black's space advantage even more.

But Black has a still stronger reply than 3 ... P-K4. He plays

3 ...   P-QN3

The text move has a forcing character, since it threatens to win a Pawn by 4 ... PxP, and, with best counterplay, it gives Black at least a Pawn majority in the center.

The relatively best line for White (the one in which he loses no material but only control of the center) is: 4 PxP RPxP, after which Black has an open QR-file and can continue by 5 ... P-QB4, thus building a mighty center.

But our amateur decides he can keep his Pawn by protecting it a second time. So he plays

4 P-QN4?

Although a natural try, this is the second mistake, which must cost a Pawn. There *are* positions in which White can afford P-QB5 followed by P-QN4, but generally not so early in the game.

4 ...   P-QR4!

This is the refutation. Observe:

(a) 5 PxNP BxPch 6 B-Q2 BxBch 7 NxB PxP and Black has a sound plus Pawn.

(b) 5 PxRP PxBP also wins a Pawn, because White's P/R5 cannot be defended: e.g., 6 B-Q2 N-QB3.

(c) 5 P-QR3 and Black also wins a Pawn, this time by
5 ... PxNP, because White's QR is not protected. If the
White QB were already on QN2, things would be quite different. In that case, 4 ... P-QR4 would not have won a
Pawn on account of the reply 5 P-QR3, and Black would
have tried the attack against the White center by ... P-K4
at the appropriate time.

It is interesting to note that, apart from this positional refutation, Black has another more tactical way of meeting White's unsound attempt to maintain his advanced Pawn 4 P-QN4: 4 ... PxP
5 NPxP BxP?! 6 PxB Q-B3, winning the Rook. White, however,
has some counterplay: 7 B-Q2! QxR 8 B-B3 QxP 9 BxP and anything may happen.

5 Q-R4ch

This attempt to save the Pawn makes matters worce.

5 ...   **B-Q2**

What is White to do now? If 6 P-N5 PxP, winning a Pawn.
Or if 6 Q-N3 RPxP and (a) 7 QxNP PxP 8 PxP N-QR3, winning
a Pawn, or (b) 7 PxP P-QB4 (better than 7 ... PxP, which would
leave Black with a double isolated Pawn) 8 PxP BxP, followed
by 9 ... QxP.

So White replies

6 Q-R3

Maintaining pressure along the QR-file.

Although Black cannot play 6 ... RPxP, he has an excellent line which will net him at least two Pawns.

6 ...   **N-QB3**

Now Black's QR is protected, and Black threatens to win a Pawn and obtain a positional advantage by 7 ... RPxP. What is White to do?

7 BPxP is quite out of the question because of 7 ... BxPch, winning the Queen.

If 7 PxRP NxQP, threatening 8 ... N-B7ch, so 8 Q-QB3 PxBP, and Black has a mighty center, whereas White's double RP doesn't count for more than one.

Therefore, White plays

7 P-K3

Thus White has finally protected one of his vulnerable points, the PQ4.

7 ...   **NxNP**

Threatening to win the Queen by 8 ... N-B7ch.

By 7 ... PxNP, followed by 8 ... PxBP, Black could also have won two Pawns, but the continuation chosen seems still stronger because now the Black pieces can develop more actively.

8 Q-B3   **PxP**

This wins the QBP, since the White Queen doesn't seem able to defend it.

9 PxP   **Q-B3**

Forces the exchange of Queens and after that the win of White's QBP, since the threat of ... N-B7ch revives after the exchange of Queens.

Whether or not to exchange is a question which often arises in a chess game. The decision depends on the relative activity of the Queens. In general, the attacking player will avoid exchanging Queens, and the defender will aim to exchange in order to facilitate his job of defending, but this does not apply in our game. Also, the player with the material advantage will probably want to exchange Queens, since it is more difficult for the player who is down materially to obtain initiative or attack without the Queen.

In the position at hand, White's Queen is not less active than Black's. Black has a material advantage, and White's Queen is charged with protecting its QB2-square. It is therefore to Black's interest to eliminate this strong piece. Also, the exchange entails the development of Black's KN.

10 QxQ

10 B-N2? would be a mistake, for 10 ... QxQch 11 NxQ N-B7ch! would follow.

| **10 ...** | **NxQ** |
| **11 N-QR3** | |

Parrying the threat of ... N-B7ch.

| **11 ...** | **BxP** |

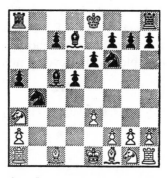

What retribution! The apparently innocent Pawn move (3 P-B5) has been punished in the most brutal way! Black has two Pawns to the good and an enormous advance in development.

| **12 B-N2** | **R-QN1** |

This move illustrates the use of the open file and the indirect attack on White's QB by 13 ... N-B7ch or ... N-Q6ch.

13 BxN

White gives Black a doubled Pawn. But in this position a doubled Pawn for Black is not a serious weakness. It is more than compensated for by the fine open KN-file it gives Black. Moreover, it is not a double isolated Pawn.

The exchange 13 BxN is not forced. White could play 13 B-Q4, after which Black would continue by 13 ... B-Q3, threatening 14 ... P-K4, and the White Bishop would come into difficulties.

If White should simply make a developing move such as 13 N-B3, Black would increase his advantage by 13 ... N-B7ch 14 NxN RxB 15 0-0-0 RxP.

13 ...	**PxB**
14 N-B3	**R-N1**

This move illustrates how an open file may be used to tie down the opponent's pieces. The pressure of Black's Rook along the file momentarily prevents the development of the White KB.

15 N-Q4

Perhaps White hopes to get some counterplay by attacking Black's QBP with 16 KN-N5.

A slightly better move would have been 15 P-N3, in order to be able eventually to develop the KB and KR. True, 15 P-N3 would create holes, but with a compromised position a player must choose the least of several evils.

15 ...   **P-K4**

Black establishes his strong center only after assuring himself that this move does not make new squares available to White. White cannot go to B5, and 16 KN-N5 is not worth much: 16 ... BxN 17 BxBch RxB! 18 NxR N-B7ch 19 K-K2 NxR 20 RxN P-B3! and then (a) 21 N-B3 RxP or (b) 21 N-B7ch K-Q2 22 N-R6 B-Q3, and the Knight is hemmed in.

16 KN-B2

What else can he do? If 16 N-B3, he has retreated with a loss of tempo. If 16 N-N3 B-Q3, threatening (a) 17 ... NxP followed by 18 ... RxN, winning a Pawn; (b) 17 ... P-R5, driving the Knight away again, and if White answers 16 ... B-Q3 by 17 NxP?, then 17 ... R-QR1 and Black wins a whole piece for his Pawn.

16 ...	B-R5!

Attacking the Knight a second time, and White cannot answer 17 NxN? for that would cost him a piece after 17 ... BxNch, attacking the Knight and King simultaneously.

17 K-Q2

17 0-0-0? loses immediately by 17 ... NxPch 18 K-Q2 BxN/R3 19 NxB BxR.

17 R-B1 could also be answered by 17 ... NxP, but still simpler is 17 ... NxNch 18 NxN R-N7 19 K-Q2, and, by a transposition of moves, we get to the game.

17 ...	NxN
18 NxN	R-N7

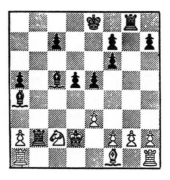

Black seizes the 7th rank with a threat. White will have to tie up his pieces in defense of the pinned Knight.

19 R-B1

If 19 B-Q3, then 19 ... P-K5 20 K-B1 PxB 21 KxR PxN with a strong passed Pawn and decisive material advantage to Black.

19 ...	**B-N5ch**
20 K-Q1	

20 K-Q3 P-K5ch loses a piece for White.

20 ...	**RxRP**

Now White cannot prevent 21 ... B-R6, attacking the defending Rook and thus depriving the Knight of its necessary protection.

21 B-Q3

The obvious reply, but the Bishop cannot maintain itself on this square.

21 ...	**P-K5**
22 B-K2	**B-B6**
23 Resigns	

White is completely tied up. He cannot move. Black continues ... K-K2, ... R-N1, and ... KR-N7, winning the whole board.

Any other reasonable Black maneuver would decide as well: e.g., ... P-QB4 and ... P-Q5 or an immediate ... RxP.

Game 10

One of the favorite moves of the weaker amateur playing Black is a defensive ... P-KR3 early in the game. This unnecessary protective move is disadvantageous for Black in two different ways: (1) it weakens his K-side Pawn structure; (2) it loses a tempo for him and allows White to secure a superior development.

The problem for White is how to capitalize on his slight advance in development.

One of the most effective methods at White's disposal is to increase his margin of development even more at the expense of a Pawn. While Black loses another move capturing the proffered Pawn, White develops one more piece. From then on, White must try to combine his developing moves with threats, molesting Black as much as possible, so that the latter will have to make defensive moves rather than developing his pieces.

In this game, once White's pieces are all in play, he eliminates most of Black's developed pieces by a series of well-considered exchanges. Then, making the maximum use of his own remaining pieces, which are active, he overwhelms his opponent's vulnerable King before Black can do anything effective himself.

Semi-Italian Opening

Master	Amateur
1 P-K4	P-K4
2 N-KB3	N-QB3
3 B-B4	P-KR3 (?)

This is a favorite move of the weaker amateur. He fears some future attack by the White QB (B-KN5, for instance) or by the White KN (N-KN5), and, before the White QB is even able to move, he plays the precautionary 3 ... P-KR3. In certain positions, such a precautionary move is occasionally necessary, but in this position, not only is it not necessary, but it consumes valuable time. This puts Black one move behind White in the type of opening where tempi are of greatest importance. Instead of meeting the enemy's rapidly mobilizing forces with armed soldiers (i.e., by bringing out his pieces), Black only loses time and force, and, without realizing it, even weakens his defensive wall.

Black would have done better to contest White's command of the center by a move such as 3 ... B-B4 (see Game 25) or by 3 ... N-B3, threatening the White KP, after which White would have to do something to meet this attack on his Pawn. With the text, there is no direct threat, and White can play at will.

Therefore, White makes an aggressive bid for complete control of the center by playing

    4 P-Q4

White now has his initial advantage of moving first, and, in addition, he has won a tempo because of Black's ineffectual 3 . . . P-KR3. Because he now has an advantage of two tempi, he decides to play for open positions, since the value of the tempo is greatest in these kinds of positions.

4 ...   **PxP**

Black must take, as we shall see by an analysis of the most plausible alternate reply 4 . . . P-Q3: 5 PxP PxP 6 QxQch and (a) 6 . . . KxQ 7 BxP, etc., or (b) 6 . . . NxQ 7 NxP. White could act even more energetically by playing 6 BxPch KxB 7 NxPch, and Black is in great trouble, for (a) 7 . . . NxN? 8 QxQ or (b) 7 . . . K-K2 8 N-N6ch, or (c) 7 . . . K-K1 8 Q-R5ch K-K2 9 N-N6ch. After (d) 7 . . . K-B3, the continuation is less clear. This does not mean that the sacrifice would be incorrect, since after 8 N-Q3, White has two Pawns for a piece and the Black King is badly placed. On the other hand, a safe win of a Pawn, as in the other variations, might be preferable.

5 P-B3

White offers to give up a Pawn in return for more rapid development. In open positions such as this one, development is of paramount importance, and it is often worth a Pawn or two to obtain it. White not only threatens to build an ideal center by 6 PxP, but he has also opened an avenue for his Queen, which could now jump to QN3.

White could also have answered 5 NxP, after which the game might have continued 5 . . . P-Q3 6 0-0 N-B3, and White certainly has a good game.

It cannot be stated objectively which of the two methods (5 P-B3 or 5 NxP) is the better. But by the sacrifice of a Pawn, White can demonstrate more convincingly the futility of Black's . . . P-KR3.

However, if Black could win the extra Pawn and then hold the position, his Pawn plus might count in the end. White must therefore play very accurately in order to make the best possible use of his superior development before Black can consolidate and make the Pawn plus count.

5 ...   **PxP**

Black accepts the Pawn. He cannot do much else. If he tries to continue his development by 5 ... N-B3, the game continues 6 P-K5 P-Q4 (6 ... N-K5 7 B-Q5 N-B4 8 PxP leads to an overwhelming game for White) 7 B-QN5 N-K5 8 NxP B-Q2 9 P-K6! PxP 10 Q-R5ch and because of Black's weakening move 3 ... P-KR3, Black now loses his right to castle and finds his King in a compromised position.

6 NxP

Compare the development of the two sides. White has three pieces developed and a Pawn on his K4; Black has one piece developed and a Pawn on his KR3. White's QB is free; Black's QB is not. White's Queen can develop to his N3. White is at least three tempi ahead, depending on the method one uses to count the tempi.

6 ...   **P-Q3**

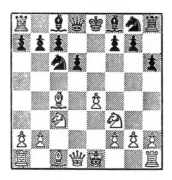

If Black tries to develop his KN (6 ... N-B3), he comes into difficulties after 7 P-K5.

If he replies 6 ... B-N5, we get a game of the nature of Game 18, with this difference: in that game, the Black KN is on KB3; here, the KRP is on KR3, certainly a disadvantage for Black by comparison. After 7 0-0 BxN 8 PxB P-Q3, White can prepare for an eventual P-K5 by 9 R-K1, and the game might continue 9 ... KN-K2 10 B-R3 0-0 11 P-K5 PxP 12 NxP, and Black cannot avoid the loss of the exchange. For instance, 12 ... NxN 13 RxN QxQch 14 RxQ N-B3 15 KR-K1 B-N5 16 P-B3. If 11 ... P-Q4 12 B-N5 and White also has a fine game and many possibilities of regaining his Pawn and more. For instance, 12 ... B-K3 13 BxQN PxB 14 N-Q4 and

> (a) 14 ... R-K1 15 BxN and 16 NxP leads to no more than equality. But White must play 15 P-KB4, maintaining the pressure and preparing a K-side attack. White has sacrificed a Pawn temporarily, therefore has a strong position. He can win this Pawn back at any time but should not do so too soon.

> (b) 14 ... B-Q2 15 P-K6 PxP 16 NxKP BxN 17 RxB R-B2 18 Q-K2 N-B4 19 RxBP and White has the better position.

7 Q-N3

White attacks the Black KBP twice and brings pressure to bear on the Black QNP, which temporarily ties the Black QB down to its defense. In general, a quick attack is not so wise, but here White wishes to take advantage of his lead in development.

White could also have played 7 P-K5, after which the game might have continued along lines outlined under Black's 4th move.

After 7 Q-N3, Black has the possibility of 7 ... N-R4, as in Game 7 (see comments after Black's 5th and 6th moves), but in the present game if Black tries for simplification immediately and plays 7 ... N-QR4, the game continues 8 BxPch K-K2 and (a) 9 Q-Q5 P-B3 10 Q-R5 N-B3 11 Q-N6, or, slightly better, (b) 9 Q-R4 KxB 10 QxN. In either case, White has recaptured the Pawn and the Black King is unsafely posted. So Black plays

7 ...   Q-K2

Black protects his KBP twice with this move, but 7 ... Q-Q2 would have given the same protection more effectively, since

Black would then threaten the simplification ... N-QR4, as the check 8 Q-R4 is out of the question. Moreover, White would not have at his disposal the attacking move 8 N-Q5. After 7 ... Q-Q2, the game might have continued 8 B-QN5 P-R3 9 BxN QxB and White has laid a good foundation for a later attack by 0-0, B-K3, QR-B1, and N-Q5.

8 N-Q5

It is important to retain the initiative in open games where one side has the advantage of a tempo or more. Therefore, White abandons his KP and threatens the Black Queen.

When a player has an open game and is tempi ahead, he can generally afford to attack, even though all his pieces are not developed.

8 ...   Q-Q2

Black does not answer with the counterattack 8 ... QxPch, because after 9 K-Q1, White threatens both 10 R-K1, winning the Queen, and 10 NxPch, winning the Rook. If Black tries to meet these threats by 9 ... K-Q1, White would do nothing special, just strengthen his position by 10 R-K1 Q-B4 11 B-Q2 (preventing ... N-R4), and now Black is at a loss. White has all his pieces developed; Black, practically none. White can do various things, such as N-K3 or N-B4 and BxP. But the game is not easy. White must play carefully to maintain his superiority.

9 B-Q2

Prevents Black's simplifying move ... N-QR4. Such preventive moves can constitute an important part of the problem of how to maintain the initiative. One should not hesitate to play them, despite the fact that they cost a tempo and seem to slow down the force of the initiative.

White could also have played 9 B-QN5, but 9 B-Q2 is stronger because it develops another piece, avoids the exchange BxN (which would be necessary after 9 ... P-R3), opens the QB1-square for the Rook, and maintains the battery Q/QN3-B/QB4.

9 ...   B-K2

To prepare for the development of the Black KN, which he cannot easily play at once, since after 9 ... N-KB3 10 NxNch PxN, Black's Pawn formation is seriously damaged and his castling possibilities are reduced.

10 0-0   N-B3

Black is now developing his pieces normally, but his 3 ... P-KR3 has cost him time, and he is still behind in development.

11 B-B3!

Again threatening to double Black's Pawns by 12 NxNch BxN 13 BxB PxB.

In positions where a player is being subjected to violent attack, he should try to simplify by exchanging pieces, but here Black cannot simplify by exchanging Knights because of 11 ... NxN 12 PxN N-Q1 13 BxP R-KN1 14 B-Q4 Q-R6 15 P-N3 and White has the advantage, since he has regained his gambit Pawn, and the Black King is very exposed in the center, and the Black pressure against the White K-side is of a temporary nature, since it cannot easily be increased.

11 ...   NxP

In for a penny, in for a pound. This leads to a quick catastrophe, as the position is becoming more and more open. Altogether, castling is probably the best for Black here, notwithstanding the possibility of White's mutilating his K-wing after 11 ... 0-0 12 NxNch, etc.

12 KR-K1

White at once takes possession of the open file, which will surely give him some sort of attack on Black's uncastled King.

If, instead, White should play 12 BxP, then 12 ... R-N1 gives Black counterchances: e.g., 13 BxP? Q-R6. Compare this with the comment after White's 11th move, and note how much better off Black is here because his KN takes part in the attack.

12 ...   **NxB**
13 NxB!

The Black Knight on White's QB3 can wait. First, White sets out to demolish the Black King position.

13 ...   **NxN**
14 BxPch

The first concrete result of the White strategy. Black must give up castling, and this is undoubtedly worth the Pawn Black still has to the good.

14 ...   **K-B1**

14 ... K-Q1 and the Black King is still worse off. White simply plays 15 PxN and already threatens the knockout blow N-K5, and if 15 ... PxN 16 QR-Q1.

15 PxN   **P-Q4**

Black must block communication between the White Queen and Bishop as soon as possible, before White strengthens his position by a move such as N-Q4, threatening N-K6ch.

16 N-K5	Q-Q3
17 QR-Q1	

Always the same principle: Bring up new forces if you have an advance in development. Compare games 14 and 24.

Here White attacks Black's QP with the newly developed Rook and even constitutes a latent threat to Black's Queen. Whenever your King or Queen is in line with your opponent's Rook or Bishop, there is latent danger even if there is an intervening piece or Pawn.

17 ...	P-B3
18 P-QB4	

Not only to direct a new attack against the Black QP, but also to open a horizontal line which will enable the White Queen to go to the other side of the board. Open lines are an advantage to the side which has the attack.

18 ...	B-B4

Note that 18 ... PxP? loses immediately after 19 RxQ PxQ 20 R-Q8 mate.

19 PxP	NxP
20 BxN	PxB
21 RxP	

White has recaptured his Pawn and stands marvelously. His attack is maintained, and the Black pieces are still fighting for development.

| 21 ... | Q-KB3 |
| 22 R-Q7 | |

Threatening 23 R-B7ch, followed by an early mate.

The possession of the 7th rank by a Rook is always strong. Here it is especially so because of the triple attack on Black's KB2-square.

| 22 ... | B-K3 |

If 22 ... BxR? 23 NxBch, winning the Queen.

White now has the initiative and certainly a much better game, even though the pieces are even.

But such positions often pose the problem of how to maintain the initiative or how to convert the advantage in tempi into an advantage in force or even how to give mate with the number of developed pieces available.

In this position, if Black could exchange certain pieces or if he could get his Rooks into play, he might be able to turn the tide. This would be difficult, however, because of the vulnerable position of the Black King. Nevertheless, White must analyze carefully and find forcing moves.

So he continues

23 N-N6ch

By this move, White forces the exchange of his Knight with the Black Bishop, thus eliminating Black's most important defensive piece. Note that Black must take.

23 ...   QxN
24 RxB

Not 24 QxB? After the exchange of Queens, White has only a *small* advantage. Without this exchange, White wins immediately, as will be seen below.

24 ...   R-K1

A last attempt. Black is hoping to administer the corridor mate by 25 RxQ? R-K8 mate.

He had nothing better, since 24 ... Q-N4 25 R-K8ch leads to 25 ... KxR 26 Q-B7 mate; and 24 ... Q-B4 25 R/6-K7 is no better.

25 Q-N4ch

This in-between check protects White's K-square and, by giving check and forcing Black to play his King, enables White to capture the Black Queen on the next move.

25 ...   Resigns

For 25 ... K-N1 (forced) 26 RxQ, etc.

Game 11

The Philidor Defense

Surrender the center

Time vs. material

The combined KB + KN attack against the hostile KBP

Pressing the advantage

Exchange to remove a well-posted piece

Morphy's great contribution to chess is his strategy and his technique of handling the open game. From an examination of his technique in the open game, one might summarize his method as follows: "Get an advantage in development; open up the game, if necessary by sacrificing Pawns or even pieces; then overwhelm your opponent with all the forces at your command before he can equalize or strike back."

In this game, the amateur makes the mistake of striving for material superiority at the expense of development. He wins first one Pawn, then a second. This gives the master an enormous edge in development. But this temporary advantage of time and space must be used at once, or it will disappear. The master must first choose the most propitious squares to which to bring his pieces; he must then decide how to maneuver the pieces so as to give mate or come out with a material superiority—a question of tactics.

In the solution of the tactical problem, all kinds of factors may arise. The perfect method would be to calculate all possibilities, but this is, in general, not practical. So the master has to examine one or two moves of different lines and evaluate the final positions of these variations. The bases of such evaluations can be different. In one instance, the basis may simply be material re-lationship; another time, the fact that the hostile King is exposed to an overwhelming number of attacking pieces; in a third case, a combination of these two elements, etc. From these evaluations the master judges the position, chooses the most favorable line, and decides which way to follow up his advantage.

The Philidor Defense

Master	Amateur
1 P-K4	P-K4
2 N-KB3	P-Q3

The Philidor Defense.

Black builds up a solid defensive wall, which is an advantage, but he shuts in his KB, which is a slight disadvantage, and he elects to play a somewhat passive and defensive game, rather than striving for an eventual ... P-Q4, which would give him a more active game.

3 P-Q4

White opens up his game immediately and now threatens to win a Pawn by 4 PxP PxP 5 QxQch KxQ 6 NxP.

Black now has several choices. He can play

(a) 3 ... N-QB3, and the game could continue: 4 B-QN5 B-Q2 5 N-B3 N-B3 and we get the so-called Steinitz Defense of the Ruy López by transposition.

(b) 3 ... N-Q2 (in order to maintain the center KP) 4 B-QB4 P-QB3 (the Hanham variation) 5 0-0 B-K2 6 N-B3 N-B3, and, although Black's position is a bit cramped, it is very solid.

(c) The counterattack 3 ... N-KB3 4 PxP NxP 5 QN-Q2 NxN 6 BxN and White stands a little better.

Instead, he plays

3 ...   PxP

This move is slightly inferior to the above alternates, because it constitutes *surrendering the center:* that is, being content with a Pawn on the third rank when one's opponent has a center Pawn on the fourth rank.

The game could now continue:

(a) 4 NxP N-KB3 5 N-B3 B-Q2 6 B-QB4, and White has more freedom, which is, in general, valid for all the variations resulting from 2 ... P-Q3.

(b) 4 QxP N-QB3 5 B-QN5 (in this way White does not lose a tempo and the Queen remains in her good central position) 5 ... B-Q2 6 BxN BxB 7 N-B3 N-B3 8 B-N5 B-K2 9 0-0-0.

But he decides instead to give up the Pawn in return for an extra tempo, and plays

4 B-QB4

Black has no pieces developed and might well continue 4 ... N-KB3 or 4 ... N-QB3. Instead, intrigued by the idea of maintaining the Pawn just captured, he plays

4 ...   **P-QB4?**

If Black could hold this formation, it might be worthwhile to play for it, but he cannot hold it, and, moreover, he has no pieces developed, so that White's superiority in development and in

control of squares is already considerable. On the other hand, Black has maintained his plus Pawn.

5 P-B3

In order to give Black a Pawn weakness, White attacks the formation, threatening 6 PxP and 7 NxP. If Black plays something like 5 ... N-QB3, then 6 PxP, and whichever way Black retakes, he ends up with a bad Pawn formation and equal Pawns. He therefore plays what is perhaps least bad under the circumstances:

5 ...   **PxP**

White could now get a good game by 6 NxP, for Black would remain with a backward QP and a hole on his Q4 in return for an extra Pawn. Masters preferring positional chess might well play this line. But White decides to carry the struggle of time versus material still farther. (Read Introduction § 9—Styles of chess play.) He plays

6 0-0   **PxP?**

Black would have done better not to have accepted the additional Pawn, but to have begun his development by 6 ... N-QB3.

7 BxP   **N-KB3?**

Because White could exploit the position after this move, it might have been better for Black first to play 7 ... N-QB3, which would have been an excellent preparation for an eventual defense of the weak point KB2, since a later N-N5 could be answered by ... N-K4, both protecting the Black KB2 and attacking the White KB.

White has now castled, has three minor pieces developed to Black's one, and has a Pawn on his K4 as contrasted with Black's bad Pawn formation PQB4-PQ3. With this overwhelming advantage in development and in control of space, White can expect to attain something more than equality: that is, he can afford to look for a big advantage, and he must look for a big advantage. If he fails to make the most of his temporary advance in time, Black may catch up with him in development and still retain his two plus Pawns. So White plays

8 N-N5

White threatens to take Black's KBP. This type of combined KB and KN attack on Black's KBP is often found in amateur KP games; and in the Two Knights Defense, where it is theory, it is also played by masters. In this position, there is no easy defense. All replies force Black to give back one of his Pawns.

8 ...   **B-K3**

If 8 ... P-Q4 9 PxP opens the K-file dangerously: e.g., 9 ... P-KR3? 10 R-K1ch B-K2 11 P-Q6, etc. (or 11 NxP).

9 BxB

White exchanges his Bishop rather than his Knight, because in this position the Knight is a more valuable piece than the Bishop, since it can make annoying threats and checks.

9 ...   **PxB**
10 P-K5

In order to answer 10 ... PxP by 11 QxQch, followed by 12 N-B7ch, winning the Rook.

It is important to see how and why the master presses his advantage here. He could have played 10 NxP Q-Q2 11 N-KN5,

117

but the text opens up the game, which makes White's advantage in development better felt.

10 ...   **KN-Q2**

10 ... N-Q4 would lose a piece after 11 NxKP.

11 NxKP

White's Knight now occupies a very commanding position in Black's territory.

11 ...   **Q-N3**

Black decides to counterattack. As a matter of fact, he does not have much choice. It would be natural to drive the White Knight away by 11 ... Q-K2, but then 12 N-B7ch wins the Rook.

White now has an overwhelming position, and yet an amateur might not know what to do with it. How can the attack be continued while at the same time protecting the attacked White Bishop? Part of the key lies in the fact that if Black takes White's Bishop, White can win Black's QR.

12 N-B3

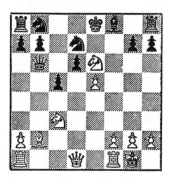

The struggle of time vs. material continues. If now 12 ... QxB 13 N-B7ch K-Q1 14 QN-Q5 NxP 15 NxR N-R3 16 R-N1, followed by 17 RxP, freeing the Knight so that White maintains the advantage in material and also has attacking possibilities.

12 ...   **N-R3**

Black decides first to protect against White's N-B7ch, but this brings his Knight to a rather ineffective square. It exercises little influence on the center.

13 R-N1   **NxP**

Black is once more interested in material gain, but this time rightly so, for, along with getting material, he eliminates White's KP, which is a dangerous weapon.

14 N-Q5

White brings his Knight to this important, strong center square with tempo, for he attacks the Black Queen.

14 ...   **Q-B3**

Here again arises the question: Given his strong position, how can White continue so as to make the most of it?

15 BxN

White exchanges here in order to remove Black's one well-posted piece and make best use of his lines to bring more pieces into dominating positions.

15 ...   **PxB**
16 Q-R5ch   **P-N3**
17 QxKP

Threatening 18 QxR, much as in Game 2.

With all the center files open and three White pieces directed like pistols against the Black King, Black stands hopeless.

17 ...	R-KN1

In this position, White is so strong that he can win the game in a number of ways. For instance, 18 N-Q4 dis ch wins the Queen and forces a resignation. But this game was played in a simultaneous exhibition, and the master, aware of the tendency of some amateurs to play on even against hopeless odds, decided to give mate instead. So he played

18 N-B6ch	K-B2

Or 18 ... K-K2 19 QR-Q1 (threatening 20 N-N5 dis ch, etc.) and (a) 19 ... QxN 20 R-Q7 mate or (b) 19 ... B-R3 20 N-N5 dis ch K-B1 21 N/6xP mate.

19 N-N5ch	K-N2
20 N-R5 db ch	

Mate is in the air. Also possible is 20 N-N4 dis ch Q-B3 21 QxQ mate.

20 ...	K-R3
21 N-B7 mate	

Game 12

Ruy López

Motives for exchange

Reducing the attack by neutralization

Center pressure by a Pawn

Cutting the communication between the sides

Exploiting the weakened side

The all-out attack against the King

The current variations of the openings are not the only correct variations, for there is a factor of fashion involved. If a certain opening is often played in tournaments, it becomes the subject of much theoretical analysis, and consequently a great many players use that opening. This does not mean that lines which are seldom played are necessarily inferior. It is a merit of World Champions such as Steinitz, Lasker, and Alekhine that from time to time they came up with very solid openings which no one knew because they were so seldom played.

In this game, Black, a coffeehouse player, chooses a rarely played defense of the Ruy López. It is not the strongest theoretical line of that opening, and he will certainly not get an overwhelming game with it, but it is a solid line, and the master will not be able to overrun him in a few moves. On the contrary, at the beginning of the middle game, nothing seems to be wrong with the amateur's position.

But this is precisely where the master shows his skill at first creating, then exploiting a weakness. He comes up with a fine move which, to the untrained eye, looks strange, but which leads to the splitting up of the Black defense system into two parts, with the communication between the parts interrupted and made difficult. This is the point. If the communication between the Queen- and King-wing is such that the opponent cannot easily and rapidly bring his pieces from one side to the other, it can and must occur that at some time or other he has a minority of forces on an important part of the board.

This is what occurs in this game. Black, through lack of communication, is unable to defend his Q-side. Having created the weakness, the master then deftly proceeds to exploit it.

Ruy López

Master	Amateur
1 P-K4	P-K4
2 N-KB3	N-QB3
3 B-N5	

The Ruy López, an opening which affords White more possibilities than most others.

With 3 B-N5, White exercises indirect pressure against Black's position, for by BxN, he threatens eventually to win Black's KP. He cannot do so immediately, since 4 BxN QPxB 5 NxP? is answered by 5 ... Q-Q5 or 5 ... Q-N4, either of which leads to regaining the Pawn and gives Black at least an even position. But Black must continually take into account the possibility of White's playing BxN under more favorable circumstances, as we shall now show in two examples where he first protects his KP so that Black cannot regain the Pawn with his Queen after White has played NxKP:

(a) 3 ... N-B3 4 P-Q3, threatening 5 BxN QPxP 6 NxP and Black cannot regain his Pawn with 6 ... Q-Q5.

(b) 3 ... P-QR3 4 B-R4 N-B3 5 0-0 B-K2 6 R-K1 and White again threatens to play BxN to advantage, as for instance, 6 ... 0-0 7 BxN QPxB 8 NxP, and White has won a Pawn.

3 ...	KN-K2

The idea behind this move is to reinforce the QN so that in case of BxN, Black could reply ... NxB, thus protecting his KP.

The theoretically strongest move here is 3 ... P-QR3. Since the coffeehouse player in this simultaneous match did not make this move, we shall not concern ourselves further with the theory of the opening at this time.

4 0-0

White castles at this point in order to gain complete freedom for all kinds of actions in the center.

4 ...   **P-Q3**

A solid defensive move, which again has the disadvantage of less mobility (see Game 11). This move is more or less a consequence of Black's previous play.

5 P-Q4

White again tries to open up the game, threatening to win a Pawn by 6 PxP. Also, 6 P-Q5 could be unpleasant for Black.

5 ...   **B-Q2**

Black now has a cramped but solidly defensive game.

6 N-B3

A simple developing move.

6 ...   **P-B3**

This move looks amateurish, but in many variations of the Ruy López it is the right way to strengthen the center.

The move may be played both by amateurs and by a World Champion. In a Lasker-Steinitz game, Moscow, 1896, White played 6 B-N5 (instead of 6 N-B3), and Black obtained a very good game by replying 6 ... P-B3 with tempo.

White, who now has better center control and therefore a slight advantage, tries to profit by the situation by playing

7 PxP

White now exchanges in order to have more freedom of action. As long as the tension (see Game 9, Black's 3rd move) Q4 vs. K5 exists, White has to take into account, after his PxP, the possibilities ... QPxP, ... BPxP, and ... NxP. This exchange frees him from the necessity of looking into these from now on.

If Black could attain ... N-N3, ... B-K2, and ... 0-0, his position would be excellent although cramped. Alekhine had a clear preference for such positions.

Note that 7 B-QB4 to prevent Black's castling, which is good strategically, is poor tactically because Black would answer by 7 ... N-R4.

7 ...   **NxP**

The alternates 7 ... QPxP and 7 ... KPxP are just as good.

8 NxN

This time White exchanges in order to free the diagonal Q1-KR5 for the Queen.

8 BxBch is not so good, for White's KB is better situated than Black's QB. The text gives the Black player the opportunity to exchange Bishops himself, it is true, but he would exchange them under conditions less favorable to himself. See (b) under Black's 8th move.

8 ...   BPxN

This opens up the K-side suspiciously. Yet

(a) 8 ... QPxN 9 B-B4 and Black has greater problems. The formation QBP2-QP3-KP4 is more natural than KBP3-PK4.

(b) 8 ... BxB could be answered by 9 N-B7! (he has to lose the Knight anyway) 9 ... KxN 10 NxB and White has succeeded in displacing the Black King; or 9 ... Q-Q2? 10 NxPch! PxN 11 Q-R5ch followed by 12 QxB, and White has won a Pawn.

9 B-QB4

White places his Bishop on the important diagonal which has been opened. Given Black's restricted position and White's open lines, there should be something in the position for White.

9 ...   Q-B1

Black plans to neutralize White's control of the dangerous diagonal by ... B-K3—an excellent idea.

10 Q-B3

Developing the Queen and threatening 11 Q-B7ch.

To be considered is: 10 Q-R5ch P-N3 11 Q-B3 B-K3 12 Q-B6, but then 12 ... BxB 13 QxR BxR with equality.

10 ...   B-K3

Certainly, this is the only way to stop White's attack.

11 BxB

The alternates 11 B-K2 or 11 B-N3 would lose a tempo for White and leave the Black Bishop in a place which is not inferior to that of the White Bishop.

11 ...   QxB

One may well ask at this point, "Now that Black has succeeded in cutting down White's attack through neutralization, what does White have? Wherein does his advantage lie?"

Actually, White has only a little more than equality here: namely, his advantage in development and a Bishop which is slightly more mobile. The fact that Black's inferiority is so slight is due to the following conditions: (a) Black has built up a solid defensive position; (b) Black was able to neutralize White's attack; (c) Black really has no Pawn weaknesses.

Under those conditions, not even a master can get an advantage over a coffeehouse player. To a certain extent, he must wait for a weak move or an error.

12 N-Q5

Why does White play the already developed Knight when his QB and his QR are still undeveloped? He wishes to force the following exchange, after which the White QP will press against the Black position and will divide the Black camp into two parts between which communication will be difficult. Moreover, White's K4-square will then become free for a piece.

12 ...   NxN

Practically forced. After 12 ... 0-0-0 13 B-N5 R-K1 14 Q-QN3 (threatening 15 N-N6ch, winning the Queen) 14 ... NxN 15 PxN, and thus ... NxN is forced anyway.

13 PxN

At this point, the position is slightly in favor of White, for Black has an open K-wing and a vulnerable Q-wing, which are potential weaknesses. As already noted, the communication between the Black K- and Q-wing is made difficult by this Pawn. However, this need not play too great a part, because too few pieces are left on the board.

13 ...   **Q-N3?**

The decisive error!

Black should have played 13 ... Q-Q2. Then the game might have continued 14 Q-K4 B-K2 (better than 14 ... 0-0-0 15 B-K3 and White might try to start an attack against the Black King, which is motivated by the pressure of White's QP and is certainly not without chances) 15 B-Q2 0-0 16 QR-K1 Q-B4 and White is only a little better off—he has the Good Bishop and possession of his K4-square—17 QxQ RxQ 18 R-K4 QR-KB1 19 P-KB3. The White Rook can go to either side of the board. This does not mean much because of the reduced material.

14 Q-QN3

127

Protecting his QBP and attacking Black's QNP. This forces Black to make some sort of disadvantageous or weakening move.

14 ...   P-N3

As a result of this move, Black now has a disadvantageous Pawn position in which he opens diagonals for White. Let us look at the alternatives.

(a) 14 ... 0-0-0 15 B-K3 K-N1 16 Q-R4 P-QR3 17 P-QN4 with a strong attack or 16 ... P-N3 17 Q-R6, followed by 18 P-QR4. (17 ... QxP makes things worse.)

(b) 14 ... R-QN1 15 Q-R4ch and 16 QxP.

Now that Black has created the weakness, White has a right to play for a bigger advantage. He starts by wrecking Black's K-position and castling possibilities.

15 Q-N5ch   K-B2

Black visualizes 16 Q-Q7ch B-K2 17 QxBP KR-QB1, with full development.

If 15 ... K-K2, which is a poor move because it blocks the Bishop, 16 Q-B6, etc.

16 P-KB4

White first makes this move, opening lines for attack, in order to prepare for Q-Q7ch.

16 ...   PxP

The alternatives are equally bad.

(a) 16 ... K-N1? 17 PxP PxP 18 P-Q6, threatening Q-Q5ch or Q-B4ch or Q-N3ch.

(b) 16 ... QxP? 17 Q-Q7ch B-K2 18 PxP dis ch K-N1 19 Q-K6 mate.

(c) 16 ... P-K5 17 P-B5 Q-B3 18 Q-B4 Q-K2 19 B-K3, after which Black's development has not improved and White can prepare the deciding blow at his leisure: e.g., R-B4, QR-KB1, P-B6.

17 Q-Q7ch

White makes this in-between move in order to immobilize the Black Bishop.

17 ...   **K-N1**

For 17 ... B-K2 loses the Bishop after 18 RxPch.

18 RxP   **P-KR3**

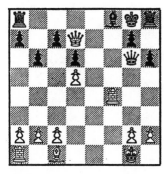

In view of the immobile position of the Black King, it is wise to create a flight square. For instance, if 18 ... QxP?? 19 Q-K6 mate.

19 B-Q2

To increase pressure against Black's KN2 by B-B3.

19 ...   **QxP?**

Don't go Pawn hunting when your house is on fire!

A better move would be 19 ... K-R2, after which White continues the attack by 20 QR-KB1.

20 B-B3

The pressure is building up.

20 ...   **Q-N3**

21 QR-KB1

White now threatens 22 R-KN4, and the Queen must give up the protection of its KN2. On the other hand, 21 R-KN4 at once would be met by the neutralizing 21 ... Q-B2.

21 ...   K-R2

Black overlooks the threat, but even so there is nothing better.

22 R-KN4   Q-K1

Hoping to neutralize by an exchange of Queens. But White's pressure is too overwhelming.

23 QxPch

23 RxPch is also sufficient.

23 ...   BxQ

24 RxB mate.

Game 13

The nature of fianchetto play

The importance of Black's having influence in the center

     when playing the fianchetto

The wing attack (P-KR4-KR5) against the fianchetto

The demolishing of a weakened Pawn position by sacrifice

The development of the NP on either side to its third square is the beginning of a maneuver known as a fianchetto, that is, a flank development. Usually the N2-square is then occupied by the Bishop, which exercises considerable pressure along the whole diagonal and particularly on the center squares which form a part of the diagonal.

Around 1940 chess masters considered this fianchetto as insufficient to obtain equality *unless* the Black player first took measures to prevent White from obtaining full superiority in the center.

The approved method of playing a fianchetto then was, for instance, 1 P-Q4 N-KB3 (preventing 2 P-K4) 2 P-QB4 and now 2 ... P-KN3, or, on the other side, 1 P-Q4 N-KB3 2 N-KB3 P-QN3. The Black player feared 1 P-Q4 N-KB3 2 P-QB4 P-QN3? on account of 3 N-QB3 B-N2 4 P-B3, followed by 5 P-K4.

On the other hand, the Black player did not fear 1 P-Q4 N-KB3 2 P-QB4 P-KN3 3 N-QB3 B-N2 4 P-K4, because he was convinced that he could obtain counterchances in the center by 4 ... P-Q3 and later by ... P-QB4 or ... P-K4.

Thus, the ability to decide when an opponent's center must be considered unassailable and when it is not so strong that it cannot be destroyed or neutralized is, in the eyes of a master, a matter of experience in practical games. The master concludes from his own games and those of other masters that in some cases he can permit his opponent a strong center, and in other cases he cannot.

Lately, some relatively unknown players have been playing the fianchetto without first taking the precaution of preventing White from taking complete possession of the center, and, strangely enough, their White opponents could not refute their play in a convincing manner.

Today, the situation is not clear. It appears that Black can play the fianchetto immediately, but he must be sure that he has counterplay in the center at the right time and in the right way.

In both of the following games, Black, the amateur, plays the immediate fianchetto, but in Game 13 he plays the fianchetto at random, without attempting to exert any influence in the center, whereas in Game 14 he tries to bring some influence to bear in the center.

It is a principle of chess established by Steinitz that once the center has become stabilized and is secure, a player can safely and profitably start a flank attack. The fianchetto, with its protruding PN3, is particularly vulnerable to an attack by his opponent's P-R4-R5. Such an attack is stronger when the attacking side is ahead in development, for that player can then hurl everything he has against the points weakened by his flank attack.

The Double Fianchetto

Master	Amateur
1 P-Q4	P-QN3
2 P-K4	

When Black plays an immediate fianchetto, it is customary for White to take complete possession of the center by occupying it with two center Pawns, the KP and QP.

2 ...	B-N2

White is now obliged to protect his attacked KP, so he plays

3 N-Q2

Compare this method of protecting the PK4 with that offered by 3 N-QB3. With the text (a) the QBP conserves freedom of movement; (b) the QN cannot be pinned by ... B-QN5; (c) on Q2 the QN can hope to participate in a K-side attack eventually; for the Knight on QB3 there is less chance; (d) but the QN on Q2 temporarily blocks the Queen and QB; (e) White's QP is temporarily unprotected; and (f) White's QN does not exert pressure on the center square Q5.

The development of the QN to Q2 is found in several openings, such as the Colle system of the QP opening and in the Tarrasch variation of the French Defense.

White could also have protected his KP by 3 B-Q3, but it is an old of precept of Lasker that it is preferable to develop Knights before Bishops. The reason for this is that the best square for the Bishop depends largely on what the opponent's center formation will be. So one should wait with his Bishop until the opponent has shown his "cards," that is, his center formation.

3 ...   P-N3 (?)

A fianchetto at random—without special reason. Black plays his fianchetto without any plan in mind, simply says: "Well, we'll fianchetto on the other side as well."

Amateurs, especially those who have not studied master games, frequently use this double fianchetto in the belief that the Bishops exert tremendous pressure along their diagonals. This they do, but it must be noted that the fianchettoed Bishops are hampered by the White center Pawns and that these Bishops can exert their full strength only if the Black Pawns are able to make holes in the White center or to neutralize it. For instance, if Black at a given moment plays ... P-QB4 followed by ... BxQP, this exchange improves the scope of the fianchettoed KB considerably.

At this point, therefore, 3 ... P-N3 must be considered a slight error, as it leaves White too much freedom in the center. Instead, Black might have played 3 ... P-QB4 simply to exert a bit of pressure against the center. If then 4 P-Q5 P-K3, etc.

4 KN-B3   **B-N2**

5 P-B3

This move is not necessary at this point, but it is perfectly good. It has the following purposes: (a) it strengthens the PQ4; (b) it forms a protective bulwark on the Black KB diagonal after the White QP is removed; (c) it opens a diagonal for the White Queen to develop to QB2 or QN3; (d) it affords to the KB, which will be developed to QB4, the possibility, if its activity on QB4 should be hampered in one way or another, of going via QN3 or Q3 to QB2, on the one hand preventing it from being trapped (as it can be in many variations of the Ruy López), on the other protecting White's KP from its QB2.

White might equally well have played 5 B-B4 first and later on P-B3.

White now has a strong center; Black has only his Two Bishops developed on the flank, and he sees that 5 ... N-KB3 could be answered by 6 P-K5. Some influence in the center seems to be necessary. He therefore plays

5 ...   **P-Q3**

This type of move, the purpose of which is to prevent the opponent from pushing his center Pawns into a pawnless center and preparing a counterpush ... P-QB4 or ... P-K4, is a common way of meeting this sort of situation, not only in openings where Black fianchettoes immediately, but in certain other openings where Black deliberately allows White to set up a Pawn center, so that he can later destroy it. It is found in the Alekhine Defense, among others.

In this particular game, 5 ... P-Q3 leads to the Black Pawn formation QR2-QN3-QB2-Q3, creating holes in the Black position (compare Game 3). Such a formation is bad in general, although White cannot take advantage of it at the moment. But, after the exchange of the White Bishops on both sides, the holes created could become a serious weakness.

6 B-B4

This is the square on which to develop the KB, first because it brings pressure to bear on the relatively weak Black Pawn at Black's KB2, second because White's KB would be passive at its K2 and relatively inactive at its Q3 because of Black's K-side Pawn formation.

Moreover, in case Black should decide to play ... P-K4, White would maintain a fine diagonal for his Bishop.

6 ...   P-K3

Black neutralizes White's activity along the diagonal in the simplest way, thereby creating new holes in his K-side Pawn formation KR2-KN3-KB2-K3.

Note the complications after 6 ... N-Q2 7 BxPch KxB 8 N-N5ch K-K1 9 N-K6 Q-B1 10 NxBch K-B2. The advisability of allowing this combination is doubtful: 11 N-R5 PxN 12 QxPch. It shows the vulnerability of Black's King position as a consequence of the fianchetto. Note further that 6 ... KN-B3 could still be met by 7 P-K5.

If 6 ... P-K4, White continues his attack by 7 P-KR4 as in the game, and the fact that the diagonal QB4-KB7 is opened for the White Bishop certainly means a strengthening of White's attack.

A glance at the board will show that White now has complete control of the center and that Black cannot alter this situation in the next few moves. White therefore is now ready to undertake a flank attack. Flank attacks are an important part of chess strategy, but they should be undertaken only when the center is stabilized.

7 P-KR4

One of the popular attacks against the fianchetto, based on the vulnerability of Black's K-side Pawn position. This type of attack is certainly stronger when Black has already castled, but even here it is effective, the more so since Black fails to reply with ... P-KR4.

By playing 7 P-KR4, White wants Black to decide whether or not to permit P-KR5. The development of White's forces depends on this decision and will be quite different in one case from the development in the other.

If Black meets the attack by 7 ... P-KR4, it means a further weakening of the Black K-wing, both of his PKN3 and of his KN4-square, as we shall soon show. Still, 7 ... P-KR4 would have been the lesser evil for Black.

Another quieter plan at this point would have been 7 0-0 8 R-K1 9 N-B1, etc.

7 ...   **P-Q4**

To drive back the White Bishop. 7 ... P-KR4 now or on the next move would be better, because it prevents White's P-R5.

8 B-Q3

Note that in general 8 B-Q3 is better than 8 PxP, since if White takes, the center is even; if Black takes, White maintains his superiority in the center by 8 . . . PxP 9 NxP. We have already learned that one should aim at maintaining the tension in the center as long as possible, if one has greater influence and space there.

8 . . .   N-KB3

Black makes this move, which permits 9 P-K5, because his Knight can then go to K5. The best move is still 8 . . . P-KR4.

8 . . . PxP 9 NxP would give White the possibility of continuing with 10 B-KN5, thus taking advantage of the holes in the Black position.

9 P-K5   N-K5
10 Q-B2

The additional pressure of a third piece forces Black to simplify, which entails the liquidation of White's K4-square.

10 . . .   NxN

If 10 . . . P-KB4 11 PxP e.p. NxP, followed by 12 P-R5 or N-K5 or even BxPch.

11 BxN

At this point, it is already too late for Black to try to prevent White's threatened 12 P-R5 by 11 . . . P-KR4, for then 12 BxP

PxB 13 QxPch K-B1 14 N-N5 Q-K2 (14 ... Q-K1 15 NxPch) 15 NxPch K-N1 16 R-R3 Q-B2 17 QxQch KxQ 18 NxP and White has for his piece four Pawns plus the exchange still to come. From this variation can be seen what the weakening of Black's KN3 means.

Therefore, he plays

11 ...   **N-Q2**

Now comes the crucial move of White's strategy, the long-expected

12 P-R5!

Black is now in an awkward situation, for:

(a) 12 ... N-B1 13 P-R6, winning the Bishop.

(b) 12 ... Q-K2 13 P-R6 B-KB1 14 B-KN5 P-B3 15 PxP NxP 16 BxPch PxB 17 QxPch, etc., winning back the piece with a couple of Pawns.

(c) 12 ... 0-0, and Black castles into a storm of oncoming Pawns: 13 PxP RPxP 14 BxP PxB 15 QxP and White's attack is decisive: (1) 15 ... Q-K2 16 N-N5, or (2) 15 ... Q-K1 16 Q-R7ch.

The importance of White's flank attack by P-KR4-KR5 now becomes clear. It threatens 13 PxP, after which Black's KNP is protected only once and therefore open to a sacrificial attack by BxP.

Were Black's Pawn still on its KR2, Black's KNP would still be protected by his BP and RP and the sacrificial attack by BxP would not work. You cannot sacrifice a piece against a doubly protected Pawn.

12 ...   **P-QB4**

Since Black has no good defensive moves, he has to find some counterattack.

13 B-KN5

Bringing more force in such a way that Black must move his Queen out of danger before he can pursue his counterattack. White could also have played 13 PxNP immediately. The text is just a transposition of moves.

13 ...   **Q-B2**

13 ... P-B3 costs a Pawn or more: (a) 14 KPxP BxP 15 BxB and 16 PxNP; or even (b) 14 BxNPch PxB 15 QxPch K-B1 16 P-R6 BxP (forced) 17 BxBch RxB (forced, for 17 ... K-K2 18 Q-N7ch) 18 QxRch and mate in a few moves.

14 PxNP   **RPxP**

After 14 ... KBPxP, there follows a typical *"petite combinaison":* 15 RxP RxR 16 BxPch, winning back the Rook with two extra Pawns.

15 RxRch   **BxR**

Let us stop to examine the position here. We note that, although the material is equal, (a) all the Black pieces are ineffective; (b) the Black K-side Pawn formation is weakened to the point where Black's KNP is protected by only one Pawn; (c) the White QB controls the Black squares of an important diagonal, thereby shutting the King from flight; (d) the White Queen and KB are on the same diagonal, poised for action; (e) as a consequence of the fianchetto of Black's QB, the Black KP could become weak (as will be shown later).

How could White amass this accumulation of power and so effectively paralyze Black? First of all, Black's fianchetto of the QB lost him two moves; second, he permitted White to weaken his K-side by P-KR4-KR5.

White's accumulation of power is imposing, yet his advantage could disappear if he allowed Black to catch up in development, or, through a series of exchanges, to come to an end game. Taking all elements into account, a sacrifice must be in the making.

16 BxP!

Black cannot afford to accept the sacrifice, for 16 ... PxB 17 QxPch K-B1 18 B-R6ch K-K2 19 Q-R7ch, winning the Bishop. So he plays:

16 ...   **PxP**

Best here would have been 17 ... N-B1. White continues 18 B-R5 PxP 19 Q-R4ch B-B3 19 QxQP, and (1) White has a sound Pawn plus; (2) Black is prevented from castling; (3) *but* there is no mating attack.

17 BxPch!

You won't take me? You must!

17 ...   **KxB**

The strength of White's position lies in the fact that White's three pieces—Queen, Knight, and Bishop—are all highly mobile and that his PK5, a spearhead Pawn, exercises a powerful restraining influence on whatever Black does, whereas Black's King is out in the open and none of his pieces is placed so that it can do anything. The situation is the consequence of the accumulation of force on the part of White.

The White PK5, the spearhead Pawn, is very powerful under these circumstances, since it prevents the King from escaping. This KP would not live long under normal circumstances—it is attacked three times, defended once—but here circumstances are *not* normal.

18 Q-R7ch	**B-N2**
19 B-R6	**R-KN1**

The only move.

White is down a piece, but all his remaining pieces except the Rook are in action, whereas Black's pieces are passive.

20 N-N5ch	**K-K2**

Forced, for if 20 ... K-B1 21 NxPch, winning the Queen.

Too bad. Since the QB was fianchettoed, Black's KP is no longer guarded and must therefore be protected.

21 BxB

Now the Bishop protects White's valuable spearhead KP and threatens the deadly double check 22 B-B6 db ch, etc.

Note that a move like 21 QxR would lead to 21 ... QxPch
22 K-B1 BxB, and a win by White is very doubtful.

| 21 ... | RxB |
| 22 QxRch | |

White now has the exchange and, a very important factor in an
attack, the initiative. The naked King is defenseless against the
combined attack of Queen and Knight.

| 22 ... | K-K1 |

Postponement of execution. Forced because of White's threat
of NxP.

23 Q-B7ch	K-Q1
24 NxPch	K-B1
25 Q-K8ch	

White prefers giving mate to winning the Queen immediately.

| 25 ... | Q-Q1 |
| 26 QxQ mate | |

Game 14

There is no problem more vital in chess than how to develop a win from an approximately equal opening position. What is the proper procedure? Often, amateurs simply play along, hoping that the opponent will make a mistake on which they can capitalize. The idea is sound—that is what the master does, too—but with several fundamental differences. First of all, the master is much quicker to recognize even a small mistake, and, in the second place, he is much more skilful in taking advantage of it. Moreover, as the game proceeds, the master plans his strategy to suit the requirements of the ever-changing position.

Most chess games pass through a series of strategic phases. Each phase emerges as a result of the preceding phase. In each phase, a player may have a different aim, and, once that aim is attained, he then turns to the next phase of the game.

This game is a marvelous example of how to develop a win through strategic planning in a series of successive phases of a game. Black plays a K-side fianchetto. He is mindful of the necessity of acquiring some influence in the center, but he chooses the wrong way. His error is almost imperceptible, but because of it White gains in development and, through a series of successive

143

stages of different types of strategy, pushes on to a win. The strategic phases are so clear-cut that they can be outlined by moves:

(a) Moves 5-9: White wins tempi and forces Black to weaken his position.

(b) Moves 10-11: White builds up his attack against Black's QP.

(c) Move 12: White completes the building-up of an accumulation of power against Black's KP.

(d) Moves 13-15: White undertakes a sacrificial attack against Black's KP.

(e) Moves 16-23: White liquidates the situation in such a way as to emerge with four Pawns plus the initiative in return for his sacrificed piece.

(f) Moves 24-27: Through a series of checks which keep Black from developing his pieces, White brings his Queen into a more favorable position.

(g) Moves 28-31: Through a series of Knight maneuvers, White wins the Black Bishop.

(h) Moves 32-33: With equality of pieces and an overwhelming Pawn majority, White forces the exchange of Queens.

The King-side Fianchetto

Master	Amateur
1 P-Q4	P-KN3

This time Black starts with a fianchetto on the K-side.

In general, the K-side fianchetto has more promise than the Q-side fianchetto, because the helping move ... P-QB4 can be played in conjunction with the K-side fianchetto, whereas the helping move ... P-KB4, which would be played in conjunction with the Q-side fianchetto, is much less likely, since it would constitute a serious weakening.

2 P-K4	B-N2
3 N-KB3	

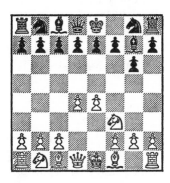

This is just a developing move, but it is one which controls important center squares.

White does not play 3 N-QB3, because he wishes to maintain the possibility of playing P-QB3.

He does not play 3 B-K3, because Black could answer 3 ... P-QB4 4 P-QB3 Q-N3 with *counterchances,* e.g., 5 Q-Q2 P-Q3 6 N-B3 N-KB3, and White has several difficulties—protecting his PK4, preventing ... N-KN5 with the exchange of his QB, which has been brought into play too early in the game—and White is a bit on the defensive.

By counterchances, we mean giving the opponent an opportunity to seize initiative. One seeks the line which will give one's opponent the least opportunity to become active. Compare the above variant 3 B-K3 with the game itself, where Black does not get this opportunity.

3 ...   P-Q3

As pointed out under Black's 5th move of Game 13, it is of importance for Black to have some influence in the center in order to be ready to execute a counteraction at a given moment.

Note that in the present game ... P-Q3 comes two moves earlier

145

than it did in Game 13 and that it creates no holes in the Black position.

If, instead of 3 ... P-Q3, Black tried to bring out a Knight at this point, he would lose time. Such a move illustrates the danger of having no Pawn center. For instance, 3 ... N-KB3 4 P-K5 or 3 ... N-QB3 4 P-Q5. At this point, it is impossible for Black to maintain the Knights in the center.

If, after 3 ... P-Q3, the game should now continue 4 P-QB4 N-KB3 5 N-B3, we would have a regular King's Indian. But White plays

4 B-QB4

White continues his development in a logical way, by bringing out pieces and at the same time controlling the center, but he does not worry too much about preventing Black from building up his center.

According to the general principles of King-fianchetto play, Black should now try to get a foothold in the center either by ... P-K4 or by ... P-QB4. But, unfortunately, neither of these two moves is satisfactory at this point.

(a) 4 ... P-QB4 has its drawbacks, as will be shown in this game.

(b) After 4 ... P-K4? 5 PxP PxP 6 BxPch K-K2, White has won a Pawn and disrupted the Black position. If Black should try to prepare ... P-K4 by 4 ... N-Q2, then 5 BxPch KxB 6 N-N5ch and wins as follows: (1) 6 ... K-K1 7 N-K6 wins the Queen; (2) 6 ... K-B1 7 N-K6ch wins the Queen; (3) 6 ... K-B3 7 Q-B3 mate.

From these two tries, it is clear that Black cannot gain control of the center and obtain counterchances by ... P-K4 at this point.

But Black must somehow find counterchances in the center. The best he can do is either 4 ... P-QB3 or 4 ... P-K3, followed by 5 ... P-Q4 to neutralize the effect of White's KB.

The neutralizing process usually means that equality is attained in the center and that an inferiority in command of space has been remedied. That is why White will try to avoid the exchange of Pawns in the event that a Black Pawn appears on its fourth rank.

Let us go through the moves of the neutralizing process:

4 ... P-K3 5 0-0 P-Q4

(a) 6 PxP PxP 7 B-N3, at which point the center is neutralized, but White has won a tempo and disposes of possibilities of exploiting the open K-file.

(b) 6 B-Q3, which may be still stronger: 6 ... PxP 7 BxP N-KB3 8 B-Q3 0-0 9 B-KN5, at which point the center is not neutralized and White rather maintains superiority in space, since he has a Pawn on his 4th rank against Black's Pawn on his 3rd rank.

4 ...   P-QB4?

The mistake! Black attempts to neutralize the center in another way, but this, too, is unsuccessful. Here White outplays Black strategically, not tactically, as he does in the case of 4 ... P-K4 and 4 ... N-Q2.

5 PxP

An important strategic decision! White gives up the center in order to accelerate the development of his pieces.

After considering Black's principal replies (5 ... PxP and

5 ... Q-R4ch), White decides that he will have the better of it, no matter which way Black replies.

Moreover, the alternatives are not promising for White. After 5 P-B3, Black will neutralize in the long run: 5 ... PxP 6 PxP P-K3, followed by, say, 7 N-B3 N-K2 8 0-0 P-Q4, and after (a) 9 B-Q3 PxP, White has an isolated QP; (b) 9 PxP PxP, both players have an isolated QP, so that White has the more reason to exchange by 5 PxP in order to avoid coming out with an isolated Pawn.

5 ...   Q-R4ch

If Black had replied 5 ... PxP? then 6 BxPch, winning the Queen. This would be a tactical refutation of 4 ... P-QB4. Instead, Black plans to win back his Pawn by checking the White King and then retaking on his QB4. That is the point of Black's whole setup.

6 P-B3

As a general rule, it is better to make a move which develops a piece than to move a Pawn, but in this specific case the Pawn move opens the diagonal for White's Queen, and presently we shall see what this will mean. General principles may be violated when there are specific reasons.

6 ...   QxP/B4

Now Black has attained his goal—the elimination of one of White's center Pawns. But in exchange White has a still more important advantage which is of immediate value—advance in development. Let us see how he uses it.

Black could have answered 6 ... PxP, but after 7 0-0, look at Black's development and the lack of cooperation of his pieces. His Queen is quite out of the game.

7 Q-N3

The first consequence of the strategic decision taken with 5 PxP. This is a move with a threat. It protects White's KB and forces Black to protect his KBP, so that White can win an extra tempo by 8 B-K3.

7 ...   P-K3

The only reply, and it has the disadvantage of weakening Black's QP. To make a move which forces the opponent to reply by a weakening move is the very essence of positional play. Moreover, again there are holes in Black's position. Compare Game 13.

8 B-K3

The second step in White's strategy. This move not only develops the White QB to a square where it controls two important diagonals, but, by forcing Black to move his Queen, it gains a tempo for White.

8 ...   Q-B2

9 N-R3

An aggressive move which continues the attack. This is the third step in White's strategy.

Normally, Knights should be developed toward the center, where the number of squares they control is the greatest. Here, however, the flank development of the Knight is justified because it threatens 10 N-QN5 with several attacking possibilities.

If Black should answer 9 N-R3 by 9 ... P-QR3, White would block Black's Q-side completely by 10 B-N6. Black therefore continues:

9 ...   B-Q2

Up to now, White's strategy has been to win tempi and force Black to weaken his position. The game now enters a new phase during which White's strategy will be the exploitation of the newly created weakness—the Black QP.

An important consideration here is the order of moves. For instance, 10 0-0-0 looks very strong, stronger than the text, but after 10 ... N-KB3 11 B-B4 NxP 12 KR-K1 P-B4, it is difficult to find a sharp continuation. Therefore, White plays

10 B-B4

The move is contrary to the rule not to play the same piece twice in the opening, but here this procedure is justified because White is following a sharply outlined plan: attack on Black's weak QP. Moreover, Black's Queen is now on a diagonal with an enemy Bishop, and, as already pointed out, this always portends danger, even though the Queen is separated from the enemy Bishop by Pawns or pieces of either color.

10 ...   **N-K2**

Now 10 ... N-KB3 would elicit the strong reply 11 P-K5 PxP 12 QBxP. Besides, 10 ... P-K4 is impossible because of 11 BxPch.

11 0-0-0   **N-B1**

The Knight is available just in time to protect the attacked QP, but Black's pieces are not being developed.

12 N-Q4

Another tactical detail of the general strategy. White now threatens (a) 13 KN-N5 and the winning of the QP, and (b) 13 NxP, a sacrifice in order to get an attack on the uncastled Black King.

Note that instead of playing 12 N-N5 immediately, White first brings up his KN so as to be able to answer ... BxN by NxB, thus continuing the threat to the Black QP. The attacking player must not give the defender the opportunity to exchange the important attacking pieces.

150

If Black now plays

(a) 12 ... BxN, then 13 RxB P-K4? 14 BxPch K-B1 15 B-R6ch, etc., giving White a Pawn and the attack. Although 13 ... P-K4 was not immediately necessary, it seemed to be dangerous for White, and therefore it should be considered. Without ... P-K4, Black has exchanged his strong Bishop for nothing.

(b) 12 ... 0-0 13 KN-N5 BxN 14 NxB, winning at least a Pawn.

(c) 12 ... P-K4 13 BxPch K-B1 (13 ... K-K2 14 B-N5ch) 14 N-K6ch BxN 15 QxB (threatening mate) 15 ... QxB 16 QxNch, with material advantage to White.

So Black decides to prevent the threat to his QP, but that is even worse than the above alternatives.

12 ...   P-QR3

Let us now stop to look at the position. White has six pieces developed actively; Black has three developed, at the most. White has complete control of the center; Black controls only one long diagonal. White has castled, bringing his QR into the active conflict; Black has not yet castled, and his Rooks and Knights are all relegated to the back row. The Black King is still in the center. After only twelve moves, White has his pieces attacking Black's QP and KP directly and Black's King and Queen behind them indirectly.

White's strategy has led to a tremendous concentration of power. His pieces penetrate into the very heart of the Black position. With such a concentration of power, a combination *must* exist for White.

The fact that White can decide the game by a sacrifice is not accidental. Whenever the difference in development between the two sides exists, the side which has the development must look for a combination, especially when the King of the opposing side is not yet castled. In such positions, the indicated procedure is to try to sacrifice material in order to open the position and expose the enemy King to the direct attack of one's pieces.

Even with such a majority as White has in this position, it is difficult to find a forced win. White has to play very carefully and exactly. This makes chess so difficult and at the same time so attractive.

But either you make the sacrifice and of necessity find the right moves to follow up, or you neglect your opportunity and never get it again.

13 BxKP

13 NxKP would be inadequate, because after 13 ... PxN 14 BxKP, Black need not recapture on his K3.

13 ...	PxB
14 NxP	**BxN**

What else is there to do? The White Knight was threatening the Queen and Bishop simultaneously.

15 QxBch	**K-B1**

Or (a) 15 ... Q-K2 16 QxNch, etc.; (b) 15 ... K-Q1 16 RxPch! NxR 17 B-N5ch, etc.; (c) 15 ... N-K2 16 N-B4! K-B1 (otherwise NxPch, etc.) 17 NxP.

16 RxP

16 BxPch would give up the attack but still maintain three Pawns for the piece with good chances.

16 ...	N-B3

For if 16 ... NxR 17 BxNch, winning the Queen.

17 KR-Q1

Notice that White could not move his QR from its square because of ... QxBch. But now he is threatening 18 R-Q8ch.

White should consider 17 P-KN3 (protecting the Bishop and threatening 18 R-Q7), but this could be answered by 17 ... N-Q1! 18 Q-Q5 N-K2.

17 ...	Q-K2
18 RxN!	

Other moves are less convincing—they involve the exchange of Queens and lead to an ending in which White has three Pawns for a piece, which might win—but this is not at all certain.

18 ...	PxR
19 QxBP	

White now has four Pawns and the initiative to compensate for his temporarily sacrificed Rook. Without the initiative, even four Pawns would not be sufficient, for practice has shown that if Black should succeed in exchanging Queens, he would have the better ending.

19 ...	Q-B3

What else? If 19 ... Q-R2 20 R-Q8ch wins.

20 QxR	QxBch
21 K-N1	Q-QB2

21 ... K-B2 is no better for Black: 22 R-Q7ch N-K2 (22 ...
K-K3? 23 Q-Q5ch, or 22 ... K-B3 23 QxPch followed by 24 RxB)
23 Q-Q5ch wins.

White now has four Pawns, a fifth Pawn to take, and the
initiative in return for his Bishop. Let us see how he uses them.

22 QxP   K-K2

To bring his Rook into the game and to prevent 23 Q-K6 followed by 24 R-Q7. White finally brings his Knight into play—
with tempo.

23 N-N5   Q-N3

Considering the large number of White passed Pawns, exchange is hardly indicated but is still the best chance, since the
Black King is very unsafe as long as the White Queen is on the
board.

If White should now exchange 24 QxQ NxQ, he might win by
25 P-QN3, followed by the advance of Pawns on the Q-side
(26 P-QR4, etc.). But, since his win will be easier with Queens
on the board, he avoids the exchange. With his next move, he
brings his Queen nearer and into a more favorable position by a
series of checks—a typical example of "step-check." The technique
is frequent in problems.

24 Q-R3ch   K-K3

154

After 24 ... K-B3, the continuation is difficult, but 25 P-K5ch entices the King into the open field. After 25 ... KxP 26 P-QB4! and White threatens, for example, 27 Q-B3ch.

25 Q-N3ch   **K-K2**

After 25 ... K-B3, the same type of continuation as in the previous note.

26 Q-N4ch   **K-K3**

If 26 ... K-B2 27 R-Q7ch.

27 Q-B4ch   **K-K2**
28 N-B7

Threatening to win the Queen by 29 N-Q5ch.

28 ...   **R-Q1**
29 RxR

To win the Bishop. Or he could have won the exchange by 29 N-Q5ch RxN 30 RxR.

29 ...   **KxR**
30 N-K6ch   **K-Q2**
31 NxB   **QxP**

The only try—to disturb the quiet of the White King.

32 Q-Q4ch

Forcing the exchange of Queens. White could have played, for instance, 32 Q-K6ch, but at this point, where White's Pawn majority is overwhelming and White has already regained his piece, the simplest course is to exchange Queens and advance the Pawns.

32 ...   **QxQ**
33 PxQ   **K-K2**

Black's last hope—to win the Knight by ... K-B2.

34 P-Q5

To allow the Knight to escape via K6.

34 ...   Resigns

Game 15

In a given position, the evaluation of the relative strength of the two sides in the various aspects of chess power can be only approximate. Even the comparison of material strength by counting pieces may be rough. But counting tempi, as we do to arrive at a measure of development, is a very rough means of measure, which can vary from valuable to worthless.

In many of the preceding games, we have emphasized the importance of an advance in tempo. Yet tempo is not an absolute quantity. The tempo has different values:

(a) In wild positions, it may be decisive.

(b) In open positions, it is generally worthwhile.

(c) In closed positions, it doesn't mean much.

(d) In very closed positions, it doesn't mean anything.

(e) In the ending, it may mean the difference between a win and a loss in either direction (i.e., a tempo may even lose the game).

In the present game, tempo figures in a very peculiar way because White's Bishops require two moves to develop to their most effective squares. We speak of White's winning two tempi because twice in the opening a White Knight is developed with an attack on the Black Queen. But if we examine the position after Black's 10th move, it appears that White's two tempi consist in White's Bishops moving to their K2 and Q2. Are these Bishop moves half-moves or no moves at all? White's Bishops have to make another move to get to their most effective squares (in this case KN5 and QN5). If then, as in this game, one first plays B-K2 and then later the same Bishop B-QN5, can we say this counts as only one move? Sometimes no, sometimes yes.

There are two aspects to such moves: (a) Generally, one cannot know at the outset of the game which is the best square for the Bishop—it depends on the course of the game. Therefore, B-K2 is a kind of waiting move. But (b) B-K2 is a developing move even if the Bishop does not do any work at K2, because by playing B-K2, castling and the development of the KR become possible. All this we find in this game.

Summarizing the question of tempi in the game:

(a) The Black Queen comes out very early.

(b) This gives White the opportunity to develop with tempo (N-QB3, N-KB3, R-K1).

(c) On the other hand, Black's threats with his Queen force White to "half" development (B-K2, B-Q2).

(d) The final balance, however, is a slight plus for White, which gradually increases to an important advantage.

This process is characteristic in chess: an advantage increases if you use it well. In this game, B-KN5 and B-QN5 leads to simplification and an ending where Black has a pair of double isolated Pawns.

The Center Counter Game

Master	Amateur
1 P-K4	P-Q4

Not content to play toward equality slowly, Black immediately contests White's possession of the center and opens a file for the development of his pieces.

This opening, the Center Counter Game, is theoretically weaker than the Sicilian or the French Defense, because after 2 PxP QxP 3 N-QB3, White wins an important tempo for development in an opening where an extra tempo counts. Also to be considered is the fact that in the Sicilian and the French the building up of the center is different in character for White and for Black, which means that each side has specific chances. In the Center Counter Game, on the other hand, the situation is equivalent—the White KP and the Black QP have disappeared, which means that Black could hardly have chances which White would not have all the more so. The only factor in favor of Black in this opening is a tactical circumstance: the Black Queen could be dangerous—but only if White plays carelessly.

2 PxP

White normally exchanges at this point, for, as will be seen, he thereby gets a slight advantage, no matter how Black answers.

If, instead of exchanging, he continues 2 P-K5, White loses a tempo rather than gaining one, and after 2 ... B-B4 3 P-Q4 P-K3 Black has a kind of French Defense in which the QB is better placed than it usually is. He continues with ... P-B4 and ... N-QB3 and has a marvelous game.

2 P-Q4 leads to the Blackmar Gambit, which is doubtful but full of possibilities. The Blackmar Gambit is more commonly reached by 1 P-Q4 P-Q4 2 P-K4.

2 ...   QxP

This move would be fine if the Queen could maintain herself in the center of the board. But she is too vulnerable to attack. Time will be wasted getting her out of danger, and during this time White will develop pieces.

Also played here—and a little better—is 2 ... N-KB3, the Scandinavian line, in which White also succeeds in coming out somewhat better than Black after 3 P-Q4 NxP. At this point, White can make Black lose a tempo and gain an excellent center for himself by 4 P-QB4 N-N3 5 N-QB3, or he can continue

4 N-KB3 B-N5 5 B-K2 P-K3 6 0-0, reserving P-QB4 for later. If, however, after 2 ... N-KB3, White plays 3 P-QB4, trying to hold on to the gambit Pawn, then 3 ... P-B3 4 PxP NxP appears to give Black better development, which might compensate for White's plus Pawn. Finally, White, after 3 P-QB4 P-QB3, can continue by 4 P-Q4, just to reach the Panov variation of the Caro-Kann after 4 ... PxP 5 N-QB3. This position is usually reached as follows: 1 P-K4 P-QB3 2 P-Q4 P-Q4 3 PxP PxP 4 P-QB4 N-KB3 5 N-QB3.

3 N-QB3

White wins a tempo by compelling the Black Queen to move.

3 ...   Q-QR4

By moving to the diagonal in line with the White King, Black hopes to exert some pressure, even though for the moment that diagonal is completely closed. More passive would be 3 ... Q-Q1. Here, Black simply withdraws the Queen without anything whatever to compensate for the lost tempo.

4 P-Q4

White now opens up *his* center at the expense of giving Black a little more pressure on the diagonal.

4 ...   P-K4

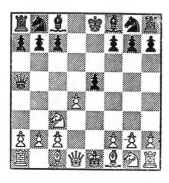

In order to equalize in the center. Enterprising but doubtful. It causes Black to lose one more tempo. More solid here would be 4 ... N-KB3 5 N-B3 B-N5 6 P-KR3 BxN 7 QxB P-B3 8 B-Q2 QN-Q2 9 0-0-0 P-K3 10 B-QB4 Q-B2 and White is a bit better off because of a freer game.

5 PxP

A bit sharper than 5 N-B3, which White could also play and after which the game could continue: 5 ... B-QN5 6 B-Q2 B-N5 7 B-K2 and after 7 ... N-QB3 8 P-QR3, Black must simplify and White maintains his advantage.

5 ...	QxPch

This loses another tempo, but Black had scarcely anything better.

He might try a premature attack 5 ... B-QN5, and theory gives 6 B-Q2 N-QB3 7 P-QR3 N-Q5 (a better move is 7 ... QxPch and Black is just as badly off as in the game) and White cannot take the Bishop: 8 PxB? QxR 9 QxQch NxPch, etc. White can, however, continue 8 KN-K2 with an excellent game, maintaining his plus Pawn.

6 B-K2

The text is superior to 6 B-K3, since then, after 6 ... B-QN5 7 KN-K2. White does not gain his second tempo by KN-B3.

Naturally, White does not offer the exchange of Queens by 6 Q-K2. Reasons: (a) in positions without Queens a tempo generally does not mean much, so after 6 ... QxQch 7 BxQ, the position is about even; (b) White does not want to exchange his "good" Queen for Black's exposed Queen.

6 ...	B-QN5
7 B-Q2	N-KB3

After 7 ... B-KN5 8 N-N5! BxBch 9 QxB, White threatens 10 NxPch QxN 11 BxB winning a Pawn. So Black has to simplify: 9 ... BxB 10 QxB QxQch 11 NxQ N-QR3 12 0-0-0, and, just as in the game, White is a few tempi ahead, which does count here, notwithstanding the exchange of Queens, because of the aggressive position of the White pieces.

8 N-B3

Developing and gaining another tempo.

8 ...	Q-K2
9 0-0	0-0

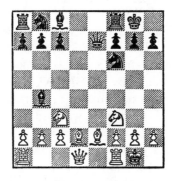

Look at the position. White is tempi ahead, but those tempi do not make a big impression. For one thing, White's Bishops are on Q2 and K2, and they must lose a tempo each to come into action. Still, White's advance in time has some significance, as will be shown. One of the reasons is that Black's Queen is still vulnerable on its K2.

10 R-K1

White occupies the open file and thereby threatens to gain another tempo by moving his KB. Now Black will not feel secure as long as his Queen is in direct line with the White Rook.

10 ...	N-B3

White has a somewhat better position. His KR is better placed, and his QB is somewhat developed. He looks about for a plan and decides that he will bring his QB to KN5, pinning the Black

KN, and then play N-Q5 with the intention of breaking up Black's K-side Pawns.

11 P-QR3

Before playing B-KN5, White plays 11 P-QR3 in order not to be inconvenienced by a double Pawn after ... BxN. But he must look into the tactical aspects of this move, which may lead to positions in which he will not be able to carry out the strategy upon which he has decided. If Black answers 11 ... BxN, White will reply 12 BxB, which is also favorable for him, leaving him with the Two Bishops and a free game. If Black then tries to eliminate the Two Bishops by 12 ... N-K5, White cannot avoid the exchange of one of his Bishops. However, White maintains in this case an advantage by 13 B-N5 NxB 14 RxQ NxQ 15 BxN NxNP 16 B-Q5. White now threatens both N-N5 and RxQBP. Black is bound to lose his plus Pawn, and it will be difficult even to avoid the loss of a second Pawn: (a) 16 ... N-R5, withdrawing the Knight as soon as possible, 17 N-N5 wins two Pawns, White thus having at least one to the good; (b) 16 ... P-QB3 17 B-N3 B-K3! freeing the game at the cost of his extra Pawn, 18 RxNP N-B5 19 N-Q4, and White will perhaps win another Pawn, but Black keeps drawing chances.

The plausible 11 B-QN5 (instead of the text) would be answered by 11 ... Q-B4, threatening to win a piece by 12 ... BxN and 13 ... QxB/N5. White could continue: (a) 12 B-K3 Q-R4 13 BxN BxN 14 PxB PxB, and White has nothing; or (b) 12 BxN QxB 13 N-K5 Q-R3 with equal chances.

11 ...   B-Q3
12 B-KN5

Carrying out his plan, White now threatens by 13 N-Q5 to direct a second attack against the pinned Knight and thus force the weakening of the Black K-wing. The threatened attack is the more serious in that it would threaten the Queen at the same time that it put double pressure on the Knight.

The attack on the pinned N/KB3 by N-Q5 arises in a standard position against which the defender must carefully guard. The consequences of such an attack are often catastrophic within a few moves. This position occurs in some variations of Game 17.

Observe that White does not play his KB, for this would simply bring the Black Queen to a less exposed square, although in the continuation it does not make much difference.

12 ...   Q-Q1

The Black Queen retreats on her own.   Black must parry White's threat. If now 13 N-Q5 (or 13 N-K4, which amounts to the same thing), Black can unpin by 13 ... B-K2, the standard way. In this particular position, after 13 N-Q5, Black has an even stronger reply: 13 ... BxPch 14 KxB QxN 15 BxN QxQ 16 QRxQ PxB, and Black has an extra Pawn.

13 B-N5

One can see that these positions cannot be evaluated exclusively by counting the tempi. White is now fewer tempi ahead than after 10 ... N-B3, but his Bishops now stand better.

White has opened his K-file and has the mild threat of 14 BxQN, thus giving Black double isolated Pawns and himself assuming greater control over his Q4- and K5-squares. Another goal of White's move becomes clear after 13 ... B-Q2? White would answer 14 N-Q5 B-K2 15 BxQN BxB 16 NxBch, winning a piece, since the exchange 15 BxQN deprives the Black KB of its double protection.

Let us examine White's threat further by asking what White would do if he could move once more: 14 BxQN PxB (the double Pawn does not count too much as long as Black has the Two Bishops to compensate—unless White can take advantage immediately) 15 N-K4 B-K2 (forced) 16 QxQ and (a) 16 ... RxQ 17 NxNch BxN (17 ... PxN 18 RxB PxB 19 NxP) 18 BxB PxB 19 QR-Q1—two double Pawns without compensation; or (b) 16 ... BxQ 17 NxNch BxN (17 ... PxN? 17 B-R6) 18 BxB PxB—about the same). The point is that one of the two Black Bishops disappears, after which the double isolated Pawns do count against Black.

13 ...	B-K2

Unpinning and simplifying.

After a move such as 13 ... B-KN5, White continues 14 BxQN as indicated above.

14 BxQN

White exchanges in order to give Black double isolated Pawns. In Games 17 and 18, the side with the attack does not fear the isolation of his Pawn because he still has the attack. In this game, Black has no attacking chances, and, moreover, through the exchange he gets double isolated Pawns, which are a much more serious disadvantage than a single isolated Pawn. The disadvantage comes from White's next attacking move, which soon leads to the exchange of one of Black's Bishops.

14 ...	PxB

14 ... QxQ? would lose a piece after 15 QRxQ PxB 16 RxB. If, in making an exchange, a player wishes to interpolate another exchange, it is wise to analyze the consequences accurately.

15 N-K5

The logical continuation. White takes possession of the conquered K5-square and exploits the double isolated Pawns.

15 ...	B-N2

(a) 15 ... B-Q2 loses a piece after 16 BxN BxB 17 NxB, or after 16 NxB; (b) 15 ... QxQ 16 QRxQ loses a Pawn after 16 ... B-N2 17 NxQBP because Black's KB is loose. Very comical is the continuation 17 ... BxP. (The Bishop is what we call "desperado." The point is that after the obvious 18 PxB BxN, Black would *not* have lost a Pawn.) 18 N-R5! BxQNP 19 N-R4! Look at the Knights! Black must lose one Bishop or the other.

16 N-Q7

An interesting sham sacrifice by which White succeeds in doubling the KBP as well. Notice that Black's moves are forced, since White is threatening to win the exchange by 17 NxR. Therefore:

(a) 16 ... NxN 17 BxB Q-B1 18 BxR wins the exchange.

(b) 16 ... QxN 17 QxQ NxQ 18 RxB N moves 19 RxP wins a Pawn.

(c) 16 ... R-K1 (text) results in the isolation of the second pair of Pawns.

16 ...	R-K1
17 BxN	BxB

If instead 17 ... PxB 18 Q-N4ch K-R1 19 QR-Q1 with a strong attack for White.

18 RxRch	QxR
19 NxBch	PxN

Black now has two pairs of isolated Pawns, very serious positional weaknesses. Let us see how White proceeds to exploit these weaknesses.

Often, such positions can be won in the attack because the Black K-wing is seriously damaged and the Black Bishop does not have very much scope. For instance, after 20 Q-B3 Q-K3? 21 N-K4, Black is practically lost: 21 ... K-N2 22 N-B5 Q-B1 23 R-Q1 followed by 24 R-Q4 or R-Q7 wins at once. But Black plays 20 ... Q-K4! temporarily immobilizing the White Knight, and then things are not so easy. The Black pieces begin to play.

That is why White decides to exploit Black's weakness in the ending.

20 Q-Q4

This move brings the Queen into an attacking position, prepares the development of the Rook, threatens QxP, and prepares N-K4, which attacks Black's KBP a second time and threatens in turn N-B5.

20 ...   **Q-K4**
21 R-Q1

Now all the White pieces are in play.
21 QxQ would strengthen Black's Pawn position.

21 ...   **R-K1**

Threatening 22 ... Q-K8ch, followed by mate.

22 QxQ!

And now White does play what one move earlier would have favored Black. Unfortunately for Black, the natural 22 ... PxQ, undoubling the KBP, does not work: 23 R-Q7 R-QB1 24 N-K4 with all sorts of threats, e.g., (a) 25 N-B5 awkward for Black; (b) 25 N-B6ch K-N2 26 N-N4 (winning a Pawn); (c) 25 N-N5,

winning a Pawn. So Black has to retake with his Rook, and his
two double isolated Pawns remain.

22 ...   RxQ

What strategy will White now follow?

Black has *three* weaknesses: (a) Pawns (two sets of double
isolated Pawns); (b) Bishop (it is badly placed and can possibly
be trapped); (c) King (it is restricted on the one hand and
unprotected by its Pawns on the other). Each of these weaknesses is the result of the double isolated Pawns. If the Pawn on
Black's QB3 were on QN3 and the one on his KB3 on KN3,
Black would be all right, even better off than White, because an
active Bishop is, in general, superior to a Knight.

What plan can White conceive, given these weaknesses? It is
not always possible to outline a single winning scheme. Moves
often depend on the opponent's possibilities of defense. Here,
the win will be based on opportunities arising from each subsequent position, but all of Black's weaknesses will figure in the
strategy.

White looks at three types of possibilities: (a) the difficulties
into which the Black Bishop will come through N-QB5 combined
with several Pawn moves (the continuation will show what this
means); (b) the possibility of winning Black's Pawns, all of
which are very weak—though, if the White Rook makes a sally,
the Black Rook can do the same, and this may mean that White

will exchange his sound Pawns for Black's unsound Pawns; (c) the possibility of playing for direct mate.

So it is understandable that White does not confine himself to a single scheme. He simply waits for his opportunity.

23 P-R3

Providing a flight square for the White King. Now White threatens 24 R-Q7.

23 ...   **R-K2**

To be considered is 23 ... K-B1 24 R-Q7 R-K2, but, as a matter of fact, after the exchange of Rooks, the Knight would be still more powerful against the Bishop than it is now.

24 N-R4!

Threatening to win the Bishop by 25 N-B5 B-B1 or B-R1 26 R-Q8ch, a well-known type of position.

24 ...   **B-R3**
25 P-QN3

In order to restrict the Bishop. White threatens 26 P-QB4, which would shut in the Bishop and might lead to its capture.

25 ...   **B-K7**

To escape being hemmed in.

26 R-Q2

26 R-K1 looks stronger, since it pins the Bishop and threatens to win it by 27 N-B3. Black, however, protects his Rook by 26 ... K-B1 and then withdraws his Bishop. However, after the exchange of Rooks we have the same type of situation as after 23 ... K-B1, favorable to White.

But the text seems to give still more.

26 ...   **K-N2**

To get out of the range of the Rook check and to protect P/KB3.

27 P-KB3

To allow the King to enter the struggle and to restrict the Bishop still further. One more move (P-QB4) and the Bishop would be lost after K-B2.

27 ...   B-N4
28 N-B5

Threatening to win the Bishop by P-QB4 or P-QR4. The Knight is now posted in front of Black's isolated Pawns and cannot be driven away except by pieces.

28 ...   R-K4

Black drives away the White Knight in order to save the Bishop.

29 N-Q7

The Knight goes away—but with tempo.

29 ...   R-K8ch

The attacked Rook also goes away, but in its turn with tempo.

30 K-B2   R-B8ch

Winning a tempo.

The fact that the Black Rook can move away from the White Knight with a check simply means that Black has not lost anything (i.e., has not lost a tempo) because of White's Knight move with tempo.

31 K-N3

Now White again threatens N-B5 and the win of the Bishop by
P-QB4 or P-QR4.

31 ...   **B-R3**
32 N-B5

Once more from his powerful position the Knight restricts the
Bishop.

32 ...   **B-B1**
33 K-B4

The King takes from the Black Bishop its KB4-square and now
there threatens 34 R-Q8 B-K3 35 NxBch PxB 36 R-Q7ch, etc.,
winning at least a Pawn. Moreover, the White King will cooperate
in the attack against the Black King, which will soon follow.

33 ...   **R-K8**

To parry 34 R-Q8 B-K3 35 NxBch (35 ... RxB!)

34 N-K4

To bring the Knight to the K-wing in order to attack, as we
shall see.

34 ...   **B-K3**
35 N-N3

According to plan.

35 ...   **R-QR8 (?)**

An amateur move. White can afford to lose this Pawn, because he has a mating attack. A better move is 35 ... R-K4, after which White continues his attack with 36 R-Q8.

36 N-R5ch	K-N3
37 P-KN4	RxP
38 R-Q8	

Taking advantage of the bad position of Black's King.

| 38 ... | R-R7 |

If 38 ... P-KR3 39 R-N8ch K-R2 40 NxP mate, and if 38 ... P-KB4 39 R-N8ch K-R3 40 N-B6, threatening 41 P-N5 mate, which cannot be parried.

| 39 R-N8ch | K-R3 |
| 40 NxP | Resigns |

White is threatening 41 P-N5 mate.

As a general rule, in a Knight vs. Bishop ending, the superiority of the Knight or Bishop depends on the Pawn structure, where the Bishop is "good" or "bad." Moreover, the Knight being able to advance only by short steps, Pawns on only one wing prove better for the Knight, whereas Pawns on both wings seem to be better for the Bishop.

But these rules do not find application here—the Knight works on both sides. The special feature of this end game is that the Bishop does not find a good square on the whole board. It is continually driven by the White pieces—Rook, Knight, Pawns. This is the direct consequence of the double Pawns.

Game 16

The theory of the Queen's Gambit Accepted

Attempts to hold the gambit Pawn in the Queen's Gambit Accepted

The freeing move ... P-QB4 in the Queen's Gambit Accepted

The accumulation of power

Attack against the uncastled King

The strategy of planning mate

Strengths and weaknesses of the Queen alone versus Rook
    and minor pieces

One of the characteristic positions in chess is that in which the attacking player has such a decisive advantage that mate is lurking around the corner, although no clear mate is in sight. In such positions, a well-developed chess imagination is of the greatest help.

The attacking player can often look beyond the immediate position and say: "I could give mate *if* ..." Once this *if-position* is determined, means of accomplishing the mate often suggest themselves. At times, one can bring about the *if-position* by a simple sacrifice. At other times, moving toward the *if-position* can be converted into a threat which may force the opponent into making further weakening moves. In still other positions, there may be several near-mates in the offing, and the combined threats of these several near-mates can become so menacing that they soon overwhelm the hapless opponent.

The Queen's Gambit Accepted

Amateur	Master
1 P-Q4	P-Q4
2 P-QB4	PxP

The Queen's Gambit Accepted.

The acceptance of the gambit leads to the exchange of a center Pawn for a side Pawn. In itself, this is not to be recommended, but there are other aspects of the Queen's Gambit Accepted which motivate the strategy followed by Black, as will be explained below and during the course of the game.

Compared with the various lines of the Queen's Gambit Declined, the Queen's Gambit Accepted has the advantage that the development of the Black Queen's Bishop does not constitute a problem. On the other hand, the Queen's Gambit Accepted has the disadvantage of leaving the center to White, at least temporarily.

In general, Black gets a free game in the Queen's Gambit Accepted if he succeeds in neutralizing White's superiority in the center, a superiority which Black has given him by exchanging the center for a side Pawn. This neutralizing move is ... P-QB4 played at the right moment. Without this move, White would get an ideal center (PQ4-PK4), from which a K-side attack might result (moves like P-K4-K5—see Game 19), and Black would remain in a cramped position.

The Queen's Gambit is not a gambit in the proper sense of the word: that is, White does not permanently sacrifice a Pawn in return for an advantage in development, for he can always recover the Pawn. Compare with Games 17 and 18, where the side offering the gambit gives up the Pawn permanently.

Since many amateurs play 2 ... PxP in the hope of holding on to the extra gambit Pawn, it will not be amiss to discuss the various attempts to keep the Pawn under the moves that follow.

3 N-KB3

This move develops an important piece to the proper square, prevents the Black ... P-K4, and theory shows that after 3 N-KB3, Black cannot hold the extra gambit Pawn.

More direct for an immediate winning back of the gambit Pawn would be 3 P-K3, but this could be answered by 3 ... P-K4 4 BxP (4 PxP QxQch 5 KxQ N-QB3 6 P-B4 P-B3 7 PxP NxP 8 BxP, and, although White has an extra Pawn, this line is cer-

tainly not favorable for him because of 8 ... N-K5 or 8 ...
B-N5ch, followed by 9 ... 0-0-0, and Black has a considerable
advance in development) 4 ... PxP 5 PxP, and White's isolated
Pawn is compensated for by a greater command of space. But in
this position also, Black has adequate possibility of activating
his pieces.

The Black amateur who is not aware of the resources of 3 ...
P-K4 often tries to hold on to the gambit Pawn by 3 ... P-QN4?.
Since this move is fairly common in amateur play, we shall show
the possible continuations:

> (a) 4 P-QR4 P-QB3 (4 ... P-QR3 5 PxP and Black cannot
> retake) 5 PxP PxP 6 Q-B3! and Black loses his Rook or, if
> Black interposes, his Knight or his Bishop.
>
> (b) 4 P-QR4 B-Q2 5 PxP BxP.
>> (1) 6 N-QR3, regaining the Pawn with a positional ad-
>> vantage.
>> (2) 6 P-QN3, regaining the Pawn with a fine center.

Sometimes after 1 P-Q4 P-Q4 2 P-QB4 PxP 3 P-K3, the inexperienced Black player tries to hold the gambit Pawn by 3 ...
B-K3, which is strategically very bad because it blocks Black's
center development. White can win the Pawn back immediately
by 4 N-QR3, or he can simply complete his development and
attain great advantage in comparison with the Black position,
which remains cramped as long as the Bishop on K3 hinders the
development of the Black pieces.

3 ...   N-KB3

A simple developing move. If Black now plays the neutralizing
move 3 ... P-QB4 at this point, White can simply continue with
4 P-K3, or he can play 4 P-Q5, and his center Pawn acts as a
restraining force on Black's movements and poses him some
problems in his search for equality.

If Black tries to hold the gambit Pawn by 3 ... P-QN4, White
regains it by 4 P-QR4 P-QB3 5 P-K3 followed by (a) 5 ... B-N2
6 PxP PxP 7 P-QN3!, the typical way of regaining the gambit

Pawn; or (b) 5 ... Q-N3 6 N-K5 (threatening 7 RPxP PxP 8 Q-B3 with the double threat of 9 QxPch and QxR) 6... B-N2 (or 6 ... N-B3) 7 P-QN3! (again this strong move) 7 ... PxNP 8 QxP with the double threat of QxPch and PxP.

4 P-K3   **P-K3**

Again a simple developing move to open lines. Black shuts in his QB, but he later plans to fianchetto it. At this point, 4 ... P-QB4 could be answered by 5 BxP PxP 6 PxP, and, as compensation for his isolated Pawn, White has a freer development, just as in the similar variation already mentioned.

5 BxP   **P-B4**

The key move of the Queen's Gambit Accepted, the purposes of which are to free Black's game, to neutralize White's center, and to afford freedom of movement to the Black pieces. Without this move, Black would have a cramped game, and White would be able to develop his pieces at will and emerge from the opening with a superior development, especially if White could realize the move P-K4, which, in general, means the triumph of White and the relegation of Black to passive play in a cramped position.

6 N-B3

Developing the QN to its natural square, which looks logical enough, is nonetheless fraught with certain dangers in this variation and at this point. First of all, it delays White's castling, and the game will show how postponing castling too long will mean that White will never get to castle. Second, if Black succeeds via ... P-QR3 in bringing his QNP to its 4th square, he may then continue ... P-QN5 at the right time, driving away White's QN. Thus, at such a time, the Knight would no longer be safe at its QB3, and the protection of the White K4-square by this Knight becomes dubious. One must keep in mind, however, that the postponement of the development of the QN is valid only in this special case of the Queen's Gambit Accepted, not in general.

6 ...	P-QR3

The first of a series of two moves which aim to drive back the Bishop, to open up Black's Q-side for the development of his QB at N2, and to threaten ... P-N5, thus attacking White's QN.

Instead, Black could have played 6 ... PxP, and, just as in an analogous line played earlier, after 7 PxP, White would have greater development and mobility to compensate for his isolated Pawn. True, White's advantage is temporary in nature; Black's, permanent as long as White's Pawn remains isolated. But in positions of this sort it is not difficult for White to force a Pawn exchange by P-Q5, in which case he keeps some superiority in space and has liquidated his only weakness.

If White answers 6 ... PxP by 7 NxP and Black attempts to control the center immediately by 7 ... P-K4, then 8 KN-N5 with threats such as 9 QxQch followed by 10 BxP, and if Black exchanges Queens, White's threat of N-B7ch is annoying. Therefore, after 7 NxP, Black would also continue 7 ... P-QR3, preparing both ... P-QN4 and ... P-K4.

7 B-Q2 (?)

An amateur move, the purpose of which is the simple development of the QB without any appreciation of the strategic requirements of the position. It has the additional disadvantage of depriving the QP of one of its defenders. Yet the move is not entirely bad. In many variations, as in this game, White can bring his QB into the game via QB3. The move also vacates the QB1-square for the QR, which might mean something.

7 0-0 is the logical move, or White could play 7 P-QR4, preventing Black from carrying out his Q-side maneuvers.

If White should try to dominate the center immediately by 7 P-K4, then Black answers 7 . . . P-QN4 and there follows 8 B-Q3 (9 B-N3 loses a Pawn after 8 . . . P-N5) 8 . . . PxP 9 NxQP and 9 . . . B-N2 or 9 . . . P-K4 (9 . . . QxN?? 10 BxPch, winning the Black Queen) and White's position is certainly not better than Black's.

| 7 . . . | P-QN4 |

Black continues his plan. The problem of his QB is solved. His threat of P-N5 means that there is indirect pressure on the center.

| 8 B-Q3 | QN-Q2 |

So that the Knight can eventually go to its QB4 to attack the White Bishop. It is very important usually for Black to retake with the Knight after White plays PxP.

In this variation, Black's QN is best developed to its Q2, which leaves the diagonal open for the QB. This may also be important in order to prevent White from playing P-Q5, which in many variations is a dangerous move for Black.

In this special position where White has played the bad move 8 B-Q2, leaving his B/Q3 unprotected, 8 . . . N-B3 would also have been good, for White would have been obliged to play 9 N-K2 to avoid the loss of a Pawn. The latter move does not do much harm to White, however.

177

The position at hand could arise from the Meran Defense of the Queen's Gambit Declined after the following moves: 1 P-Q4 P-Q4 2 P-QB4 P-QB3 3 N-QB3 N-B3 4 P-K3 P-K3 5 N-B3 QN-Q2 6 B-Q3 PxP 7 BxP P-QN4 8 B-Q3 P-QR3 9 B-Q2? P-B4. One more move is necessary to reach the same position in the Meran Defense, because in this variation White loses a tempo by B-Q3 followed by BxP, and Black by . . . P-QB3 followed by . . . P-QB4.

9 N-K4 (?)

This move has the advantage of making room for the White QB on QB3, but the disadvantage of White's losing a move to exchange his Knight for the Black Knight. It is preferable that he should castle here and then continue by moves such as Q-K2 and PxP followed by P-K4. Amateurs often postpone castling too long. A practical principle is: Castle first, then think of your attack or strategy.

From 9 N-K4, it is evident that White has no definite strategy in mind, no plan, that he is swimming in the whirlpool of the middle game, playing from move to move without any idea of the direction in which he should go.

True, White has more pieces developed than Black, but consider *how* they are developed!

9 ...   B-N2

Black carries out his strategic plan of fianchettoing his QB and with tempo, since he is now threatening to win White's N/K4.

10 NxNch

If White does not exchange, he loses a move. For instance, 10 Q-B2 P-B5! 11 NxNch NxN 12 B-K2 and White has been compelled to withdraw his Bishop, leaving Black with full power over his K5-square.

It is true that, after Black retakes, White will have as many pieces developed as Black, but Black's fianchettoed Bishop is much stronger than White's poorly developed QB.

10 ...   QxN

Threatening to mutilate the White Pawn structure by 12 ...
BxN 13 QxB QxQ 14 PxQ PxP 15 PxP and also, under certain
circumstances, to attain ... P-K4 with greater domination of the
center.

10 ... NxN, putting additional pressure on White's K4-square
and preventing White from playing P-K4, is also good. But the
text had the additional advantage of preventing White from playing PxP because of Black's reply ... QxQNP.

11 B-K2

To prevent Black from carrying out the exchange described
under Black's 10th move. But it loses White a tempo.

11 ...	B-Q3

A continuation of Black's development and the beginning of an
accumulation of power: Bishops at QN2 and Q3.

To be considered is 11 ... PxP 12 PxP B-Q3, but in that case
White's QB has the diagonal Q2-KN5 at its disposal.

12 PxP

This exchange has the advantage of allowing White to bring
his QB to a better diagonal, but the disadvantage of bringing
Black's Knight to an ideal square.

12 ...	NxP

13 B-B3

The Bishop stands better here than on Q2, but it is not yet
ideally placed, since Black has at his disposal moves such as
... N-K5, ... P-K4, and, under certain circumstances, also
... P-N5.

13 ...	Q-K2

The Queen retreats temporarily in order to come out again at
the right time with greater force. It also now protects the Bishop
at Q3.

Black now has the better game. His pieces are more active.
Compare the relative position of the White and Black Bishops
and Knights.

Now White should play 14 0-0 and, if possible, simplify by 15 B-K5, in order to exchange Bishops and thus reduce Black's concentration of power. 14 B-K5 at once would cost a Pawn after 14 ... BxB 15 NxB BxP for if 16 R-KN1 B-K5 17 RxP B-N3.

Note that 14 BxKNP would not work after 14 ... R-KN1 15 B-B3 (15 B-K5 BxB followed by 16 ... RxP) 15 ... RxP. (Compare this with the above reverse combination.) Both sides lose their KNP, but Black ends up with his Rook on his KN7, where it is in an excellent attacking position.

14 Q-Q4?

Not understanding the requirements of the position, White tries for a greater concentration of power himself. His Queen is not safe here; it will soon be driven to another square, where it will not be safe either. White's attacking chances are nil—a Queen plus one Bishop is too little. But perhaps White was hoping for 14 ... 0-0??

14 ...   P-B3
15 R-Q1

White's pressure along the Q-file is illusory. He forces Black to play 15 ... R-Q1, a move which he would have played anyway. A better move would be 15 0-0 R-Q1 16 Q-KR4 N-K5 17 B-K1, which does not leave White with a marvelous position, but White is not too well off in any case.

15 ...   R-Q1

16 P-QN3

To make room for his QB in view of a possible ... N-K5 (or ... N-R5), but the text move does not work.

Let us examine the position a little more closely. The point to be noted is Black's indirect threat against the White Queen by his QR. This means that White cannot castle because of ... BxPch. On the other hand, Black cannot move his KB at random with an attack against the White Queen because of the simplifying White QxRch. For instance, after 16 P-QN3, 16 ... B-K4 would be bad: 17 QxRch QxQ 18 RxQch KxR 19 NxB, etc.

Although White's Queen is in some danger, there are no direct threats. Yet White must play very cautiously and, for instance, must take into account Black's move ... B-B2, defending his QR and attacking the White Queen. However, after 16 B-R5 (instead of 16 P-QN3), White need not fear 16 ... B-B2, since he can still continue by 17 QxRch! BxQ 18 RxBch and White reaches an almost equal ending. This means that after 16 B-R5, Black would have continued 16 ... R-Q2, thus protecting his Rook once more by his Knight, so that he now would threaten to move his KB anywhere.

16 ...   **0-0**

Threatening 17 ... B-K4.

Not convincing is 16 ... N-K5 17 B-QR5 B-B2 18 QxRch, with the same combination as above.

17 Q-KN4

17 Q-KR4 would put the Queen in a somewhat less exposed position and would be slightly better. Why the Queen is more exposed on its KN4, we shall see.

Black, looking for the proper strategy in a position where he has a considerable accumulation of force and pressure over many points on the board, notes two weaknesses in White's position: (a) his uncastled King; (b) his loose Bishop on QB3. He therefore takes the opportunity to drive away the Bishop (and then attack the uncastled King) by playing

17 ...   **N-K5**

18 B-N2

White postponed castling on his 7th and 14th move, perhaps because he feared an attack. This was bad strategy, for after Black's next move he can no longer castle at all.

After 18 B-Q2 NxB 19 NxN B-N5, the same situation obtains: White cannot castle.

White cannot hold the diagonal by 18 B-R5 either, for 18 ... B-N5ch 19 BxB QxBch loses a piece after 20 R-Q2 or N-Q2 and so 20 K-B1 gives up castling, as in the continuation of the game.

18 ...   **B-N5ch**

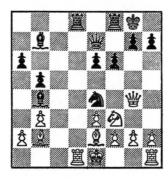

In order to prevent White from castling, which is an important adjunct of Black's plan. The catastrophe resulting from White's inability to castle will become clear!

19 K-B1

Forced, since Black controls his Q7-square with too many pieces for White to be able to interpose successfully.

19 ...   **RxRch**

Black eliminates White's active Rook and brings his own KR into play with tempo within a few moves. White's KR, on the contrary, remains out of play.

20 BxR   **R-Q1**

The remaining Rook is placed on the vital Q-file with a threat to the White Bishop.

From now on, one blow follows another. All the Black pieces

cooperate, constituting a maximum concentration of force. The White pieces, on the other hand, have very little activity. There is no cooperation at all from the White Queen and Rook.

21 K-K2

A relatively good move in a bad position. There is now some hope that the White Rook may be brought into play.

If 21 N-Q4?, White's Rook remains undeveloped, the White Knight can be driven away, and Black will gain possession of his Q7-square: 21 ... P-B4 (in order to try to deprive White's KB of its protection by the Queen) and

(a) 22 Q-K2 P-K4 23 NxBP? (better 23 N-B3—see [d]) 23 ... Q-Q2! attacking both Knight and Bishop and winning a piece.

(b) 22 Q-R3 P-K4 23 NxBP RxBch 24 K-K2 R-Q7ch, winning a piece.

(c) 22 Q-B3? N-Q7ch, winning the Queen.

(d) 22 Q-R5 P-N3 23 Q-K2 P-K4.

(1) 24 N-B3 N-Q7ch and (a) 25 NxN RxN, winning a piece; (b) 25 K-N1 NxNch 26 PxN R-Q7, winning a piece all the same.

(2) 24 N-B2 R-Q7, winning the Queen (25 Q-B3 RxPch, etc.).

If 21 B-B2 N-Q7ch and (a) 22 K-K2 NxN followed by 23 ... R-Q7ch, winning a piece; (b) 22 NxN RxN and if 23 BxBP QxB 24 QxB QxP mate.

All these variations show why 21 K-K2 is forced.

21 ...   P-B4

To displace the White Queen in order to reduce her possibilities of engaging in further play.

22 Q-R5   P-N3

23 Q-R3

If White tries 23 Q-R4 in order to reduce the attack through exchanges, Black replies 23 ... R-Q7ch with all sorts of threats which compel a direct decision, and White cannot reply 24 NxR without losing his Queen.

23 ...	Q-Q3

Black thus threatens 24 ... Q-Q6 mate and obtains complete control of the Q-file and of his Q7-square.

24 B-B2

If 24 N-Q4 P-K4; if 24 N-K5 (to prevent 24 ... Q-Q6 mate) 24 ... Q-Q7ch.

24 ...	Q-Q7ch!

This sound Q-sacrifice is the result of the accumulation of power. Black's goal is twofold: (a) to drive the King back to his 1st rank, again immobilizing the White Rook; (b) to take possession of his own 7th rank.

25 NxQ	RxNch
26 K-B1	

If 26 K-B3 RxP mate; if 26 K-K1 RxB dis ch, winning at least two pieces.

26 ...	RxPch
27 K-N1	RxB
28 Q-R4	

White prepares a counterattack, since he cannot save his remaining Bishop: e.g., 28 B-Q4 R-B8 mate.

| 28 ... | RxB |
| 29 Q-Q8ch | B-B1 |

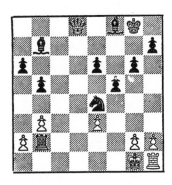

The material result of Black's combination is in favor of Black: three pieces and a Pawn against the Queen. Moreover, Black has a tremendous attack. He now threatens 30 ... R-N8ch, followed by mate. What can White do against it?

(a) 30 K-B1 R-N8ch, winning White's remaining Rook.

(b) 30 Q-Q1 N-B6 31 Q-Q3 R-N8ch 32 K-B2 N-K5ch, winning the Rook.

White cannot hold his 1st rank. He therefore plays

30 P-KR4

This is a bit better than 30 P-KR3, because it puts the KR3 at the disposal of the White King.

| 30 ... | N-N6 |

Black now threatens 31 ... RxP mate.
If 31 K-R2? RxPch 32 K-R3 NxR, etc. So White answers

31 R-R2

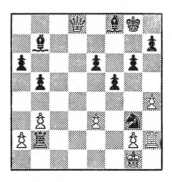

The analysis of the position arising at this point in the game is rather involved and difficult to follow. It is included here in order to give the reader an impression of the extent of a complete analysis of a complicated chess position, as an illustration of the richness of the possibilities and the surprising turns which may exist in such a position, and of a method which may be used to analyze certain types of positions.

The reader should not be concerned if he does not grasp the details of the following analysis at once, but should rather simply play over the variations a few times to enjoy the variety of turns which they produce. Those desiring can explore the analysis more deeply on subsequent readings.

Black has given up his Queen in return for three pieces and a Pawn. He has complete control of his 7th rank and the long diagonal. In addition, he has absolutely immobilized the White Rook, which must remain on its KR2 because of Black's attack on White's KNP. Only White's Queen can play. But this Queen is a powerful piece, especially because it can simultaneously give check and attack other pieces. This makes the problem in this position much more difficult than it appears at first glance.

Yet, in positions where the enemy King is seriously restricted, a player can think in terms of giving a not too distant mate or of winning considerable material.

Often, in positions such as this one, no absolute mate is in sight, only a mate *if* the position were just a bit different. When a player is that near to mate, this *if* can be a valuable clue as to how to proceed, and one should make the most of it. Let us see how it can be applied in the position at hand.

Black notices that he could give mate in not one but three ways—*if*:

Mate A—*if* there were no White Pawn on White's K3 and *if* Black's KB were not pinned, Black could play ... B-B4 mate.

Mate B—*if* Black's Knight were protected, Black could give mate in two by 31 ... R-N8ch 32 K-B2 R-B8 mate.

Mate C—*if* the White Rook plays, Black has mate in one by ... RxNP.

Black also considers 31 ... N-K5, threatening mate in one, but rejects it, since after 32 K-B1 there is no positive continuation. The White King simply has more freedom than before. He therefore thinks along the lines of mates A, B, and C.

He reasons: I could play 31 ... P-B5, threatening mate in two (mate B). This practically forces 32 PxP, for if 32 Q-Q1 B-K5, threatening 33 ... R-N8 winning the Queen.

If I then play 32 ... K-N2, threatening 33 ... B-B4 (mate A), White answers 33 Q-Q4ch, winning my Rook, but this would be followed by 33 ... K-R3 34 QxR B-B4ch 35 Q-B2 BxQch, winning Queen for Bishop. But the ending of Bishop and Knight against Rook may be a difficult one. Let's see whether there isn't something better. The principal problem here is how to mobilize the KB.

Is there any way that I can unpin my KB without moving the King? I could play 31 ... R-B7 to continue later by ... R-B1, driving the Queen away and unpinning the KB. The direct threat here would be 32 ... P-B5 33 PxP R-B1, followed by 34 ... B-B4ch (34 Q-Q4? N-K7ch) or by 34 ... B-B4, winning the Queen in either case. After 31 ... R-B7, White's retreat 32 Q-Q1 does not work on account of the role played by the K-Q forking attacks by the Knight, here and also in what follows. For instance, 32 ... R-B8! 33 QxR N-K7ch.

White's only defense against 31 ... R-B7 seems to be 32 P-N4, protecting his QB5-square, but it has the disadvantage of freeing Black's QB5-square for my QB, and after 32 ... B-Q4, which both protects my KP and brings my QB into active play, there must be something in this position. In view of the very limited space at its disposal, the White King cannot stand alone against the combined attack of all the Black pieces.

31 ...   R-QB7!

White now has various replies at his disposal.

(a) 32 Q-N8 (simultaneously attacking Black's QB and his Knight) 32 ... P-B5! 33 PxP (33 QxP? N-K7ch, again a K-Q forking Knight attack) 33 ... R-B1 and White cannot parry the 34 ... B-B4 mate without giving up his Queen.

(b) 32 Q-Q1 R-B8 33 QxR N-K7ch, again winning the Queen by the K-Q forking Knight attack.

(c) 32 Q-Q7 B-Q4 33 Q-Q8 P-B5 34 PxP K-N2 (after a check by the White Queen the Black King will go to R3, where it cannot be checked further, and then White cannot effectively prevent ... B-B4 mate).

(d) 32 P-R5 (or 32 P-R3) 32 ... P-B5 33 PxP and Black carries out the threat 33 ... R-B1, followed by ... B-B4 mate (mate A).

(e) 32 P-N4 B-Q4 and Black now threatens a variation of mate B: 33 ... R-B8ch 34 K-B2 N-K5ch and (1) 35 K-B3 R-B8ch 36 K-K2 B-B5 mate or (2) 35 K-K2 B-B5ch 36 K-B3 R-B8 mate. Therefore 33 P-K4 (after any other move, Black carries out the threat) 33 ... P-B5! and Black can now execute mate B, beginning 34 ... R-B8ch, which works even after 34 R-R3 (34 ... R-B8ch 35 K-R2 R-R8 mate).

So far, Black's plan seems to succeed. White, however, finds the one move which poses an entirely new problem. He plays

32 Q-K8

This is to some extent an improvement over line (c) 32 Q-Q7. It should be noted that if the Black King now tries to escape,

32 ... K-N2, unpinning the Bishop, White can simply play 33 QxKP, because Black does not now have "one move threat." This might lead to the idea of reviewing the order of the moves and playing 31 ... P-B5 first, forcing 32 PxP and then 32 ... R-B7. But then variation (e) no longer works: 33 P-N4! and, because of changed circumstances, the White King now has his K3-square as a flight square, and there is no clear decision. We are therefore now faced with an entirely new problem. Since we cannot afford to lose our KP because of the many checks involved, we have practically nothing better than 32 ... B-Q4.

32 ...	B-Q4

The unpinning can now be realized only by playing the King in one of the following moves. For the moment, White has a little breathing space, since he now has no "one move threat" to fear. White can therefore try—and he has practically no other choice—to mobilize his dormant Rook to some extent.

33 P-R5

Not 33 P-K4, after which 33 ... P-B5, followed by 34 ... R-B8ch and mate B.

33 Q-N8 is easily met by 33 ... P-B5 34 PxP (forced, for if 34 QxP?? N-K7ch wins the Queen) 34 ... K-N2 35 Q-K5ch K-B2!, followed by mate A.

33 ...	PxP

Here there is no point to 33 ... P-B5 34 PxBP and unpinning the Bishop by 34 ... K-N2 because of 35 P-R6ch.

Black now threatens to protect the Knight by ... P-R5, and if RxP then ... RxP mate.

34 Q-Q8!

The only move, but a strong one which both attacks and defends, threatening 35 Q-N5ch, 36 QxN, and parrying ... P-R5.

34 ...	P-B5!
35 Q-N5ch	

If 35 PxP K-B2 (threatening 36 ... B-B4 mate) 36 Q-Q7ch K-N3 37 Q-K8ch (37 P-B5ch K-R3!) 37 ... K-N2 (a peculiar zigzag—it is very instructive to observe how Black escapes White's check) 38 Q-Q7ch K-R3! and there are no more checks so that ... B-B4 decides. (39 RxPch NxR costs too much material.)

35 ...	B-N2
36 Q-Q8ch	

If 36 QxBP N-K7ch.
If 36 PxP? R-B8ch 37 K-B2 N-K5, winning the Queen by the K-Q forking attack.

36 ...	K-B2
37 Q-Q7ch	K-N3
38 Q-K8ch	K-R3!

Black again takes refuge in a flight square from which he cannot be checked, and now all three mates are still in the position. White can choose:

Mate A—39 PxP B-Q5 mate.
Mate B—39 Q-B7 R-B8ch 40 K-B2 R-B8 mate.
Mate C—39 R-R3 RxNP mate.

There is only one way to postpone the mate:

39 RxPch	NxR

Now the position is no longer either difficult or instructive— only amusing.

40 Resigns

The game might have finished: 40 Q-B7 RxPch 41 K-B1 N-N6ch 42 K-K1 B-QB6ch 43 K-Q1 B-B6ch 44 K-B1 B-N7ch 45 K-N1 B-K5 mate.

Game 17

The nature of the gambit
Ideas behind gambit play
The target of attack
Creation of positional weaknesses to further attack
The power of a direct attack against the King by Queen and Rooks
Rule of thumb for double Pawns

A gambit is, in general, the giving up of a Pawn or a piece in return for an extra tempo which will be used to obtain a greater development in pieces, or sometimes for a majority in the center. A real gambit leads the game into quite a new direction, for one is in the presence of two entirely different units: *time* against *material*. One can never say which is superior, for it is almost impossible to compare two entities so different in nature. One can only prove which is better in a given position of a variation. Moreover, there is considerable difference between theory and practice. Even if a gambit is not theoretically correct, it works fairly well in practice because of two very important factors: (a) the task of the defender is, in general, more difficult than that of the attacker; (b) the player who accepts the gambit is beset with a psychological problem—he has won material, which makes him think that he has the moral obligation to play for a win. Practice has shown the importance of this second factor as well. It should be pointed out that the defender of the gambit should not set his goal too high. He should be satisfied with some simplification and equality, for only in this way can he be freed from the bad consequences of the psychological disadvantage which he has incurred in accepting the gambit.

Once the gambit player has attained maximum development, he must convert this advantage of development into an attack of some kind at the right time, since a superiority in development is purely temporary in nature, and the other side can catch up in development if given time.

Successful attack must, in general, be based on weaknesses in the opponent's position. If the opponent has no weaknesses and therefore no target for attack, the only way to proceed is to maintain the balance, to continue maneuvering, putting problems to the opponent and looking for the opportunity to obtain an advantage.

In gambits, therefore, the problem of the side that offers the gambit is to find a target for attack in order to make effective use of superior development, whereas the role of the defender is to play in such a way that no target for attack exists and then eventually to make his material plus count.

The Center Counter Gambit

Amateur	Master
1 P-K4	P-Q4

The Center Counter Game. For the main lines of this opening, see Game 15.

2 PxP	P-QB3

Black offers White a Pawn in exchange for faster development. This is known in chess as a gambit.

A distinction must be made between a gambit such as the Queen's Gambit (see Games 9, 16, 19 and 20), in which Black may accept but cannot hold the extra Pawn, and the Center Counter Gambit and the Göring Gambit, in which the side against which the gambit is played can accept and hold this extra Pawn.

3 PxP

White accepts the proffered Pawn, and the battle between time and material begins.

White did not have to accept the gambit. He could have played 3 P-Q4, and after 3 . . . PxP, we get the exchange variation of the Caro-Kann. Or, after 3 P-QB4 PxP 4 P-Q4, we get by transposition the Panov variation of the Caro-Kann. (See Game 15, Black's move 2.)

3 ...   **NxP**

Instead, Black could have offered a second Pawn (3 . . . P-K4 4 PxP BxP), and in that case, since his material sacrifice was greater, his advance in development would also be proportionally greater.

If, after 3 . . . NxP, White wishes to play a solid game in which Black's advance in tempi will net him the least, he will answer 4 P-Q3, which gives him a solid position on which to begin developing his pieces. True, 4 P-Q3 shuts in White's KB, but in this case White plays a defensive role and hemming-in has the advantage that all pieces are at hand. Also to be considered is 4 P-KN3. Then the game might continue 4 . . . N-B3 5 B-N2 B-N5 6 P-KB3, and thus Black still has some compensation.

4 B-N5

White pins the Black Knight, threatening to isolate the Black Q-side Pawns by 5 BxN. If Black wishes, he can avoid the isolation of his Pawns by answering 4 . . . Q-N3, attacking the White Bishop. An amateur might even play 4 . . . B-Q2, which would also avoid the isolation of the Pawns. But this move would be completely out of harmony with the spirit of the gambit which Black has chosen: 4 . . . Q-N3 threatens and compels White to act, whereas 4 . . . B-Q2 does not. After 4 . . . B-Q2, White would not think of exchanging.

If Black has played the gambit, it was to get rapid development in the type of game where the positional disadvantage of isolated Pawns will not count too much.

4 ...   **P-K4**

Black is unimpressed by White's threat to isolate his Q-side Pawns. He is more concerned with getting an active game in order to make use of the possibilities opened to him by the Pawn sacrifice. In other words, the Pawn sacrifice has given Black one more tempo, and this he must use to further his development if he is to retain his temporary advantage in time.

5 BxNch

At this point, White might have played 5 P-Q3 or N-QB3 or N-K2. But he will be practically forced to play BxN as soon as Black has castled, since at that time the White Bishop would become the object of attack by moves such as ... N-Q5. Therefore, White makes the exchange at once, which is also all right.

5 ... PxB

As compensation for his sacrificed Pawn, Black now has the Two Bishops, two open files, and open diagonals.

Black's KP restricts White's freedom to develop. If White now plays the natural 6 N-KB3, his Knight can be driven away by 6 ... P-K5. White therefore decides to control his K4-square first by N-QB3, later by P-Q3 if necessary.

6 N-QB3 N-KB3

Black applies counterpressure to White's K4-square. Therefore, White deems it necessary to protect that square once more and plays

7 P-Q3

At this point, White might consider 7 Q-B3, attacking Black's weak QBP. It is a question of which system White wishes to follow. He has already won material, and he might try for additional material. In that case, Black might answer 7 ... B-Q2 or 7 ... Q-B2 and later play ... B-KN5, gaining a tempo by attacking White's Queen and forcing it to move.

7 ...   B-QN5

Again neutralizing White's pressure on his K4-square. For instance, if now 8 N-B3, 8 ... P-K5 could be played: 9 PxP BxNch 10 PxB QxQch 11 KxQ NxP and Black has a good game, as for instance, 12 R-K1 B-B4 13 N-Q4 0-0-0!

8 B-Q2

Breaking Black's pin, re-exerting pressure on the K4-square.

Another possibility would have been 8 KN-K2, after which 8 ... P-K5 would not mean much: 9 PxP QxQch 10 KxQ and the KP is protected.

8 ...   0-0

Black would not consider 8 ... BxN at this point, for he would not want to exchange his Good Bishop even if he could manage to advance his KP after the exchange. The advance has meaning only when it attacks.

9 N-B3?

This move is of utmost importance in the continuation of the game, because it gives Black a target for attack and compensation for his sacrificed Pawn. Up to now, he has had only a shadow of compensation—the Two Bishops and one tempo.

After 9 KN-K2, Black would not have had many chances. If the game had reached the ending, he might have drawn, notwithstanding his being a Pawn down, but he would have had to fight for a draw at the maximum. Certainly Black has mobility for his pieces, but how can he go about using it? An example: 9 KN-K2 B-N5 10 P-B3 B-K3 11 0-0 Q-N3ch 12 K-R1 QR-Q1 13 N-R4 Q-N2 14 BxB QxB 15 P-QN3 and Black no longer has attacking chances.

Black's essential difficulty in this sort of position is that every exchange improves White's game and diminishes Black's chances to take advantage of his mobility.

There are two ways of proceeding in a chess game: (1) by ordinary—i.e., logical—moves; (2) by extraordinary moves, such as sacrificing Pawns or pieces or carrying out artificial, illogical maneuvers.

Up to move 9, the White position has no weaknesses which would allow Black to undertake a direct attack. The ordinary way is too slow, and the extraordinary way is not possible here. If one plays a gambit, in many cases, one can obtain a promising game by ordinary, logical moves. In this position, Black cannot. This means that, after all, Black's gambit is not worth very much.

With 9 N-B3? will come the later pin of White's KN by ... B-KN5, and this almost always leads to a weakening of White's King position if White's KB is missing. If the KB were still on the board, White would never have to fear this weakening. Up to now, Black was merely moving pieces. From here on, Black's strategical plan is clear.

9 ...   R-K1

By threatening 10 ... P-K5, Black induces White to castle on the K-side. Only after White has castled on the K-side will Black's ... B-N5 have sufficient force. Before that, it does not mean much.

An immediate 9 ... B-N5 has no particular significance. Then comes 10 P-KR3 B-KR4 (10 ... BxN accomplishes nothing, simply gives up the Two Bishops) 11 N-K4 NxN 12 PxN BxN 13 PxB, and, although Black has weakened the White K-side, it does not greatly inconvenience White because he can still castle Q-side. In many analogous positions, after 10 P-KR3 B-KR4, White could continue the attack against the Black Bishop by 11 P-KN4, but in this case it is sensible for White to postpone this attack for one or two moves only because it drives the Bishop to the N3-square, from which it controls a very vital square in the battle, its K5.

On the other hand, an immediate 9 ... P-K5 10 PxP BxN 11 BxB NxP is not too illogical, since Black is playing for an attack with the initiative, and in many cases the push P-K5 gives the initiative. However, one must analyze the tactical details and evaluate the position resulting from the continuation. After 12 QxQ RxQ 13 B-Q4 B-N5 14 0-0-0, and Black is still a Pawn down with nothing to show for the attack. True, he has succeeded in giving White a double isolated Pawn structure on the K-side after 14 ... BxN, but that does not mean much in this position.

The rule of thumb for double Pawns is as follows: Doubling on your majority wing *does harm*, because it diminishes the chances of getting a passed Pawn. On the other hand, doubling on the minority wing does not mean much, nor does doubling on the equality side. But this is only the aspect of the double Pawn in regard to the possibility of getting a passed Pawn. The other aspect is the vulnerability of the double isolated Pawn.

10 0-0

White does castle on the K-side and Black will now be able to attack. Let us see if there was anything better.

10 Q-K2 does not look very trustworthy, as the White King and Queen are both on a file controlled by the Black Rook. Still, it would not have been easy to exploit the situation: e.g., 10 ... BxN (the necessary preparation for the following move) 11 BxB P-K5 looks killing. Then

(a) 12 PxP? RxP wins the Queen, as could be expected after such a silly continuation.

(b) 12 BxN PxN 13 BxQ RxQch 14 K-B1 RxQBP, and Black has by far the best of it.

(c) 12 N-K5! (the right move) 12 ... PxP 13 QxP QxQ 14 PxQ. This situation seems hopeless for White, and still, when Black continues 14 ... N-Q2 (or 14 ... N-N5, in both cases with the intention after 15 P-Q4 of following with 15 ... P-B3), White answers 15 0-0!

(1) 15 ... NxN 16 KR-K1 and White wins back his piece, after which he certainly cannot lose.

(2) 15 ... RxN! 16 BxR NxB 17 KR-K1 P-B3 18 P-Q4 N-N3 19 R-K8ch K-B2 20 QR-K1 B-N2 and it will be a hard fight between R + P against B + N with about equal chances.

So there remains the problem of which is the better move here— 10 Q-K2 or 10 0-0.

10 ...   **B-N5**

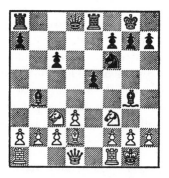

The pin. White can never get rid of this pin without incurring some other inconvenience to himself. At last, Black now has some compensation for his sacrificed gambit Pawn. Whether it is sufficient, remains to be seen.

11 R-K1

Not a bad move, considering the important role played by White's K4-square in this game. The move is made with the intention of preparing N-K4.

11 P-QR3 does not come into consideration here. The Bishop

on QN5 is not so well placed that it needs to be driven away. Black would welcome such a move in order to bring his Bishop back to B1 with tempo.

11 P-KR3 at this point is a double-edged move. After 11 ... B-KR4, nothing is improved in White's position. If White really wants to eliminate the pin, he has to continue with 12 P-N4, and then he has weakened his K-side and Black's well-known sacrificial 12 ... NxP 13 PxN BxP may be very risky for White.

11 ...   **R-K3**

Sooner or later, White's K-side will be weakened by a double Pawn or an advanced Pawn or something of that nature. The Rook will stand in readiness to attack it along its 3rd rank, which in most cases is very effective. For instance, after 12 P-KR3 B-KR4 13 P-N4 NxP 14 PxN BxP, the Rook stands ready to act and to strengthen the attack by ... R-N3 or ... R-B3.

12 N-K4

Correct. By an exchange of pieces, White hopes to eliminate Black's threats and then to attack Black's isolated Pawns and make his own plus Pawn felt.

12 ...   **NxN**

Black sees that he can weaken the White K-side by force and thus at least equalize.

13 RxN

The correct reply. After 13 BxB

(a) 13 ... N-N4! and White can no longer avoid the doubling of his Pawns, which entails very serious consequences. A Rook and a Queen against a weakened King's wing can sometimes decide the game in a few moves (see conclusion of this game).

(b) 13 ... NxP 14 KxN Q-N3ch followed by 15 ... QxB, winning back the Pawn.

It is noteworthy that if you make one weak move, combinations surge up all at once. The character of the gambit is such that if the opponent fails to make the right move, combinations develop. But if he succeeds in finding the right moves all the time, most gambits will fail.

13 ...   **BxN**

Black now proceeds in the simplest way. By exchanging, he gives White a double isolated Pawn and opens the KN-file for attack. If he should fail to do this, he would have nothing.

14 PxB

Forced, since 14 QxB costs a piece.

14 ...   **BxB**

If the Black Bishop retires, the White Bishop is not weaker in the defense than the Black Bishop in the attack.

15 QxB

Now Black's only possibility of winning is by attack, because he is a Pawn down and only heavy pieces are left, so surprises in the open field are hardly possible: that is, with minor pieces gone, double attack, pins, etc. are out.

Attack entails bringing as many pieces as possible into the battlefield so as to overwhelm the hostile King.

15 ...   **P-KB4**

First, Black tries to reduce White's defensive power by driving away the Rook; then he plans to continue with . . . P-B5 and shut off the White pieces from the defense.

16 R-K2?

This is fatal: (a) because it enables the Black Queen to enter into the attack directly via its KR5, i.e., without any preparation; (b) because it later deprives the fleeing King of the very important flight square K2.

The correct move was 16 R-QB4. Now, with accurate play, White cannot lose, since just this *one tempo* gives White time to organize his defense, that is, to protect the vital KR2, KB3 and KN2: 16 . . . P-B5 17 K-R1 Q-R5 18 R-KN1 and if (a) 18 . . . Q-R6 19 Q-K2 (to protect KB3) 19 . . . R-R3 20 R-N2, and White is protected on the K-side, or (b) 18 . . . R-KB1 19 Q-K2 R-B4 20 Q-K4 QxBP draws (21 QxR QxPch, etc., or 21 RxP R-R4! 22 R-B8ch K-B2 23 R-B7ch K-B3!).

16 . . .   **Q-R5!**

Black is threatening to win as follows: 17 . . . R-N3ch (a) 18 K-B1 Q-R6ch followed by mate; (b) 18 K-R1 Q-R6 19 R-N1 QxBPch followed by mate. It is evident from these variations that White is unable to protect both his KB3 and his KN2.

17 P-KB4

After 17 KR-K1, Black wins by 17 . . . Q-R6! (threatening 18 . . . R-N3ch) 18 K-R1 R-N3 or R-R3.

17 . . .   **Q-N5ch**

Wins by force, for 18 K-R1 Q-B6ch leads to mate.

18 K-B1   **R-N3**
19 KR-K1

To provide a flight square for his King.

19 . . .   **PxP**
20 Resigns

For there is no adequate defense against 20 ... P-B6, since the White King is trapped. After 20 P-KB3, Black wins by 20 ... Q-R6ch and 21 ... R-N7ch.

A gambit (a) makes your play easier than that of your opponent; (b) entails the risk that if the opponent solves all the problems, he has a clear advantage.

In this game, White does not solve all the problems (e.g., 9 N-B3), and this gives Black a certain grip on the position (his QB on its KN5), which under all circumstances must lead to a weakening of the White K-position. It is now only a question of a draw or win for Black: three heavy pieces against three heavy pieces. Placed in the right defensive position, they can maintain the balance. In the game, the Rook on K2 ruins the White defensive system.

Game 18

The Scotch game

Cutting down force through exchange

Finding attacking possibilities

Analyzing tactical lines

Making the most of the opponent's weaknesses

The strong Bishop radiating its power into the heart
of the hostile position

One of the hardest tasks of the chess player is to find the most favorable line in a position beset with tactical problems. To do so requires: (1) the imagination to discover the various playable lines; (2) the power to analyze each line for the necessary number of moves; (3) the judgment to evaluate accurately the results of each of the available lines.

In this game, the gambit player succeeds in building up a strong attack by sacrificing two Pawns. His opponent is quite willing to return the Pawns for the sake of simplification and in order to reduce the attacking power of the gambit player, but he chooses an inferior tactical variation, so that when equality of material is re-established, he is left with a serious weakness: a compromised King position. His King is no longer safe in the center; he cannot castle on the K-side; and by castling long he heads into serious weaknesses. At this point he again fails to find the best defense, whereupon the gambit player makes the most of the weaknesses he has induced in his opponent's position.

The Göring Gambit (Scotch Game)

Master	Amateur
1 P-K4	P-K4
2 N-KB3	N-QB3
3 P-Q4	

The Scotch Game.

White immediately occupies the center and opens up the game. After retaking, Black has no trouble in attaining equality after several more moves. Hence, the Scotch Game is not seen as frequently in tournament play as are certain other openings in which Black has greater difficulty in equalizing.

3 ...	PxP

Although Black loses a tempo by taking, this does not really entail a loss of time, for White must also lose a tempo in order to retake.

If Black does not retake at this point, he cannot equalize as easily. Let us examine some of the alternatives in order to get a better idea of the problem of gaining equality as worked out in the theory of openings.

(a) 3 ... P-Q3 4 PxP loses a Pawn or the privilege of castling after 4 ... PxP or 4 ... NxP. Or White can also play 4 B-QN5, with some pressure against Black's position.

(b) 3 ... P-B3? entails a weakening of Black's K-wing. After White's 4 B-QB4, Black cannot castle. On the other hand, 4 PxP is not conclusive, for (1) 4 ... PxP and White would not have attained much, but (2) 4 ... NxP? 5 NxN PxN 6 Q-R5ch wins immediately.

(c) 3 ... N-B3 4 PxP NxP/K5 5 B-QB4, threatening 6 Q-Q5 with a good game for White.

(d) 3 ... Q-K2 has the disadvantage of blocking the Black KB.

After 3 . . . PxP, White normally continues:

(a) The Scotch Game: 4 NxP N-B3 (attacking the center and preparing . . . P-Q4) 5 N-QB3 (protecting the KP) 5 . . . B-N5 (reattacking the KP) 6 NxN (practically forced) 6 . . . NPxN 7 B-Q3 P-Q4 and Black has attained equality.

(b) The Scotch Gambit, in which White temporarily gives up the Pawn for the more rapid development: 4 B-QB4 N-B3 5 0-0.

In this game, the master deliberately chooses a continuation which is not entirely sound.

4 P-B3

The Göring Gambit, which, despite the fact that it is not entirely sound, leads to complicated and interesting play.

4 . . .   **PxP**

Black accepts the gambit Pawn. He could have refused the proffered Pawn by 4 . . . P-Q4, which is not at all bad. For instance 5 PxP/Q5 QxP 6 PxP B-KN5, etc. Or he could refuse the Pawn by 4 . . . P-Q6, which would prevent White from building up the ideal center by PxP and thus prevent him from dominating the center. This last variation embodies an important principle: *When one must lose or wishes to lose a Pawn in any case, it is economical to lose it in such a way that one's opponent gets some positional disadvantage by taking it.*

5 NxP   **B-N5**

An enterprising move which leaves open to Black possibilities of counterattack but involves certain risks. Compare with Game 10.

The alternate 5 . . . P-Q3 is a more peaceful continuation. Black tries to build up a solid position, and, if he succeeds in withstanding the White attack, his plus Pawn must do its work in the end. But White *is* able to complicate things. For example: 6 B-B4 B-K3 7 BxB PxB 8 Q-N3 Q-B1 9 N-KN5 N-Q1 10 0-0 B-K2 11 P-B4 and anything can happen.

6 B-QB4

The right square for the White KB. White threatens moves like Q-N3.

6 ...   **P-Q3**

To control his K4-square and open a diagonal for the QB. Black feared White's P-K5.

If Black had played 6 ... N-B3, the continuation 7 P-K5 would have been very strong: 7 ... P-Q4 8 B-N3 N-K5 9 0-0 BxN 10 PxB with very difficult complications. The amateur would do better to avoid lines which entail such extremely complicated problems.

7 0-0

7 ...   **BxN**

By exchanging, Black sets out to reduce the lead in development which White has attained in return for the gambit Pawn. The exchange is especially justified here, for, since White's QN is no longer pinned, Black has to reckon with N-Q5. If, for instance, Black had replied 7 ... N-B3, then 8 N-Q5! would bring him into difficulties, since 8 ... NxN would cost a piece after 9 PxN N-K2 10 Q-R4ch.

If, instead, Black had played 7 ... B-N5 and pinned White's KN now that White has castled, the game could have continued 8 Q-N3 Q-Q2 9 N-Q5 B-QR4 10 QxP, threatening 11 B-QN5. Black therefore plays 10 ... R-N1 and after 11 Q-R6 BxN 12 PxB with equal Pawns, and both sides have chances.

At this point, we take the opportunity to give an example of a typical amateur combination based on the unsound sacrifice of White's KB on his KB7 after 7 ... B-N5: 8 BxPch? KxB 9 N-N5ch, and it looks as if White is going to regain his piece plus a Pawn by 10 QxB. But Black plays 9 ... QxN! and wins a piece after 10 BxQ BxQ 11 QRxB.

8 PxB

White now has an isolated Pawn, but this does not mean much under the given circumstances. White is a Pawn down, and he must find some compensation for it. The isolated Pawn is compensated for by the fact that White now has the Two Bishops against Bishop and Knight, and, moreover, he has open lines for his Bishops and Rooks. Most important here are White's attacking possibilities, not the special positional features such as Pawn structure. If a general liquidation should occur, then these positional factors would again count. But White has based everything on winning by attack. If the attack fails, he is likely to find himself at a disadvantage with or without isolated Pawns.

8 ...	N-B3

9 P-K5

To open up the game and try to find some compensation for the sacrificed Pawn in attacking possibilities. With this move, White gives a second Pawn.

The quiet continuations 9 R-K1 and 9 B-KN5 (which is playable despite the fact that the King has not yet castled—compare Game 17) are not so bad, either, but perhaps they are less direct.

9 B-R3 B-N5 seems to be inferior, and White has no promising continuation of his attack.

9 ...   PxP

9 ... NxP is followed by 10 NxN PxN 11 Q-N3 0-0 12 B-R3, winning the exchange as compensation for White's two lost Pawns, which in many cases is a doubtful bargain, but here seems at least to guarantee a draw.

10 N-N5

White violates the general principle of moving a piece only once until the other pieces are developed, but here again there are special circumstances which justify such a move. By moving his Knight to N5, White threatens 11 NxBP, winning the Rook. The fact that it is not simple for Black to parry this threat justifies the violation of the above-mentioned rule. If Black plays 10 ... 0-0, then 11 B-R3 wins the exchange. This does not mean that White would then have a won game, for Black would have two Pawns as compensation, but in any case the game would then enter a new phase of the struggle, with all its possibilities and all its chances.

10 ...   B-K3

Rather than lose the exchange, Black prefers to give up his extra Pawn and allow White to isolate the KP. The idea is to accelerate the development at the price of one or two of the gambit Pawns.

After 10 ... QxQ 11 BxPch K-B1 12 RxQ, White is still a Pawn down, but he threatens 13 B-R3ch N-K2 14 R-Q8 mate. After 12 ... P-KN3 13 B-R3ch K-N2, White has good chances after 14 B-N3, notwithstanding the fact that Queens are no longer on the board. With threats such as 15 N-B7 or 15 N-K6ch, depending on Black's counterplay, White certainly has chances by which to compensate for the Pawn.

With the text, however, Black offers to return the gambit Pawns, thus hoping to eliminate White's most dangerous pieces and to enter an end game in which he would certainly not have the worst of it. These are the proper tactics when playing the defensive side of the gambit, as has been pointed out in the early moves of the game. For example: 11 BxB PxB 12 NxKP QxQ 13 RxQ K-B2 14 NxBP QR-Q1 and Black stands well. Pawns are even, but one of White's Bishops has disappeared, and now the isolated Pawns may count in favor of Black.

11 NxB

Special tactical possibilities favor 11 NxB over 11 BxB. No generalization is possible in a tactical position such as this.

If now 11 ... QxQ 12 NxBPch K-Q2 13 RxQch KxN 14 BxP, the ending is a little better for White because he has maintained his Two Bishops. True, White's QBP is weak, but in this variation White has full compensation, in that the Black KP is also isolated. So Black plays

11 ...   PxN

If White now simply plays the obvious 12 BxP, the game could continue 12 ... QxQ 13 RxQ K-K2 14 B-N3 KR-Q1, and White would find himself in a simplified position with a Pawn down. He must, therefore, look for a stronger reply. With this in mind, he plays

12 Q-N3

With this move, White attacks the QNP and threatens BxP with greater force, since the possibility of Black's exchanging Queens no longer exists, and since the side that has less material should not exchange Queens. White's 12 Q-N3 is so strong that Black must carefully analyze all possibilities. His reply here will prove the turning point of the game.

12 ...	N-R4?

Black protects his QNP and hopes by a series of exchanges to reduce White's attack, but he has underrated the fact that, even after the simplification, White's initiative remains strong.

It appears that after 12 ... 0-0 13 BxPch K-R1 14 QxP Q-Q3 15 B-N3 QR-N1 16 Q-R6, Black can hold his own. This line is better for Black than the text—his pieces are more centralized, more cooperative, but White has the Two Bishops and the threat of B-R3.

But Black has still better. After 12 ... N-Q4 13 QxP N-R4 14 B-N5ch K-B2 15 Q-R6 P-B4 16 B-R3 Q-N3, Black has the best of it, because the Black Knights are well posted and the White Bishops have no lines. Tarrasch said: "A Bishop is stronger than a Knight only when it can run along open lines."

From this, we conclude that at this point 12 ... N-Q4 was the strongest continuation, and that it was at this point that the

amateur went wrong for the first time. This is the more noteworthy since the position is so complicated.

13 Q-N5ch	P-B3
14 QxKP	NxB
15 QxPch	Q-K2
16 QxQN	

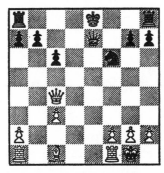

Thus, at the end of the liquidation invited by Black, the sides
are equal in pieces, and White's isolated Pawn, a weakness, is
compensated for by open lines for attack, by the fact that White
has a Bishop whereas Black has a Knight, and by the fact that
Black cannot castle on the K-side. White certainly has the best
of it.

16 ...   **0-0-0**

Although Black's Q-side is not an extremely safe place for the
Black King, considering the open lines at White's disposal, neither
is Black's King safe in the center. Black had no alternative. Castling was forced in view of the eventual threat R-K1.

17 B-B4

The idea behind this move is to take from the Black King his
QN1-square. Surprising combinations could evolve, as we shall
see later. The Black King is unsafe.

17 ...   **N-Q4**

Black hopes to reduce White's attack by exchanges. The idea
is correct, but the means of execution is imperfect.

211

Despite its centralized position, the Black Knight does not succeed in eliminating the White Bishop. Correct for forcing the exchange of pieces would have been 17 ... Q-K5, and after 18 QxQ (forced) NxQ 19 B-K5, White is a little better off because of the centralized position of his Bishop, to be strengthened by P-KB4 and the unsafe position of the Black King, which, it is true, does not count too much after the exchange of Queens. These two factors more than compensate for the disadvantage of White's isolated Pawn.

18 B-N3

The Bishop is just as strong on KN3 as it was on KB4.

18 ...   **P-KR4**

An attempt to drive away the Bishop, which is easily met. It would have been preferable to bring pressure on the center by a move such as 18 ... KR-K1, possibly followed by 19 ... Q-K5.

19 P-KR3

To provide a refuge from which the Bishop can continue to control the diagonal.

19 ...   **P-KN4**

Black wishes to exploit the weakness of the KRP, but White has various possibilities of attack which must be met. The text is a weakening and, to a certain extent, an unmotivated attack. Still preferable was 19 ... KR-K1, the centralizing move. But White already had some attack anyhow. After White moves such as Q-QR4, Black cannot protect his QRP by ... K-N1, so he must weaken his position by ... P-QR3. One sees the enormous force of White's Bishop along the diagonal.

20 KR-K1

Development with tempo.

With White's superior command of space and the open lines at his disposal, Black's position is already precarious. Although there is nothing definite yet, White can feel confident that there must be promising lines in the offing, and Black must be very careful. For instance:

(a) 20 ... Q-Q2 21 QR-N1 KR-K1 22 KR-Q1! R-K3 23 Q-R6! PxQ? 24 R-N8 mate.

(b) 20 ... Q-KB2 21 Q-QR4 P-R3 (forced) 22 QR-N1 and
    (1) 22 ... NxP? 23 QxBPch PxQ 24 R-N8ch K-Q2
    25 R-N7ch K-B1 26 RxQ R-Q2 27 RxR KxR 28 B-K5, etc.
    (2) 22 ... KR-K1! the best continuation, and now the sacrifice of the Queen leads only to a draw: 23 QxPch PxQ 24 R-N8ch K-Q2 25 R-N7ch K-B1 26 R-N8ch, etc., but White need not draw; he can play 23 B-K5, for example, and maintain the initiative.

20 ...   Q-R6?

A mistake in a very difficult position. The Queen should not leave its K-position undefended. In general, one should not go Pawn hunting in critical positions in which the opponent has the attack.

21 Q-K4

Wins. The threat is 22 Q-B5ch R-Q2 23 Q-K5 with the double threat of 24 Q-N8 mate and QxRch.

21 ...   QxBP

Black puts his Queen and Rook on the same diagonal—a combinational motif to be exploited with a Bishop.

Let us examine some alternate possibilities:

(a) 21 ... KR-K1? 22 Q-B5ch R-Q2 23 RxR mate.

(b) 21 ... Q-B1 22 Q-K5 and the penetration of the Queen to N8 is catastrophic.

(c) 21 ... N-B2 22 Q-B5ch K-N1 (22 ... R-Q2? 23 BxN KxB 24 Q-K5ch wins the KR) 23 Q-B7 R-QB1 24 R-K7 Q-R4 25 R-Q1 KR-KB1 26 BxNch wins, for (1) 26 ... RxB; 27 QxRch or (2) 26 ... K-R1 27 BxQ.

(d) 21 ... N-B3 22 Q-K5 wins (22 ... N-Q2 23 Q-B7 mate; 22 ... Q-Q3 23 QxQ wins the Rook).

22 Q-B5ch

Forces Black to interpose his QR, and then his KR remains unprotected.

If first 22 B-K5, White wins only the exchange, for the Black KR would still be protected.

Note that more than 80 per cent of all these possibilities hinge on the phenomenal position of the White Bishop, which controls squares such as its QN8, QB7 and K5.

22 ...	R-Q2

The only move.

23 B-K5

Winning the Rook.

23 ...	Resigns

In this gambit, White had attacking chances from the very beginning, and Black had to choose between a number of possible defenses. This made the defense difficult for Black.

As regards both the manner of defending against a gambit and the psychological factor mentioned in the introduction to Game 17, Black behaved properly in this game. He continually tried to give back his extra gambit Pawn and find his happiness in the end game. He didn't quite succeed; he could have, but he still had to overcome difficulties in positions where material was even, but White had a better placed Bishop. After Black missed the opportunity to force the exchange of Queens, White was able to maintain his attack, and this attack proved to be killing, thanks to White's well-posted Bishop.

Game 19

The Marshall variation of the Queen's Gambit Declined

Surrender of the center without compensation

Attack on the castled King position with all pieces

The standard sacrifice BxKRPch

One of the most glittering types of chess is that in which a player surprises his opponent with an all-out mating attack against the relatively undefended castled King. Bringing one piece after another to bear on that area of the board, he overwhelms his opponent before the latter has an opportunity to do anything about it.

Of the combinational attacks against the castled King, none is easier to execute than the well-known Bishop sacrifice on KR7. This attack, good for either White or Black, can be undertaken whenever the following situation exists on the board:

(a) The attacker must have his KN and Queen posed for action and his KB on the proper diagonal for an immediate sacrifice at KR7.

(b) This KN must be able to maintain itself on its KN5 without danger of being exchanged.

(c) Usually a spearhead Pawn at the K5-square of the attacker is useful both for preventing the enemy King from getting away and for preventing enemy pieces from going to their KB3.

(d) The defender's pieces must be far enough away from the K-side that they cannot give effective aid at the right time.

(e) The defender's King must not have available sufficient flight squares to be able to escape.

The attack starts with BxKRPch. Whether the defender accepts or refuses the sacrifice, he is in for trouble. But in order to succeed the attacking player must follow up with just the right moves. If he chooses the right moves, he will either mate or emerge with material superiority. If he does not find the correct continuation, he can find himself down a piece and his attack dissipated, in which case he may go down to eventual defeat.

The Queen's Gambit Declined—Marshall Variation

Master	Amateur
1 P-Q4	P-Q4
2 P-QB4	

The Queen's Gambit, which we have already encountered in Games 9 and 16.

| 2 ... | N-KB3 (?) |

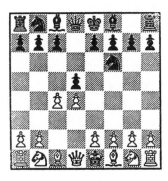

One of the favorite positional errors of amateurs.

Apparently, 2 ... N-KB3 is a developing move which adequately protects Black's QP. Actually, after 3 PxP Black is compelled to give up the center for nothing: that is, without securing any counterchance to attack the White center.

True, once in a very great while 2 . . . N-KB3 is found in master games. For instance, the American grandmaster Marshall sometimes used it with success. One must differentiate between 2 . . . N-KB3 (a) as a move played by an amateur who makes it without realizing that he has committed a strategical error by giving White the opportunity to build up a strong center; (b) as a move played very infrequently by a master, in the spirit of challenge, with the aim of enticing White to play a premature 4 P-K4. In this latter case we could speak of tactical considerations.

3 PxP

White reasons: "If 3 . . . QxP, I will answer 4 N-QB3 (compare Game 15), and the Black Queen will be forced to move again, thus gaining a tempo for me and also allowing me to threaten to take possession of the center by 5 P-K4. If 3 . . . NxP, then P-K4 will become possible very soon."

3 . . .   NxP

Black now occupies the center temporarily, but he cannot remain there because his Knight can be driven away by P-K4. Yet an immediate 4 P-K4 would be premature. Black would reply 4 . . . N-KB3 and

(a) 5 N-QB3 P-K4! and Black has counterchances, for

(1) 6 PxP QxQch 7 KxQ N-N5, winning back the KP, for White must protect against the threatened 8 . . . NxPch: 8 K-K1 NxKP 9 P-B4 N-N3, and, although White occupies the center, his King cannot castle and is vulnerable to attack in this open position.

(2) 6 P-Q5 B-QB4 and Black has satisfactory development, being one tempo ahead.

(b) 5 B-Q3 is better than 5 N-QB3, but Black here also gets chances to attack the White center: 5 . . . N-B3 (Black cannot play 5 . . . QxP because of 6 B-N5ch, winning the Queen) and

(1) 6 N-KB3 B-N5; (2) 6 N-K2 P-K4; (3) 6 P-Q5 N-K4
7 B-B2 P-K3

4 N-KB3

This simple move prevents Black from playing ... P-K4 for the present and at the same time conserves for White the possibility of playing P-K4 himself.

4 ...   P-K3

Black might have replied 4 ... B-B4 in order to prevent the White P-K4 and post pieces centrally on the board. White could then answer 5 QN-Q2 with the strong threat of 6 P-K4! After 5 ... N-KB3 6 Q-N3 Q-B1 7 P-N3 P-K3 8 B-N2, White threatens 9 N-R4 followed by BxP, with a superior game because he has more space and controls more central squares.

5 P-K4

Now White occupies the center completely, forcing Black to retreat.

5 ...   N-KB3

Inferior to 5 ... N-N3, because after 5 ... N-KB3 the Knight is exposed to the advance P-K5.

6 N-QB3

Look at what a fine position White already has—possession of the center, mobility, better development, etc.

6 ...   B-N5

To neutralize White's control over his K4-square. The pin of White's QN is not very effective, as the White King will castle sooner or later, thus eliminating the pin. Since the exchange ... BxN only strengthens White's center and leaves White with the Two Bishops, it can be stated in general that this pin is effective only if Black succeeds in a successful pressure against the center squares Q4 or K5.

Perhaps a better move would be 6 ... P-B4, attacking the

219

center in a more efficient way. In that case, White has the possibility of (a) 7 P-Q5; (b) 7 P-K5; or (c) a move such as 7 B-Q3 (7 ... PxP 8 NxP QxN?? 9 B-N5ch and the Black Queen is lost).

7 B-Q3

By this one move, the White KB is developed to its most powerful diagonal, the K-side is cleared for castling, and the White KP is protected.

7 ...   **QN-Q2**

A weak move. It does very little against White's overwhelming superiority in the center. But the position is already difficult. From the following alternate tries, it is evident that White's center is so strong that even direct attacks will not destroy the strength of White's center, the force of which is exemplified in this game.

(a) 7 ... P-B4 8 0-0 PxP 9 NxP 0-0 (9 ... QxN 10 B-N5ch, winning the Black Queen) 10 P-K5 with a strong attack for White (again 10 ... QxP? 11 BxPch wins the Queen).

(b) 7 ... N-B3 8 0-0 0-0 (8 ... NxQP? 9 NxN QxN?? 10 B-N5ch, winning the Queen!) 9 P-K5, as in the game.

One must see this kind of attack as a direct result of the strong White center: P-K5 drives away Black's only defensive piece.

8 0-0   **0-0?**

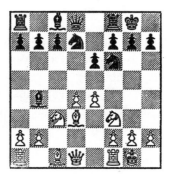

This is fatal! At this point, Black's position is already ripe for exploitation. Black should never castle when White has such a concentration of force against his K-side and the possibility of eliminating the defensive N/KB3 by advancing his KP.

Let us examine the position. White's Queen is on its original square, ready to go to KR5; his KN is on KB3, ready to go to N5; the KB is on Q3, ready to be sacrificed on KR7; the QB guards the KN5 from its home base; and the KP is on the point of going to K5 and driving the Black Knight from its KB3. Once this Knight is driven away, the Black K-side will be devoid of protecting pieces, therefore ripe for attack.

This type of position often arises in variations of the Queen's Gambit Declined, the French Defense, and certain other openings. Whenever the K-side is without defenders, the attack which follows is in the air.

Black should have played 8 ... P-B4 in order to break up the White center. After 9 P-K5 N-Q4 10 NxN PxN 11 N-N5! White also has great superiority, with threats such as 12 Q-B3. Let us try: 11 ... P-KR3. White can answer 12 Q-R5 and then

(a) 12 ... Q-K2 13 NxP 0-0 (13 ... QxN? 14 B-N6) 14 Q-N6, etc.

(b) 12 ... P-KN3 13 BxP PxP 14 QxPch, followed by mate.

(c) 12 ... 0-0 13 P-K6 N-B3 14 PxPch K-R1 15 Q-N6 Q-K2 16 N-R7!

9 P-K5

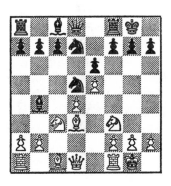

(See next page for N-Q4 move.)

The simple key.

9 ...   N-Q4 (Diagramed on page 221)

Now everything is set for the all-out attack.

10 BxPch

The well-known Bishop sacrifice on KR7.

The first move of a combination which leads either to mate or to an overwhelming attack culminating in more than equality for White.

Yet White must play with care, calculating the moves carefully. Once a piece is sacrificed, it is everything or nothing. Unless White can move up his forces and overwhelm Black, he may find himself short of the desired mate and with a piece down.

10 ...   KxB

Black, not realizing that he is in mortal danger of a blitz attack, accepts the Grecian gift. He erroneously believes that his extra piece will insure him an eventual win. Pieces count only when they are active. In this special situation, few of Black's pieces can act at all, and none at once because of White's checks.

Even if Black had declined the proffered Bishop, White's attack would have been successful, as we shall show later.

11 N-KN5ch

Preparing 12 Q-R5 and mate in a few moves. Notice that White's KN is protected by its QB.

In all-out attacks which entail the sacrifice of a piece, the attacking player must find moves which limit the squares accessible to the enemy King. Here, White's spearhead PK5 already denied the King access to his KB3, and now the White Knight controls Black's KR2 and KB2.

11 ...   K-N1

If 11 ... K-N3 12 Q-Q3ch P-B4 13 NxP (forcing the Black Queen to move) 13 ... Q-K2 (after 13 ... Q-K1, the answer 14 NxN is also decisive) 14 NxN (again forcing the Black Queen to move) 14 ... QxN 15 N-B4ch (winning the Queen).

12 NxN

If 12 Q-R5 immediately, Black can give back his extra piece and temporarily stop White's attack: 12 ... KN-B3 (or 12 ... QN-B3) 13 PxN NxP, and Black posts his Knight on his KB3 and White's attack is at an end for the time being.

12 ...	PxN
13 Q-R5	R-K1

The only move.

The following forced moves illustrate how White systematically takes squares from the Black King until mate is inevitable. Notice that all Black's moves are forced; he has no time to bring up any pieces for defense.

14 QxPch	K-R1
15 Q-R5ch	K-N1
16 Q-R7ch	K-B1
17 Q-R8ch	K-K2
18 QxP mate	

Two factors are important in this mate: (a) the continual checks gave Black no opportunity to mobilize his pieces; (b) White's PK5 and N/N5 effectively prevented the Black King from slipping out of the mating net.

Black Declines the Proffered Bishop

Now we shall consider what would have happened if Black had not accepted the Bishop sacrifice. The variations which follow give an excellent idea of numerous possibilities rising from these kinds of attacking positions. White has two very strong continuations, which we shall call A and B.

10 ...   K-R1

Continuation A

11 B-B2

White withdraws the Bishop, keeping open every possibility and, among other things, preventing 11 ... NxN, for then 12 PxN BxP? 13 Q-Q3! winning a piece, since it threatens simultaneously to give mate and to capture Black's Bishop.

Continuation A-1

11 ...   P-QB4

Black finally makes the important move (see comments under Black's 6th move), but it was more important to secure the K-wing by 11 ... P-KN3 (see A-2), although the latter move was not sufficient either. It is only a question of time now how long the loss can be postponed.

12 B-N5

To drive the Queen from the K-side. The point is that Black can no longer answer 12 ... P-B3, which would be met by 13 Q-Q3 and mate in a few moves.

12 N-KN5 wins as well: 12 ... P-KN3 13 NxN PxN 14 NxPch RxN 15 P-K6.

| 12 ... | Q-B2 |

12 ... Q-R4? loses a piece: 13 NxN PxN 14 P-QR3 and the Bishop has no retreat.

12 ... Q-K1 13 Q-Q3 P-KN3 14 B-R6 wins (14 ... R-KN1 15 NxN PxN 16 N-N5 and 17 Q-R3).

13 NxN

By exchanging pieces, White eliminates a well-posted Knight in exchange for a Knight which, for the moment, does not participate in the struggle.

| 13 ... | PxN |

One of the basic problems in positions of this sort is to vacate squares so that the key pieces can come out and do their work. Therefore, White plays

| 14 B-K7 | R-K1 |

Offering to give up the exchange would certainly have been better. Perhaps the relatively best line (although completely hopeless with the exchange and a Pawn down) would have been 14 ... K-N1 15 N-N5 P-KN3. Other moves are inferior and cost more material. For instance: 14 ... PxP? 15 BxB; or 14 ... NxP 15 NxN! QxB 16 Q-R5ch and mate on the next move.

| 15 N-N5 | P-KN3 |

If 15 ... RxB 16 Q-R5ch K-N1 17 Q-R7ch K-B1 18 Q-R8 mate.

16 Q-N4

Again mate in three threatens, so that moves like 16 ... NxP, threatening the Queen by discovery, fail.

| 16 ... | K-N1 |

16 ... K-N2 loses as well after 17 N-K6ch! PxN 18 QxNPch, followed by mate.

| 17 Q-R4 | N-B1 |

What else?

18 B-B6

Followed by mate.

Continuation A-2

See diagram on page 224 and play the move 11 **B-B2**.

11 ...	P-KN3
12 Q-Q2	

Forcing the penetration into Black's K-side position.

12 ...	R-K1

To make room for the Knight.

13 Q-R6ch	K-N1
14 B-N5	B-K2
15 NxN	

In order to continue 15 ... PxN 16 P-K6!

15 ...	PxN
16 P-K6	

To undermine Black's KNP.

16 ...	N-B1
17 PxPch	KxP
18 BxPch	

White temporarily sacrifices the Bishop in order to be able to drive the Black King out into the open.

18 ...	NxB
19 Q-R7ch	K-K3
20 QxNch	K-Q2
21 N-K5 mate	

Continuation B

See diagram on page 224.

11 N-KN5

Bringing the Knight into the fray and threatening 12 Q-R5, which is also very strong.

11 ...   **P-KN3**

The only move; 11 ... QN-B3 would lose a piece; 11 ... P-KB3 leads to 12 Q-R5 PxN 13 B-N6ch, followed by mate.

12 Q-N4

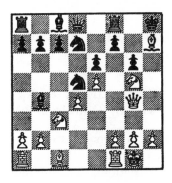

Continuation B-1

12 ...	K-N2
13 Q-R4	R-R1

At first glance, it looks as if Black has been able to protect adequately. But through threats White can open lines and make the superiority of his active pieces felt.

14 NxPch	PxN
15 Q-R6ch	K-B2
16 QxPch	

The game continues:

(a) 16 . . . K-K2 17 Q-N7ch K-K1 18 B-N6 mate.

(b) 16 . . . K-B1 17 B-R6ch K-K2 18 Q-N7ch, followed by mate.

Continuation B-2

See diagram on page 227.

12 . . .   Q-K2

13 Q-R4 and wins, as will appear from the following possibilities:

(a) 13 . . . K-N2 14 NxPch followed by the win of the Queen or an early mate; if 14 . . . QxN 15 Q-R6ch K-R1 16 BxP dis ch K-N1 17 Q-R7 mate.

(b) 13 . . . P-KB4 14 NxN PxN 15 BxP dis ch K-N1 16 P-K6 N-B3 17 B-B7ch RxB 18 PxRch, with great material advantage.

(c) 13 . . . P-KB3 14 BxP dis ch K-N1 15 B-R7ch K-N2 16 KN-K4 and wins by Q-R6ch or B-R6ch.

These combinations are very instructive because the Black position is so bad that White has a great many possibilities and there are only a few variations, with the moves almost forced.

The student should try to follow the combinations, first working out the moves on the board, later without moving the pieces. Such practice enhances combinative power.

Game 20

Exploiting a deviation from theory

Gaining a preponderance in space

Violating chess rules with a purpose

The unsafe center King position

Taking advantage of a temporary preponderance
of pieces in a given area

Concentrated attack on a weak point

There is one chess rule which says, "Move a piece only once during the opening," and another which states, "Do not undertake attack or other action until your development is completed." These are excellent general precepts, for certainly many games have been lost because players failed to get enough pieces into the battle at the right time.

They are, however, generalities, and they apply mainly to strategic positions. Only such positions lend themselves to a more or less automatic following of rules. There are naturally positions in which these rules must be broken in order to attain the strongest play. A master cannot blindly follow the precepts set down for learners but must evaluate every position according to its merits.

Positionally, the rules of development may be disregarded when the strategic plan requires other action. For instance, in a position where the player's development is incomplete, it may look as though the development of the QN, as yet on QN1, is obvious. Yet in that position there may be an imperative reason for moving an already developed piece a second time, in order to take command of some vital square or to prevent the opponent from doing so.

The rule of "development first" may also be broken when the opponent has made a weak move or an error which must be taken advantage of immediately. In such cases, the entire game must be focused on the point of the error, rather than on "strategic development as usual."

If the tactical situation is clear-cut, it is often easy to see that the development rule must be broken, but this is much more difficult when it is necessary to define the exact weakness of the opponent and then to study how to go about exploiting it.

In this game, White does not complete his development in the usual way, but from time to time makes a sharper sally. The consequence of this well-directed handling of the position is that very soon the whole board is on fire and the Black player is faced with very difficult tactical problems.

The Queen's Gambit Declined—Marshall Variation

Master	Amateur
1 P-Q4	P-Q4
2 P-QB4	N-KB3 (?)

This move, which we have already met in the previous game, is somewhat questionable, because it allows White to build up a strong center which Black cannot easily weaken. On the other hand, one must not forget that a master of the strength of Marshall often played the move and that he won with it, once from Reti, once from Nimzovich.

For further discussion of the move, see Game 19.

3 PxP

White must exchange immediately in order to take advantage of Black's slight deviation from theory. Otherwise, Black can protect his Pawn center on the next move with 3 ... P-K3 or 3 ... P-B3.

3 ...	NxP
4 N-KB3	

White makes this move in order to prevent ... P-K4. An immediate 4 P-K4 would give Black some counterchances, as is shown in Game 19.

| 4 ... | P-K3 |
| 5 P-K4 | N-N3 |

Superior to 5 ... N-KB3, where the Knight is exposed to the advance P-K5 (see Game 19).

6 B-Q3

Although it might seem natural to play 6 N-QB3 first, since there is no doubt that this is the best square for the QN, White plays his KB to Q3 at this point, because after 6 N-QB3 P-QB4, White cannot play 7 PxP without giving Black the opportunity to exchange Queens and thus lessen White's advantage.

| 6 ... | P-QB4 |

Black plays this move at this point for various reasons: (a) Black's game is cramped, and it will remain so until avenues are opened for his pieces; 6 ... P-QB4 opens Black's game and thus constitutes a freeing move, without which his game would continue to remain cramped; (b) Black wants to attack and thus neutralize White's strong center setup as soon as possible.

7 PxP

White takes in order to keep control of the square K5. For instance, after 7 O-O PxP 8 NxP, Black would play ... P-K4.

Black was not actually threatening to win a Pawn here. After 7 ... PxP 8 NxP QxN? (the correct move is 8 ... P-K4) 9 B-N5ch, and Black loses his Queen.

| 7 ... | BxP |

At this point, the only advantage White has is that he has a Pawn on his K4, whereas Black has a Pawn on K3. If Black were able to play ... P-K4, White would have no advantage whatever.

231

It is of great interest to see how the master makes the most of this very slight advantage during the remainder of the game.

8 0-0

Here, the amateur might make the plausible developing move 8 N-B3. The master, on the contrary, looks into possibilities such as 8 ... P-K4 9 NxP BxPch 10 KxB Q-Q5ch. One of the big differences between the strong amateur and the master is that the latter sees more, considers more.

8 ...   **Q-B2**

This amateur, who understands the nature of White's advantage, prepares for 9 ... P-K4 and complete equality. For that reason, the text is better than 8 ... 0-0, which is a solid developing move without a specific purpose, in that the text is a strategic move which stems from a purpose.

9 P-K5!

Absolutely necessary to prevent Black from freeing his game with ... P-K4. The text has the disadvantage of giving Black free access to his Q4-square, but this does not weigh so heavily. Besides, the text has the advantage of freeing the diagonal for the KB.

An amateur intent on developing pieces might expect a move such as 9 N-B3 and condemn the text as a loss of time. Yet the text has the advantage of cramping Black's development and of making it difficult for him to bring pieces to his K-side.

9 ...	N-B3

Black attacks White's advanced outpost, and if White tries to defend with 10 B-B4, Black can play 10 ... N-Q4, after which Black's minor pieces develop a reasonable degree of activity.

The advance of White's KP has opened the diagonal and has given White more mobility and control of more space, but it does have the disadvantage of handing over to Black White's Q4-square, as already noted.

10 N-B3!

Developing the Knight to its natural square and exerting pressure on Q5, to which Black might want to play his Knight.

Moves such as 10 Q-K2 or 10 R-K1 are also possible, but they might give Black counterchances, as, for instance, 10 R-K1 N-N5 11 B-K4 B-Q2 12 P-QR3 N/5-Q4 13 P-QN4 B-K2 14 B-N2 B-QB3, and Black has a kind of counterweight. The text is sharper and controls the pivotal square. It brings the game into the gambit sphere, which is very favorable for White in view of his superior development.

10 ...	NxP

Let us consider the alternatives:

(a) 10 ... 0-0 would invite 11 BxPch, the consequences of which we have seen in Game 19.

(b) 10 ... B-Q2 and White might continue by 11 B-KB4, preparing assaults like N-QN5-Q6ch.

(c) 10 ... N-Q4 11 NxN PxN would make things easier for White, because of Black's isolated Pawn, and White can play moves such as R-K1 and take advantage of the Pawn majority on the K-side.

11 B-KB4

White is now a Pawn down, but in return he has pinned Black's Knight and won a tempo. The pin is the more serious because

Black cannot answer 11 ... B-Q3 (12 N-QN5) to eliminate the pin. On the other hand, Black does have—and must use—the resource of taking with check. So he plays

11 ...   NxNch

Forced, for if 11 ... B-Q3? 12 N-QN5 Q-Q1 (or -Q2 or -B3) 13 NxBch and if 13 ... QxN 14 BxN; if 11 ... P-B3 12 NxN PxN 13 Q-R5ch.

12 QxN   Q-K2

Look at the position. All the White forces are in the game; it is White's move; Black has not yet castled; and Black has only partially developed. For one Pawn, White has three tempi. Most of White's pieces are very well posted, very threatening. Still, it is not so easy to take advantage of the situation. For instance, if White plays 13 N-N5 (planning 14 N-B7ch), Black can reply 13 ... N-Q4, and things are not easy.

13 N-K4

Again the master moves a developed piece instead of making a developing move such as 13 QR-B1 or 13 KR-Q1. This he does because it is important to drive the Bishop from the diagonal K2-R6. Once the Bishop has left the diagonal, one of White's pieces can penetrate to Q6. For instance, 13 ... 0-0 14 QR-B1 B-N5 15 P-QR3 and Black can prevent the direct catastrophe

234

only by 15 ... P-B4, but after 16 PxB PxN 17 QxP, Black is hopeless, for White is threatening things like QxPch or R-B7.

13 ...   N-Q4

Black also plays his Knight to a prominent center square, threatening to neutralize with 14 ... NxB.

14 QR-B1

White again threatens to eliminate Black's KB.

To be sure, Black can now exchange his Knight for the White Bishop, but after 14 ... NxB 15 QxN, he has not solved the problem of his attacked Bishop. Again, 15 ... B-N5 can be answered by 16 P-QR3, and if the Bishop leaves the diagonal, 17 N-Q6ch follows. On the other hand, the in-between move 16 ... P-K4 would allow 17 Q-N3, attacking the Black KNP.

14 ...   P-QN3

Protects the Bishop a second time and opens the diagonal for the development of the QB.

If Black tries to neutralize by exchange, the White position is so strong that he can overwhelm Black: e.g., 14 ... NxB 15 QxN B-N5 16 R-QB7 (even stronger than 16 P-QR3) 16 ... B-Q2 17 B-N5 R-Q1 18 R-Q1 and wins, for White is threatening 19 RxB.

15 RxB!

The previous phase of the game centered around the idea of White's obtaining the square Q6, and now he gets it by means of a sacrifice. If now 15 ... PxR 16 B-Q6 must win. For instance, 16 ... Q-Q2 (or ... Q-N2) 17 BxP, threatening both 18 B-N5 (18 ... QxB? 19 N-Q6ch) and 18 N-Q6ch.

Contrast the concept of 15 RxB with the superficial 15 NxB, playing for the isolated Pawn. In this case, White, who is a Pawn down, relinquishes his attack for only a small positional compensation.

15 ...   **NxB**

Black must exchange the dangerous Bishop to avoid the line beginning 16 B-Q6.

16 RxBch

This in-between check allows White to win a minor piece for the exchange.

16 ...   **RxR**
17 B-N5ch

Another in-between check is used to harass Black's uncastled King. Note the mobility White's pieces have acquired through the series of exchanges.

17 ...   **K-B1**
18 QxN

White has come out of the scuffle with two minor pieces in exchange for a Rook and a Pawn—not a big material advantage, but, in view of the bad development of Black (his KR in prison) and of his displaced King, White's preponderance is decisive.

18 ...   **P-K4**

This gives White the opportunity to open the KB-file for his Rook and thus concentrate his attacking forces against the important KBP. A better move would have been 18 ... P-KR3, since it does not create new weaknesses for Black and it opens the possibility of mobilizing the inactive KR by ... K-N1-R2. True, this whole maneuver takes three moves, and in the meanwhile

White would be able to improve his position by moves like P-KR3, in order to have a flight square, which is always important when heavy pieces are on the board, then R-K1 or R-Q1, followed by more active participation of the Rook.

If Black had tried to seize the initiative by 18 ... Q-N5, White would have continued by 19 B-Q7 and 20 BxP.

19 Q-B5	R-B2
20 P-B4!	

Strong again. White must continue to make strong moves in order to bring the game to a head before Black can bring his immobile Rook into play. Once he succeeds in doing that, White's advantage is very small.

20 ...	PxP

Forced. After other moves, Black's KP is lost.

21 QxBP

White is now threatening 22 N-Q6, followed by 23 NxP QxN 24 QxR.

21 ...	P-KR4

Black cleverly prevents the above threat, for if 22 N-Q6 R-R3 23 NxP R-KB3, or 23 N-B5 Q-B4ch.

22 B-B4!!

The only quick winning move.

22 ... R-R3 no longer works, for 23 BxP, and he cannot interpose on account of NxR: e.g., 23 ... QxB 24 QxR/B7.

If 22 ... RxB 23 Q-N8ch Q-K1 24 QxQch KxQ 25 N-Q6ch.

If 22 ... P-KN4 23 NxP Q-B4ch 24 R-B2! QxB 25 QxR! QxQ 26 N-K6ch, again coming out with an extra piece.

| 22 ... | K-N1 |

The only move.

23 N-Q6

To win the KBP.

23 ...	R-R3
24 BxPch	K-R1
25 N-K4	

In order to prevent 25 ... R-KB3.

| 25 ... | R-B1 |

With the idea of continuing by 26 ... R-B1, just immobilizing one of the important White pieces. In view of the added fact that the White Knight has to stay at his post in order to prevent ... R-KB3, this would mean a considerable reduction of White's mobility and possibilities.

26 B-Q5

It is important to have the Knight protected. After 26 B-N3 R-K1 would be troublesome, as 27 N-N5 is answered by 27 ... R-B3.

Notice that the exchange of heavy pieces would facilitate Black's play, although in the long run Black has to lose anyway.

| 26 ... | R-K1 |

26 ... R-Q1 is answered by 27 Q-B5.

27 P-KR4!

Gives the White King a flight square and, moreover, provides the strong outpost for the Knight on N5.

27 ...   **Q-K4?**

Loses at once, but Black has no good moves anyway.

28 QxQ	RxQ
29 R-B8ch	K-R2
30 N-N5ch	K-N3
31 B-K4ch	Resigns

He must give up the exchange and remains a full piece behind.

Game 21

The theory of the French Defense

The Good Bishop and the Bad Bishop

The Pawn-chain

The strong square

The well-posted Knight vs. the Bad Bishop

Planning for the end game

In this game we meet for the first time a more refined element of strategic play: the strong square in the center of the board.

The squares of the chessboard do not all have the same value. Center squares are more advantageous than side squares. They are particularly ideal as posts on which to station pieces, for from a center square a piece radiates pressure on all squares to which it can move at a given moment. Especially powerful in the center of the board is the Knight, for a Knight does not have long-range penetration. Posted at its Q4-square, for instance, a Knight exercises pressure on the opponent's QN4, QB3, K3, and KB4-squares.

A Knight can be very powerful at its Q4 or K4, but if the opponent is able to drive it away with a Pawn, the temporarily good position of the Knight does not mean much. In certain cases, however, the opponent's Pawns have advanced or have been exchanged in such a way that they are no longer available to drive an enemy piece from a given square. For the side which can post a piece on such a square, it then becomes a strong square. To have a Knight posted on a strong center square is of great strategic value in chess.

One of the questions most frequently asked of chess players is:

"Which is stronger, the Knight or the Bishop?" The strength of these two pieces is relative, not absolute. In the case of the Knights, it depends on where they are posted and whether they can be maintained in their position. In the case of the Bishop, it depends on whether the Bishop is on diagonals on which it is free to move at will, in which cases it is called a *Good Bishop,* or on diagonals obstructed by its own Pawns, in which case it is called a *Bad Bishop.*

This game exemplifies the power of a well-posted Knight as opposed to the ineffectiveness of a Bad Bishop.

The French Defense—Classical Variation

Master	Amateur
1 P-K4	P-K3

As has already been explained in Game 6, 1 ... P-K3 is the beginning of an opening called the French Defense, a *closed game:* that is, one in which the center files generally remain closed, thus enabling Black to build up a solid position in the center, as contrasted with the faster development and greater mobility of the open games beginning 1 P-K4 P-K4. In the French Defense, Black will need more time to bring his pieces into play because they are hemmed in by his solid Pawn formation.

2 P-Q4

White immediately takes possession of the center.

2 ...	P-Q4

Black contests White's attempt to command the center and threatens 3 ... PxP, compelling White to do something about the situation.

3 N-QB3

White makes another move to command the center. His QN now exerts pressure on his Q5 and K4. Tension in the center is maintained.

White has several other possibilities at this point.

(a) The Exchange Variation

He could have ended the tension by playing 3 PxP, which is known as the Exchange variation. After Black answers 3 ... PxP, the game becomes drawish because there is one open file for both players. The logical consequence of a single open file for both players is that Rooks and Queens will be exchanged along this file. If this open file is left in possession of one player, his opponent might get into trouble.

(b) The Nimzovich Variation

White could also end the tension by playing 3 P-K5, which would alter the position and the positional aims of the game completely. In the Nimzovich variation, we are in the presence of a Pawn-chain: White's Q4-K5 vs. Black's Q4-K3. The Q4 is the base of the White Pawn-chain; the K3, the base of the Black Pawn-chain. The K5 is the head of the White Pawn-chain; the Q4, the head of the Black Pawn-chain. When dealing with a Pawn-chain, the primary strategy is to attack the opponent's base. In this position, Black will try to play ... P-QB4; White, P-KB4-KB5. The secondary strategy is to attack the head of the Pawn-chain, as will be shown later in the present game. We have already seen in Game 6 how a beginner playing White can go wrong in this variation.

(c) The Tarrasch Variation

White can maintain the tension and defend the KP by 3 N-Q2. As compared to the text, it has the disadvantage of not exerting any pressure on White's Q5-square. On the other hand, the Tarrasch variation has the following advantages over the text: (a) The QN cannot be pinned by the Black KB, since 3 ... B-N5 would be quite useless on account of 4 P-QB3; (b) at Q2, the QN does not hem in the QBP, which White might later wish to play to B3, especially if Black plays ... P-QB4.

Black, by playing 3 . . . N-KB3 and controlling his Q4 and K5, protects the center and incidentally threatens to win a Pawn by . . . NxP or . . . PxP.

Black could also have played 3 . . . B-N5, the Winawer variation, which is probably safer. In this variation, Black protects his center squares by pinning White's QN. (See Game 22.)

4 B-N5

By this pin White threatens, under certain circumstances, 5 P-K5 and also neutralizes Black's pressure on the center.

If White should succeed at this point in forcing Black to give up the center by . . . PxP, he would have a superiority in space, for White would then have his Pawn on the 4th rank, whereas Black's Pawn would be on the 3rd rank.

At this point, amateurs sometimes instead play the plausible move 4 B-Q3. The following analysis will show that the move gives Black counterchances in the center after the reply 4 . . . P-B4:

(a) 5 PxBP PxKP 6 NxP NxN 7 BxN QxQch 8 KxQ BxP.
(b) 5 P-K5 PxP 6 PxN PxN.
(c) 5 PxQP NxP 6 NxN QxN.
(d) 5 N-B3 PxQP 6 NxP/4 P-K4, followed by 7 . . . P-Q5.

After 4 P-K5 KN-Q2, one gets the PQ4-PK5 formation, typical in many variations of the French Defense. White should then try to defend either his PQ4 or PK5 or both, playing 5 P-B4 or 5 QN-K2 (preparing 6 P-QB3).

4 . . .   B-K2

Black, in turn, unpins, again threatening to win a Pawn.

At this point, the McCutcheon variation, 4 . . . B-N5, is also very playable. After 5 P-K5 P-KR3 (a standard forced move in such positions): (a) 6 PxN PxB 7 PxP R-N1 8 Q-R5 Q-B3 is not dangerous for Black; (b) 6 B-Q2 BxN 7 PxB N-K5 8 Q-N4 P-KN3 is very sharp, with chances for both players.

5 P-K5

Black was threatening ... PxP or ... NxP. Here, 5 B-Q3 is inadequate, as we shall show below. White has no further good defense against Black's pressure against his center. He therefore decides to exchange his QB for Black's KB, and this will take place on the next move. As we shall also explain in detail very soon, White's QB, which is on the same color as his center Pawns, is known as the Bad Bishop, whereas Black's KB, which is on the opposite color from his center Pawns, is known as his Good Bishop.

There are two plausible possibilities other than 5 P-K5, the second of which is sometimes played by amateurs, who often do not realize why one variation is superior to another. An examination of these two variations and a comparison of the resultant positions to that of the main line will illustrate:

(a) 5 BxN

5 BxN BxB 6 P-K5 B-K2 makes things a little easier for Black —he has the Two Bishops. This means that he has retained both his Bishops, whereas White has either a Bishop and a Knight (as in this variation) or two Knights. To have both Bishops when an opponent has a Bishop and a Knight or two Knights is considered advantageous. The game might continue 7 Q-N4 0-0 8 B-Q3 P-KB4 9 PxP e.p. BxP, with considerable counterchances for Black. Note that the seemingly strong continuation 10 Q-R5 leads to the loss of a Pawn for White, since after 10 ... P-KN3! (1) the sacrifice 11 BxP PxB 12 QxPch B-N2 is unsound because White has no follow-up, whereas Black has a start in development and already threatens 13 ... Q-B3, (2) yet the White Queen cannot withdraw without loss of the QP, as, for instance, 11 Q-K2 BxP or 11 Q-N4 P-K4, and Black obtains control of the center, which is very important.

244

(b) 5 B-Q3

On the face of it, 5 B-Q3 looks like a logical developing move leading to attack, but one must examine what happens after 5 ... PxP:

(1) 6 NxP NxN 7 BxB QxB 8 BxN Q-N5, which wins a Pawn.

(2) 6 BxP NxB 7 BxB QxB 8 NxN Q-N5ch, which wins a Pawn.

(3) 6 BxN BxB 7 NxP BxP, which wins a Pawn.

Even 5 ... NxP 6 BxB NxN 7 Q-N4 KxB is favorable for Black: 8 Q-N5ch K-Q2.

| 5 ... | KN-Q2 |
| 6 BxB | |

White exchanges his relatively bad Bishop here, because it has no important work to perform. If it had, then White should not exchange. For instance, after inserting the moves 6 P-KR4 P-KR3, White would *not* exchange but would rather play 7 B-K3!, for now the Bishop has a meaningful function because of Black's weakening move ... P-KR3. The White Bishop on KN5 is only relatively "bad," because its diagonal QB1-KR6 is not blocked by White Pawns.

After 6 P-KR4, the Alekhine-Chatard attack, White develops quite another type of game, which is taken up in Game 23.

| 6 ... | QxB |

White now has (a) a Good Bishop, in contrast to Black's un-developed Bad Bishop, and (b) more space. Black, on the other hand, has the possibility of attacking the base of White's Pawn-chain by ... P-QB4 much more easily than White can attack the base of Black's Pawn-chain by P-B4-B5.

Let us now examine the situation of the White and Black Bishops. White's Bishop can move freely, since it is not hemmed in by its own Pawns; not only is Black's Bishop undeveloped, but its possible development is severely limited by its own Pawns. White's Bishop is, therefore, called the *Good Bishop;* Black's Bishop, the *Bad Bishop.*

In the opening and middle game, it is especially the center squares which make a Bishop good or bad. If, from the initial position, White has played P-Q4, P-K3, and B-Q2, that Bishop is "bad" because it is hemmed in. If, instead, he has played B-KB4 before playing P-K3, the Bishop is still "bad," because, if Black should attack White's Q-side, the White Bishop on its KB4 cannot come to the defense of the Q-side. In general, blocked Pawns cannot move, and they determine to a great extent whether a Bishop is "good" or "bad." One Pawn move sometimes changes a Bishop from "good" to "bad" or vice versa. In the end game, it is the blocked Pawns and their position which determine the value of the Bishop.

7 Q-Q2

The move 7 Q-Q2 has in itself no deep-hidden meaning; it is part of a system. White cannot maintain his complete center after Black plays ... P-QB4. He will therefore protect his KP by P-KB4 and will exchange his QP sooner or later by playing PxP after Black's ... P-QB4. 7 Q-Q2 prepares 0-0-0 and protects White's KB4-square. This square (or the Pawn which will shortly move to this square) will require protection if Black plays ... P-KB3, which White will answer by PxP and Black in turn by ... QxP.

Other moves, such as 7 B-Q3, enable Black to ruin White's center completely by ... P-QB4 and ... P-KB3.

Let us examine some of the common alternatives to 7 Q-Q2.

(a) 7 P-B4

This move is about as strong as 7 Q-Q2. The usual continuation is 7 ... 0-0 8 N-B3 P-B4 9 PxP NxBP 10 B-Q3 P-KB4 11 PxP e.p. QxP 12 P-KN3 N-B3 13 0-0, exerting pressure against Black's position as long as Black is prevented from playing ... P-K4.

(b) 7 N-N5

This constitutes somewhat of a premature attack, which does not have much force. Black answers 7 ... N-N3, followed by 8 ... P-QR3, driving back the Knight. White, however, does attain one of his goals, namely, the strengthening of the center (after ... P-QB4) by P-QB3. In the present game, this is not possible because the QN is on QB3, and White has to give up the center by PxP, which in this case is not too bad. Also see the comment under Black's 7th move in the present game.

(c) 7 Q-N4

Aggressive as it looks, this move, found in many variations of the French Defense, has no value here. It forces Black to castle, which he would have done anyway. After 7 ... 0-0 8 B-Q3, Black might continue either by 8 ... P-QB4 or 8 ... P-KB4.

7 ...   0-0

It is instructive to note that if Black had played 7 ... P-QB4 here, he would have weakened his Q3-square and 8 N-N5! might have been dangerous, since 8 ... N-N3 can now be answered by 9 N-Q6ch.

8 P-B4

The purpose of 8 P-B4 is to strengthen the White KP on K5. In many variations of the French Defense there occurs at some time or other ... P-KB3, PxP QxP, after which it might be important for White to have his K5-square defended. After certain preparations, White could then keep Black's backward KP on K3. If White succeeds in preventing ... P-K4 (after ... P-KB3; PxP QxP), Black's KP remains backward. White can prevent ... P-K4 in two ways: (a) pressure against K5; (b) pressure against Q5, i.e., Black's QP, so that Black's ... P-K4 is answered by NxQP.

8 ...   P-QB4

In the French Defense, Black's primary strategy is to attack the base of the Pawn-chain at White's Q4; then, after having eliminated White's QP, there often follows the secondary strategy of attacking the head of White's Pawn-chain by ... P-KB3.

White's possible 9 N-QN5 is not as dangerous now as it would have been a move ago, for Black's King is now safely castled. For instance, 9 N-QN5 N-QB3 10 P-B3 P-B3, and White's Q6-square is already undermined. After 11 PxKBP NxBP, White has not accomplished anything, and 11 N-Q6 is not good either, for 11 ... PxQP 12 PxQP PxP 13 BPxP? Q-R5ch, followed by 14 ... QxQP. If instead of 13 BPxP he plays 13 QPxP, even the sacrifice 13 ... QNxP might work: 14 PxN NxKP 15 NxB QRxN, and Black has a marvelous game. His whole army is mobilized—look at his Rooks!

Why does Black suddenly come to life notwithstanding the fact that his opening, the French Defense, has a rather quiet character?

One must see this as follows: Black's attitude means at the outset passivity in the center. But, as soon as he has developed a sufficient number of pieces, Black will try to obtain the initiative. This strategy will be more effective if White neglects his development, and this is the case after 9 N-QN5. Note the rule "In the opening never play the same piece twice." It is true that this is not a rule which can be applied in all cases, but it may give some help, and in this position it does.

Another example of the chances which Black can obtain after 9 N-QN5 is shown by the following variation:

9 ... P-QR3 (still stronger than 9 ... N-QB3, since 10 N-B7

now leads nowhere after 10 ... R-R2) 10 N-Q6 PxP 11 N-B3
(11 NxB RxB 12 N-B3 N-QB3 leads to about the same, while
11 QxP N-QB3 loses some tempi for White) 11 ... N-QB3
12 NxQP KNxKP! winning a Pawn: 13 PxN Q-R5ch, and 14 ...
QxN.

9 N-B3

After the exchange of the center Pawns either by PxP or
... PxP, it is important for White to have control over his strong
square Q4. A strong square, as we have already pointed out, is
one which cannot be controlled by hostile Pawns. White's KN
also assumes control over White's K5-square, which may be of
importance to keep Black's KP backward in case of ... P-KB3;
PxP QxP (as already mentioned). The entire later part of this
game evolves about the idea of the strength of the strong
square Q4.

9 ...   N-QB3

10 P-KN3

The idea of 10 P-KN3 is to continue by B-N2 (or B-R3),
PxKBP (after ... P-KB3) and 0-0-0 (Rubinstein's move) in order
to get pressure against Black's center.

If, instead, White should play 10 0-0-0 immediately, Black
might play 10 ... P-B5, followed by 11 ... R-N1, 12 ... P-QN4,
and 13 ... P-QN5, with a heavy attack.

10 ...   PxP?

Black captured in order to open the QB-file and gain possession of it. But, in doing so, he handed over to White the possession of White's strong square Q4. White now has full possession of his Q4: that is, no Black Pawn can threaten White's possession of the square, only Black pieces, which means that, in the long run, White must always be able to occupy the square. Since Q4 is not threatened and cannot be threatened by a Pawn, we call it a strong square for White. A piece on that square is like a cannon in a hidden place. It fires, and you cannot attack it.

Certainly, 10 ... P-B3 (Black's secondary strategy) is stronger here. It forces White to liquidate his center completely, but after 11 KPxP NxBP 12 PxP QxP 13 0-0-0, Black's center Pawns might become weak. White has all his pieces at his disposal and can continue by moves such as B-R3 and KR-K1.

Let us now see how White uses his strong square at Q4.

11 NxP	NxN
12 QxN	Q-B4

This is consistent with Black's previous play. Note that 12 ... P-B3 is much weaker here than two moves earlier and would represent a loss of tempi; 12 ... N-N3 leaves White's Queen in a powerful position.

Black cannot do much with his half-open QB-file, whereas on the contrary White can make full use of his strong square Q4 by posting a Knight on it, thus preventing Black's Bad Bishop from occupying many squares.

13 QxQ	NxQ
14 N-N5	

Not to bring the Knight to White's Q6, as one might think, for it could most likely be exchanged there, and its position could be undermined by ... P-B3; but rather to bring it to Q4, which is the ideal square for a Knight here. The Knight on Q4 could also be exchanged, but then the White King would move to that square and become the deciding factor in the simplifications which would ensue, namely, those leading to Pawn endings.

14 ...   P-QN3

Black, who had assumed that White planned to play 15 N-Q6, wished to answer by ... N-N2 and ... NxN.

15 0-0-0

Simply a developing move. If White had played 15 N-Q4 immediately, Black could possibly try to trade off his Bad Bishop by ... B-R3 and then obtain his K5 as a strong square for his own Knight. With the text, ... B-R3 is prevented for the time being by 16 N-B7!

15 ...   N-K5

Black now occupies *his* strong square, but this is not so important here, since White can always exchange this Knight for the White Bishop. However, Black's threat of ... N-B7 does give White some trouble.

Black might have considered playing 15 ... P-QR3, but this is bad because it takes the QR3-square from Black's Bishop.

16 R-N1   P-QR3

A better move would have been 16 ... B-Q2, which would have gained a tempo by attacking the White Knight. It is true that the

Bishop is not very active on its Q2, but it is not very effective on its N2 either.

The text move also weakens QN3 and makes Black's QB worse, since more Pawns are on its color.

17 N-Q4

The Knight now settles on its strong square, where it is very powerful. It controls many important squares in the enemy position: White's QN5, QB6, K6, and KB5; it can support a later attack by P-KN4 and P-KB5. Moreover, the Knight protects its QBP, which will be of importance in case the Black Rooks start an attack along the QB-file.

17 ...   B-N2

Black is playing from general principles instead of from a specific position. Often the Bishop is strong at N2, therefore Black plays 17 ... B-N2. At this point the White Knight blocks the advance of Black's QP. Therefore, the Black Bishop has no future at QN2 as long as the White Knight remains on his post at Q4.

Black might have played 17 ... B-Q2 and 18 ... P-B3, aiming at White's Pawn formation.

18 B-Q3

White plays to exchange his Bishop for the Knight or drive the Knight away. After the exchange, White remains with a powerful Knight against a Bad Bishop. Also after the exchange, White can maintain his Knight on his Q4-square, if necessary by P-B3. It is another question whether after BxN PxB White could have derived as much advantage from his strong Knight as he did in the game.

18 ...   N-B7

It would have been better to try 18 ... N-B4. After Black exchanges his Knight, White's advantage is too clear.

19 R-Q2   NxBch
20 RxN

20 PxN would also be good. Black's possible attack along the QB-file does not mean much, since White can oppose his own Rooks. But 20 RxN is probably better because of the possibilities on the 3rd rank.

Now the situation is clear. The White Knight is on the strong square, and it can be maintained there for the rest of the game. No power on the chessboard will be able to drive it away.

Such a permanent Knight is the most ideal basis for a plan, because the Knight can be relied on: it will always be in its place; it cannot be driven away. The question is how to take advantage of this strong Knight, how to bring the Knight into the strategic plans.

We have already seen that the Knight (a) can work on the K-side; (b) can work on the Q-side; (c) defends its QBP so that Black cannot do any harm by doubling his Rooks on the QB-file.

This last consideration especially makes it possible for us to proceed quietly, without undue haste, without being disturbed by counterplay. This is most important in general and especially here, since a careful study of the position will show that White's plans cannot be realized at once. This will soon become evident.

For the moment, we must consider two plans:

Plan A—on the K-side

The key move is P-KB5. How can it be executed? And what is its purpose? It attacks Black's KP and, under certain circumstances, permits the successful pushing of the BP to B6.

253

In most positions, Black will have to take the BP with his KP (KPxBP). If White can then answer KNPxBP, he will be able to open the KN-file, and will also be able to push his KP to K6. Under certain circumstances, this plan looks promising, but it is not necessarily decisive. So White will have to prepare P-KB5 very carefully and carry out this advance only if it can be shown to be decisive—for, if it is not decisive, it might create a weak KP.

Plan B—on the Q-side

If White had the move, he could win at once with 21 R-QN3 P-QN4 22 P-QR4, etc. But Black can easily parry the threat, and then there is no way to develop a growing attack against the Black Q-side.

Therefore, White's chances lie in still another direction: the exchange of the four Rooks, followed by a struggle between a powerful Knight and a limited Bishop (Knight vs. Bad Bishop). White has all kinds of chances in such a struggle, but he is sure of a win *only if his King can penetrate the hostile position*. Let us try:

20 ... KR-B1 (as played in the game) 21 R-N3 P-QN4 (by forcing this move, White has created holes in Black's position by which his King could penetrate later) 22 R-Q1 (22 P-QR4? R-B5!) 22 ... R-B5 23 P-QR3 (White does not want P-QN5) 23 ... QR-QB1 24 KR-Q3 K-B1 25 K-Q2 K-K2 26 QR-B3 K-Q2 27 P-N3 RxR 28 RxR RxR 29 KxR K-B2 30 K-N4 K-N3 (the Black King has arrived just in time to prevent the White King from marching in). White can still try all kinds of maneuvers, but the win is doubtful. White has simplified too soon.

This means that neither direct action on the K-side (Plan A) nor direct action on the Q-side (Plan B) will guarantee success. White has to *keep an eye on both possibilities* and make a definite choice, depending on Black's counterplay.

20 ...   KR-B1
21 K-Q2

Following Plan B. This move is necessary for the general exchange on White's QB3.

21 ...   K-B1

To counter Plan B.

22 P-KN4

This move is useful for both plans.

For Plan A—P-B5 is better prepared; the possibility of now playing R-R3 gives additional means of attack.

For Plan B—KR-KN3 is prepared, to be followed by a general exchange on White's QB3. Moreover, R-KR3 might force the Black King back to KN1 and thus favor the success of a general exchange.

22 ...   R-B2 (?)

A colorless move! Preferable was 22 ... K-K2.

23 R-KR3

A very important move. (a) 23 ... K-N1 would now favor Plan B; (b) 23 ... P-R3 would favor Plan A. It would even permit White to carry out Plan A directly: 23 ... P-R3 24 P-B5! and (1) 24 ... R-K1 25 P-B6! PxP 26 PxP P-K4 27 RxRP, etc.; (2) 24 ... PxP 25 PxP R-K1 26 P-B6 P-N3 27 RxRP, etc.—not the slightest doubt; (3) 24 ... K-K2 25 P-N5 with wild complications finally leading to convincing advantage for White.

On the other hand, after 23 ... K-N1, the advance 24 P-B5 does *not* decide. 24 ... PxP (24 ... R-K1 could be tried as well) 25 PxP R-K1 26 P-B6 P-N3 with nothing definite.

23 ...   K-N1

Still better than the text would have been 23 ... R-B5, for after 24 P-B3, Plan B would have been out of the question. This means that White would have had to rely on Plan A completely—with chances, but nothing certain.

We have already seen that the weakening Black move 23 ...
P-R3 would allow the breakthrough by P-B5.

24 R/N1-N3

Not giving up the possibilities on the K-side, at the same time
White prepares the later general exchange (Plan B).

24 ...   **P-N3?**

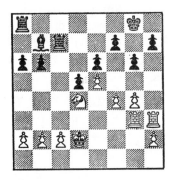

This additional weakening move makes possible the immediate
carrying-out of Plan A.

Let us see what could have happened after the preferable move
24 ... R-B5 25 R-Q3! QR-QB1 26 P-N3 R/5-B2 27 R-R5! (Plan
A—a general exchange by R-QB3 would not mean much, since
the King cannot penetrate: Black's QNP is still on its N3. Still,
there would have been chances. However, Plan A is better and
decides right away.) 27 ... P-R3 (if not, White wins by 28
R/3-R3 and 29 P-N5) 28 R/3-R3 K-B1 (White threatened P-N5)
29 P-B5! PxP 30 PxP R-K1 31 P-B6 and wins. A better move for
Black is 29 ... K-K2, but then 30 P-N5 leads to a win in the long
run. Again Plan A decides.

Or, supposing 24 ... QR-QB1 and now Plan B comes to the
front, which shows the strategic value of the strong Knight:

25 R-QN3 P-N4 26 P-QR3 R-B5 27 R/N3-Q3 (the other Rook
must hold the Black King at its KN2) 27 ... P-R3 28 P-N3 R/5-B2
29 R-QB3 K-B1 30 RxR RxR 31 R-QB3 RxR 32 KxR K-K2 33 K-N4

K-Q2 34 K-R5 (34 K-B5 is also good) 34 ... K-B2 35 P-N4 B-B1
36 N-N3 K-N2 37 N-B5ch K-R2 38 P-B3, with three variations:

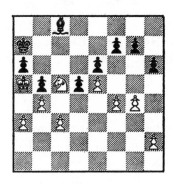

(a) 38 ... P-N4 39 PxP PxP 40 N-N3 B-N2 41 N-Q4 B-R1
42 N-B3 P-Q5(!) 43 NxQP B-Q4 44 N-B2 B-B6 45 N-K3
B-K7 46 P-QR4 wins.

(b) 38 ... B-N2 39 P-B5 B-B1 (39 ... PxP? 40 PxP and
41 P-K6) 40 PxP PxP (40 ... BxP 41 NxRP BxP 42 N-B7)
41 P-KR4 P-N3 42 P-N5 P-R4 43 N-Q3 followed by 44 N-B4.

(c) 38 ... P-N3 39 P-R3 B-N2 (39 ... P-R4 40 PxP PxP
41 P-KR4) 40 N-Q7 B-B1 41 N-B6 K-N2 wins a Pawn anyhow: 42 N-N8 P-R4 43 PxP PxP 44 P-KR4. The *Zugzwang*
(after White's 39th move) in the ending Knight vs. Bad
Bishop is most important.

We further notice that the exchange of all Rooks is to be considered only after Black's Q-wing formation is weakened by
... P-QN4. White's 26th move is necessary to prevent ... P-N5
after ... R-QB5.

Now back to the diagram on page 256.

25 R-R6   **K-N2**

The KRP was in danger.

26 R/3-KR3   **R-R1**
27 P-B5!

Plan A at last!

27 ...	B-B1

Other possibilities are: 27 ... KPxP 28 PxP and (a) 28 ... PxP 29 NxPch K-N1 30 RxNP, etc.; (b) 28 ... B-B1 29 P-B6ch K-N1 30 R-QB3, etc. White is practically a Rook up, as in the game.

28 P-B6ch	K-N1
29 P-N3	

29 R-QB3 would have been just as good, but White has another plan, that of playing N-B3-N5, and he does not wish to be disturbed by ... R-B5.

29 ...	B-N2
30 N-B3	Resigns

The game might have continued 30 ... P-Q5 (despair) 31 N-N5 (nonetheless) 31 ... R-B4 32 RxP RxR 33 RxR RxKP 34 R-N7ch K-B1 35 RxPch K-K1 36 R-K7ch K-B1 37 N-R7ch K-N1 38 P-B7ch and mate in another move.

Game 22

In chess, as in war, it is possible to carry on a battle on two fronts by dividing one's forces into two separate armies. Games in which the battle is fought on more than one front require a continuous weighing of the factors on the respective fronts and very sharp calculations as to the relative value of the fronts and whether it is worthwhile to continue the two fronts. Decentralization can have its advantages, but it should not last too long. Two separate armies should maintain points of contact, so that at any moment these armies can reunite. If a player misses the right time to reunite his forces and maintains the split of his army into two separate parts, the time may come when the opponent can successfully attack one of these armies, weakened by the absence of part of the total forces.

In chess, separate armies are sometimes created by dividing the forces into the most powerful piece, the Queen, on the one hand, and the rest of the pieces on the other. For a time, the Queen may go off for adventure on her own, but there always comes a time when it is prudent for her to go back to the rest of the forces to restore the cooperation between the pieces, a cooperation which has naturally suffered during such an isolated action.

In the game, the White Queen gets separated from the rest of the White forces and never again rejoins them. Black's task is facilitated by: (a) the very damaging self-pin which White imposes on himself; (b) the fact that White does not bring his King to safety in time. With White's forces paralyzed by the self-pin and weakened by the absence of the Queen, and with White's King still in the center of a relatively open board, Black gets the maximum opportunity to launch a forceful attack.

The French Defense—Winawer Variation

Amateur	Master
1 P-K4	P-K3
2 P-Q4	P-Q4

The French Defense once more. For the basic ideas of this opening, see Game 21.

3 N-QB3	B-N5

The Winawer Variation. Black pins the White QN and threatens 4 ... PxP, which compels White to come to an immediate decision as to what he will do about the center.

In the Winawer variation, Black plans to break up the White center and to gain the initiative at the expense of a broken Pawn position on his K-side. This defense gives Black slightly more initiative than other variations of the French. It is often played by Botvinnik.

Instead, Black could have answered 3 ... N-KB3, maintaining the tension and allowing White to neutralize in the center by 4 B-N5. This is the Classical line, which was taken up in detail in Game 21.

The Winawer variation avoids certain problems inherent in the Classical defense and eliminates the possibility of White's playing the Alekhine-Chatard attack (see Game 23).

4 P-QR3

White puts the question to the Black Bishop at once. As will be seen, this allows Black to gain a Pawn, but only temporarily.

In addition to the text, White has these alternatives: (a) 4 P-K5 (the most often played); (b) 4 PxP; (c) 4 B-Q3; (d) 4 N-K2; (e) 4 Q-N4.

4 ...   **BxNch**

Black exchanges his Bishop for a Knight, a slight disadvantage, but succeeds in return in doubling White's Pawns, an advantage.

If 4 ... B-R4 5 P-QN4 B-N3, and Black's pin on the 3rd move has not had any meaning, for 6 P-K5 or N-B3 and Black is hemmed in, completely unable to realize his freeing move ... P-QB4.

5 PxB   **PxP**

He also wins a Pawn temporarily, but he cannot hold it.

6 Q-N4

An attack by the White Queen on the Black KNP early in the game is a common theme in variations of the French Defense where the Black KB has left its original square.

Here, White attacks Black's KNP and KP/5 simultaneously.

6 ...   **N-KB3**

Black, who has the choice of defending his KNP by 6 ... Q-B3 or his center Pawn by 6 ... N-KB3, prefers to protect his center Pawn, at the same time developing an important piece and forcing the White Queen to move.

7 QxNP

In return for a broken Pawn position on the K-side, Black obtains a half-open file along which he may attack under certain circumstances. Important also is the temporary absence of the White Queen from its Q-wing, which is weak.

7 ...   **R-N1**

Not only does Black force the White Queen to move once more;

he also exercises pressure on White's KNP, thus temporarily immobilizing White's KB.

8 Q-R6   P-B4

At this point, Black makes the thematic move of the French Defense, attempting to break up White's center and perhaps attack White's uncastled King. The text move, moreover, opens the diagonal for the Queen to come to QN3 or QR4 where it can do considerable harm to the White Q-wing. By this move, Black follows the precept: "Take the initiative where the opponent is weak." It is to be noted that Black does not need to protect his QB4-square, for if White plays 9 PxP, the disadvantage of his triple isolated Pawns outweighs the advantage of having the extra Pawn.

Black's Pawn on his K5 is already exerting a restraining influence on White's movements. It prevents the natural B-Q3 and N-B3.

9 N-K2!

White hastens to develop his Knight to its K2, where it adds protection to his QP and QBP. Moreover, moves like N-B4 and N-N3 now come into the picture.

If White had played 9 PxP for the win of the Pawn, he would simply have afforded Black more freedom of action, and his extra Pawn, being one of triple Pawns, would not have meant anything. If he had played 9 B-N5ch, then 9 ... B-Q2 10 BxBch QNxB, which simply furthers Black's development and exchanges

White's Good Bishop for Black's Bad Bishop. If he had played 9 B-KN5, the threat to the Black Knight could have been parried by 9 ... R-N3 10 Q-R4 QN-Q2.

9 ...   **N-B3**

Black counters with more pressure against White's Q4.

This is much better than 9 ... QN-Q2 10 N-N3! R-N3 11 Q-K3 N-Q4 12 QxP NxP, and White is better off (Alekhine-Euwe match 1935). The material is even, but White has the Two Bishops and the possibility of castling soon, whereas Black's Rook is vulnerable at its KN3.

10 B-N2?

A typical amateur move. White tries in this way to give added protection to his Q4. The move is bad because the Bishop is exposed at QN2 and because White gives up the possibility of playing B-KN5 at some later time.

However, 10 B-N5 R-N3 11 Q-R4 PxP is good for Black as well. If 12 N-B4 Q-R4, and if 12 BxN QxB 13 QxQ RxQ 14 PxP B-Q2.

Theory gives 10 PxP with about equal chances, since White has a plus Pawn and the Two Bishops to compensate for his triple Pawn.

10 ...   **Q-N3**

Attacking the undefended White QB and at the same time applying pressure on the White Q4.

11 R-QN1

White protects his Bishop by a self-pin; the Rook's threat to the Black Queen along the file is illusory, since the Rook is unprotected and the White Bishop dare not move. We have already seen a self-pin in Game 5. However, the self-pin in this present game is still worse.

11 QxN QxB wins at least a Pawn for Black. The best move would have been 11 Q-B1.

11 ...	R-N3
12 Q-R4?	

This does not solve the Bishop pin. White should have played 12 Q-B1, unpinning.

12 ...	PxP

By this exchange, Black retains the initiative, an important consideration. Moreover, after the reply 13 PxP, the White Knight is tied down to the defense of its PQ4, which Black could take at once if that Knight should leave its position. If Black does not exchange at this time, White could play 13 PxP, unpinning his Bishop and freeing his game after 13 ... QxP.

13 PxP

After 13 NxP B-Q2, Black has considerable advantage in view of White's wrecked Q-wing Pawn structure.

13 ...	B-Q2

Although the Black Bishop cannot move far, its moving clears the way for the development of the Black QR and places the Bishop itself on a diagonal where it, too, may be useful later on.

14 N-B4

If White made this move just to threaten Black's Rook, he was too material-minded; one must not play for win of material when one's house is on fire. But if he made the move to develop the K-wing, then the move is good.

Momentarily, White is in an awkward position because on his

K-side the KB and KR are out of play, and on the Q-side the QR and QB are tied down. One cannot play a game with only half the pieces. Black must, therefore, have a favorable line.

14 ...   NxQP!

Threatening to crack the position by 15 ... NxPch.

Considering White's lack of development, it is not surprising that Black has this enterprising move at his disposal.

15 NxR??

The amateur knows that the Rook is normally worth more than the Knight. He therefore makes this exchange as a matter of course, hoping by this mechanical means to even the score somehow. At this point, White needs to (a) develop pieces, (b) unpin the Bishop and thereby activate two or more pieces: the Bishop and the Rook.

White had two better moves:

15 B-B4—to prepare for castling and thus unpin the QB.

15 BxN—sacrificing the exchange, but solving the problem of the pin in one move.

In either case, the position becomes rather complex, although naturally favorable for Black. We give one line of each of the above-mentioned moves to illustrate how the game could have continued:

(a) 15 B-B4—One must consider that as soon as White has castled, he succeeds in threatening Black in several ways

265

simultaneously. In the first place, he now has NxR (now good) followed by QxN. This means that Black has to do something to improve his position on the K-side. He could play 15 ... N-B4 16 Q-R3 R-R3 17 Q-QB3 P-K6! And now after 18 0-0, Black wins beautifully: 18 ... PxPch and (1) 19 RxP QxRch! 20 KxQ N-K5ch, which leads to material advantage for Black, or (2) 19 K-R1 N-K5, threatening mate on N6. But if Black replied 15 ... NxPch?, he would be playing into White's hands, for 16 K-Q2 and White has connected his Rooks and his QB is free to move.

(b) 15 BxN QxRch 16 K-Q2. White has given up the exchange, but now he has threats such as NxR and BxN. Black must again act positively: 16 ... P-K6ch! (making room for the Knight) 17 BxKP (other ways of retaking are no better) 17 ... N-K5ch 18 K-K2 QxPch 19 K-B3 N-N4ch 20 K-N3 N-B6 dis ch! 21 KxN B-B3ch, etc.

Now to return to the game.

15 ... NxPch

Not to win a Pawn, but to draw the King out into the open, where it can be surrounded by Black's forces and captured.

16 K-Q1

16 K-K2 would be countered with 16 ... B-N4ch, and White would not be any better off.

16 ... Q-Q3ch

Black can afford to sacrifice material to bring the White King into the mating net. Moreover, since White's pieces are either tied down or far from the field of combat, it does not matter that Black sacrifices more than a Rook.

17 KxN

If 17 K-B1 R-B1 and the discovered check is killing. For in-stance:

(a) 18 N-K5 (to interpose if possible) 18 ... N-K6 dis ch 19 N-B4 Q-Q8 mate.

(b) 18 QxN N-Q5 dis ch 19 K-Q2 N-B6 db ch 20 K-K3 Q-Q7ch 21 KxP B-B3 mate.

(c) 18 B-K5 N-K6 dis ch 19 K-N2 R-B7ch 20 K-N3 (20 K-R1 QxP mate) 20 ... Q-N3ch, followed by mate.

17 ...   B-R5ch

The encirclement continues. Because of White's lack of de-velopment, he is powerless to interpose. In general, the King alone is powerless against two major and one minor piece.

18 K-B3   R-B1ch
19 B-B4

The only move, but the interposed Bishop is pinned and has only part of its normal power.

19 ...   Q-Q6ch
20 K-N4   QxBch
21 K-R5   Q-N4 mate.

Game 23

The Alekhine-Chatard attack in the French Defense

Playing according to the strategic requirements of the opening

Bringing pressure to bear on the center

Breaking through the center

A complete scheme of variations in a complicated position

The success of certain openings depends on the extent to which the players execute the fundamental ideas on which the opening is based. In the Alekhine-Chatard variation of the French Defense, Black strives to build up a strong Pawn center, preventing White from taking advantage of the superiority in space which he always gets in this opening. By advancing his center Pawns against his opponent, Black is sometimes able to reduce his opponent's superiority in space.

The present game exemplifies what can happen when one of the players is ignorant of the basic idea behind the opening which he is playing. Black, the amateur, plays mechanically, without understanding the strategic requirements of the position. White succeeds first in neutralizing the Black center, then in building up a terrific concentration of power against that center.

The game is a striking example of how to build up pressure by bringing all available pieces to bear down on a given point, so that, once the attack is launched, the opponent is helpless to defend himself against the avalanche of power which descends on him. There is no way out!

Master	Amateur
1 P-K4	P-K3
2 P-Q4	P-Q4
3 N-QB3	N-KB3
4 B-N5	B-K2

The Classical line of the French Defense, which was taken up in Game 21.

For many years, 4 ... B-K2 was considered the logical move here. But, because of the Alekhine-Chatard variation, this move is no longer considered as safe as it used to be. This is one of the reasons for the popularity of 3 ... B-N5, the Winawer variation, taken up in Game 22.

5 P-K5	**KN-Q2**
6 P-KR4	

The Alekhine-Chatard attack, in which White offers a Pawn in order to open the KR-file for a strong attack in which the White KR will play an active role.

If Black now accepts the Pawn, White gets the half-open KR-file, and Black does not get the opportunity for the counter-play which is usually so effective in the French Defense.

The acceptance of the Pawn sacrifice by Black is so strong for White that one seldom sees it in master play. The game might continue: 6 ... BxB 7 PxB QxP 8 N-R3 (developing with tempo and leaving the Q1-KR5 diagonal open for the White Queen)

8 ... Q-K2 9 N-B4 and White now has sufficient compensation for the sacrificed Pawn in his open KR-file—his extra tempo and his greater mobility. The game might now continue: 9 ... P-QR3 (to prevent N-N5) 10 Q-N4 (an attack against the uncastled K-wing) 10 ... P-KN3 11 0-0-0 P-QB4 12 Q-N3 (White wants to make the sacrifice KNxQP but this could be met here by 12 ... PxN 13 NxQP N-N3, attacking the White Queen) 12 ... N-N3 13 PxP (13 KNxQP would also work here, but the text is stronger, since it opens the Q-file for the White Rook) 13 ... QxP 14 B-Q3 (threatening 15 BxNP BPxB 16 NxNP) 14 ... Q-B1 15 B-K4, and after 15 ... PxB 16 NxKP/4, White's attack is overwhelming, and if Black does not take the Bishop, White sacrifices on his Q5.

This is just an example, which has little conclusive force. It is difficult in a short discussion to show the full power of the White position, but with best play White gets so much activity for his pieces that his attack becomes irresistible.

6 ...   **P-KB3**

It is very difficult for Black to find a move sufficient for equality here. For a long time, the text was considered so strong that it was looked upon as the refutation of the Alekhine-Chatard variation of the French Defense, but that is no longer the case today. There are five common continuations for Black, which we are listing in order of their comparative strength. If 50 indicates full equality, then the number in parentheses after the move indicates the extent to which equality is attained according to theory today: (a) 6 ... P-QB4 (48); (b) 6 ... P-QR3 (to prevent 7 N-N5) (40); (c) 6 ... P-KR3 (35); (d) 6 ... P-KB3 (35); (e) 6 ... 0-0 (35).

7 Q-R5ch

It is this strong attacking move which almost refutes the 6 ... P-KB3 variation.

For a long time, it was customary to continue 7 B-Q3, but 7 ... PxB 8 Q-R5ch K-B1 9 R-R3 P-KN3! 10 BxP K-N2 seems to give Black a tenable position.

7 ...   **K-B1**

In the French Defense, Black often gives up the privilege of castling in return for a center majority. That is why in this game White tries to neutralize the center majority and prevent Black from taking advantage of it. If White succeeds in neutralizing the center majority, he has the best of it, because Black's King is misplaced.

If instead Black should reply 7 ... P-KN3, then 8 PxP! (this surprising move was not known until about 1950) 8 ... PxQ 9 PxB, which leads to a clear superiority for White, because after 9 ... QxP 10 BxQ KxB, Black has weak Rook Pawns, and White has the Good Bishop. White could win a Pawn right away as follows: 11 KN-K2 N-KB3 12 N-N3 R-N1 13 B-K2, followed by 14 K-B1 and 15 NxRP.

8 PxP

As soon as White has succeeded in preventing the hostile King from castling, it is in his interest to play for an open game—which means that, in the first place, the center Pawns have to disappear.

8 ...   NxP

Strategically, it would be ideal for Black to consolidate his center by 8 ... PxP, but tactically this is bad, for then 9 B-R6ch K-N1 10 Q-N4ch wins.

8 ... BxP is less good, because it entails no effective threats, and the Black Knight hampers Black's development. After 9 0-0-0, White has more advantage than in the game.

9 Q-K2!

Also commonly played here is 9 Q-B3. But the text is perhaps still better, since from the K2-square the Queen exercises pressure on the Black center. From here, it most effectively prevents Black from carrying out his aim of taking advantage of his center majority. If Black can attain ... P-K4, his position will be excellent. If he cannot, the Black Pawn at K3 remains a weakness, and Black's inferior King position is not compensated for.

Although 9 Q-K2 is in accordance with the strategic aims of the position, the move looks strange because it prevents the development of the White KB along its natural diagonal. But this KB will be developed to KR3, where it will bring new pressure to bear on K6.

9 ...   P-B4

If White should now reply 10 PxP, Black might eventually be able to play ... P-K4 and obtain a strong center. Black threatens 10 ... PxP, which might also give him the possibility of playing ... P-K4.

10 N-B3

Protecting the QP and controlling the important center squares Q4 and K5.

10 ...   N-B3

Black's countermove controls the same squares. After 10 ... PxP 11 NxP, Black's KP would be *en prise*.

11 0-0-0

This move brings White's King to a more sheltered position and at the same time brings the Rook to a center file where it defends White's QP in order to maintain the center.

Black now still has his trump in hand—the center. But a trump is of no value unless it is used. The way in which Black should use his center is to attempt to advance the KP without disadvantage to himself. If he can do that, he will obtain counterchances. At this point, the general exchange on Black's Q5 was necessary. After 11 ... PxP 12 KNxP NxN 13 RxN Q-Q3, and Black can hope for ... P-K4, and in that case he would obtain a splendid game. This is especially true because after 14 R-Q1, Black could improve his position by 14 ... P-KR3 (15 BxN BxB 16 N-K4? Q-B5ch). This last variation, however, gives the solution for White. He should play 14 R-Q2, and in that case 14 ... P-KR3 does not work, for 15 BxN BxB 16 N-K4, and Black must play 16 ... Q-K2. Or 16 ... BxPch 17 KxB Q-N5ch 18 K-B1 QxN 19 QxQ PxQ 20 R-Q8ch, and Black loses a Rook. In short, with 11 ... PxP, etc., Black would have some hope of playing his center trump sometime; his KP is not permanently immobilized in that line, as it is in the game.

11 ...	P-QN3?

At this point, then, Black should have played 11 ... PxP or 11 ... NxP.

But Black, not understanding the strategic requirements of the position, not realizing that his true strength lay in his Pawn center, made a routine move with the idea either of simply developing his Bishop to N2 or, after ... P-QR4, of playing ... B-QR3 and exchanging Bishops.

In the French Defense, after ... P-KB3 has been played, the Black KP often becomes weak. The Q-side fianchetto is all the more useless here because Black's QB is needed to defend his KP.

11 ... Q-N3 also comes into consideration. In that case, White continues 12 PxP QxP (if 12 ... BxP 13 N-R4) 13 N-N5, followed by 14 N-B7 or 14 QN-Q4.

12 P-KN3

White, taking advantage of Black's weak KP, opens the way for his KB to go to KR3 and attack it again. That is the logical consequence of White's 9 Q-K2. Now Black has to face the attack without counterchances.

12 ...   **K-B2**

In order to protect his KP doubly so as to allow the Rook to come to K1.

13 B-R3

By his attack on the Black KP, White immobilizes Black's QB and prepares for KR-K1, which will bring a third attacking piece to bear on the Black KP.

13 ...   **P-KR3**

By this move, Black hopes to force exchanges which will cut down White's pressure and attacking forces.

Another method would have been the strengthening of the weak point by 13 ... R-K1. In that case, White continues the siege by 14 KR-K1, whereupon 14 ... B-B1 fails against 15 N-K5ch NxN 16 PxN P-KR3 17 PxN PxB 18 Q-R5ch, and 14 ... Q-Q2 fails against 15 N-K5ch NxN 16 PxN N-N1 17 NxP and wins.

14 KR-K1

White pays no attention to Black's threat to his Bishop. Rather, he intensifies pressure on Black's KP and along the entire K-file. The sacrifice is sound, because White gets two Pawns for the piece and a direct attack against the King, as all his pieces are in action.

14 ...   **PxB**

If instead Black had protected his KP by 14 ... Q-Q2, then 15 Q-N5, threatening both 16 BxPch and 16 QxN! (16 ... QxQ 17 N-K5ch) would have won.

15 BxPch   **K-B1**

If 15 ... BxB 16 QxBch K-B1 17 QxQN! and White has regained the material with a Pawn interest and a splendid attacking
position.

16 NxNP

With threats such as 17 N-B7 or 17 BxB followed by 18 N-K6ch.
The Black position is tottering. This is a result of the disadvantageous position of the Black King and of Black's failure to take
advantage of his numerical majority in the center.

16 ...   **NxP**

The only move. There is no defense against all the threats, so
Black makes a move which is both aggressive and defensive.

17 RxN

White does not need this Rook for his attack and can therefore
afford to sacrifice the exchange in order to continue the attack
along the most direct line.

17 ...   **PxR**
18 BxB

Threatening 19 N-K6ch, winning the Queen. Once again, notice
the tremendous role the threat plays in chess.

18 ...   **Q-K1**

Black cannot retake the White Bishop with the Queen because
of 19 QxBch, etc., nor with the Rook because of 19 N-K6ch.

19 NxP

Threatening 20 NxB.
19 N-K6ch followed by 20 N-QB7, winning the exchange, looks
fine at first glance, but it leads nowhere. Consider the sequence
19 N-K6ch K-N1 20 N-B7 QxB 21 NxR QxN 22 QxB, and White's
attack is gone. When attacking, it is imperative to maintain the
attack and not to be drawn into a series of exchanges in which so

many pieces disappear from the board that no clear-cut decision is possible.

19 ...   B-N5!

19 ... NxN? will not work because of 20 Q-B3ch and if 20 ... N-B3 21 QxR or if 20 ... K-N1 21 B-K6ch.

In many variations, the powerful Knight on KN5 locks in the King, as, for instance, 19 ... RxB 20 NxB R-QN1 (practically forced) 21 Q-B4 and White threatens to win the Black Queen by 22 N-K6ch, since the Queen has to guard against the mate on KB2 and thus cannot run away from the danger.

With the text, Black hopes to exchange Queens at the cost of material but still maintain the advantage of the exchange for some Pawns. Thus he hopes to soften the attack. For instance, 20 NxB QxQ 21 RxQ RxB, and White is slightly better off: 22 N-K6ch, followed by 23 NxQP.

20 N-K6ch

To avoid the exchange of Queens and to continue the attack. Never exchange Queens during the attack unless you attain a clear win thereby or unless there is nothing else to do.

Look at this marvelous position. Almost all the White pieces are in the air. This means that White has to calculate very sharply, consider all the possibilities. The slightest omission could be fatal.

20 ...   K-B2
21 NxN

For White, there is nothing in 21 NxB RxB.

The complications now to follow have several implications. The player always has to take into consideration: (a) the material relationships, which may not be so important during the battle, but which determine the decision after the battle; (b) pieces in the air or pieces *en prise* (it is a good thing that one can take only one piece at a time, and this explains why White, under the given circumstances, can permit himself the luxury of having so many pieces in the air); (c) the situation is very volatile. At each move, either White or Black can completely turn the balance. The battle is taking place on a razor's edge.

Conclusion: White has a won position even if Black's defense is perfect. (See the detailed analysis of possibilities on pages 278-279.) The game itself took the course of 21 ... QxB, etc. The student might ask how it is possible for the master to analyze in such a jungle of variations. He does not analyze all the lines. He sees a few complications, then knows whether there will be a winning continuation. If he feels there must be one, he goes into the jungle. It is just a matter of intuition. The student of chess should carefully and repeatedly examine all these possibilities, for it will improve his capacity in the field of making combinations. The first time, he will be able to carry out the variations only by making the moves on the board, but eventually he must try to follow the variations without moving the pieces.

| 21 ... | QxB |
| 22 N-N5ch | KxN |

We have already seen that other moves, such as 22 ... K-B1 and 22 ... K-N3 lead to a loss as well.

| 23 Q-B3ch | K-N3 |

Not 23 ... Q-B4? on account of 24 R-K6 mate.

| 24 Q-B7ch | K-R3 |
| 25 P-R5! | |

This is still stronger than 25 R-K6ch, which "only wins the Queen," since 25 ... QxR is forced.

| 25 ... | Resigns |

For if Black plays 25 ... Q-B3, his only defense, then 26 R-K6ch! QxR 27 NxQ, followed by mate.

We now give an almost complete scheme of possibilities:

21 22 23 24 25 26 27

(a) … KxN Q-K5ch K-B2 QxP mate
                   K-N3 QxPch, followed by Q-N5 mate
                   K-K2 NxNP dis ch, winning Queen

(b) … PxN Q-N4, threatening Q-N7 mate

        R-KN1 Q-R5ch R-N3 Q-R7ch, followed by mate
                       K-K2 N-B7 dis ch, winning the Queen

        R-R2   N-N5ch PxN Q-B5ch wins the Queen

        Q-N1   N-N5ch PxN B-K6ch wins the Queen (material advantage + attack)

                       K-N3 N-B7 dis ch K-R2 B-B5ch, etc.
                                          KxN   B-K6ch, wins the Queen

                       K-N2 N-R7 dis ch? K-R3! with no mating combination
                             B-K6   Q-KB1 N-B7 dis ch K-R2 B-B5ch Q-N3 QxQ mate
                                    Q-QN1 N-R7 dis ch KxN   B-B5ch, etc.
                                                        K-R3 NxP, etc.
                                    Q-K1   N-B7 dis ch K-R2 B-B5 mate
                                                        K-B1 P-QB3

And, in the above position, White has two Pawns for the exchange plus the attack and possibilities of attaining extra material. One variation: 26 ... R-KN1 27 QxP B-B4 (27 ... B-K2 28 N-Q6) 28 QxP Q-K2 30 Q-B5.

	21	22	23	24	25	26	27
(c) ...	QxB	N-N5ch K-B1	Q-B3	PxN			
				BxR			
				QxP, followed by mate	K-K1 (only)		
				N-Q5 dis ch	Q-B7ch	K-Q1	Q-K7 mate
			K-N3				
			P-R5ch K-R3	N-B7 mate	Q-B4		
				KxN/4 Q-K5ch	K-R3		
					P-B4ch wins the Queen		
					Q-K4, followed by Q-N6 mate		
			KxN	Q-B4 R-K6 mate	K-R3	Q-B3	N-K6, etc.
			Q-B3ch	K-N3 Q-B7ch	P-R5		

(d) ... BxR NxQ with important material advantage and a mating attack

Game 24

There are gambits and gambits. In some gambits, one must play very carefully to make the tempo gained count for the material sacrificed; in others, where one has sacrificed much, one can almost throw caution to the winds in order to overwhelm the opponent before he can catch his breath. These two methods of approach apply not only to different gambits, but also to different variations of the same gambit.

In the King's Gambit, the king of all gambits, there are variations such as the Kieseritsky or the Philidor Gambit, which have a positional nature to a certain extent. On the other hand, the oldest variations of the King's Gambit, such as the Allgaier and Muzio Gambits, are highly combinational and generally lead to the wildest existing open positions, in which only the carefree adventurer can feel entirely at home. Such variations are characterized not only by the offering of a Pawn for a tempo, but, in addition, by the sacrifice of a piece at a very early stage of the game. This sacrifice of a piece is designed to bring the Black King into the open field, and White can take advantage of the resultant position only if he succeeds in opening the maximum number of lines at whatever cost necessary.

The King's Gambit which follows is an excellent illustration of this procedure. Typical in such cases is that White either wins quickly or doesn't win at all.

Master	Amateur
1 P-K4	P-K4
2 P-KB4	

The King's Gambit. As has been explained in detail in Game 17, a gambit is the offer to an opponent of a Pawn in return for a more rapid development.

By 2 P-KB4 White hopes through an exchange of Pawns to open his KB-file. Once he opens this file, the possibilities of developing a strong attack on the Black KB2 are great. Imagine the open KB-file with White's KB on QB4, his KN on K5 or KN5, his Queen on KB3, and his KR on KB1, and you will see the possibilities of the White attack. With normal resistance from his opponent, White will never be able to attain this position completely, but he will strive for it.

If Black accepts the gambit by 2 ... PxP, White will also have the possibility of attaining a strong center by moves such as P-Q4.

2 ...	PxP

Black accepts the Pawn, and now White has a clear plan to open the KB-file either by recapturing Black's Pawn himself or by some other means. Momentarily, Black has an extra Pawn, and, as we shall see, it is not easy for White to regain this Pawn. But, on the other hand, Black has exchanged his center Pawn for a side Pawn, thus giving up control of his Q5 and allowing White the possibility of occupying the center.

Black can refuse the gambit by simply replying 2 ... B-B4 or can play the interesting Falkbeer Countergambit 2 ... P-Q4, the usual continuation of which is 3 PxQP P-K5, at which point, in return for the Pawn surrendered, Black has these compensations: (a) White has not succeeded in opening the KB-file as he wished; (b) Black's KP has become an oppressive force which will prevent White from developing normally.

3 N-KB3

The KN is now developed to its natural square. This eliminates the possibility of Black's playing 3 ... Q-R5ch, which, in certain cases, might be recommended: e.g., 3 N-QB3? Q-R5ch 4 K-K2 and the White King is very exposed and moreover impedes White's development.

3 B-B4 Q-R5ch, often played during the nineteenth century, leads to violent attacks and counterattacks: e.g., 4 K-B1 P-KN4 5 P-Q4 B-N2 6 N-QB3 N-K2 7 P-KN3! PxP 8 K-N2! threatening to win the Black Queen by 9 PxP.

3 ...	P-KN4

A popular nineteenth-century continuation with three aims: (a) it protects the extra gambit Pawn; (b) it attempts to prevent White from opening his KB-file; (c) it threatens ... P-KN5 followed by ... Q-R5ch, at which point the Queen check has greater force than in other variants.

4 P-KR4

White immediately challenges Black's attempt to protect the KBP. This move has far-reaching consequences, as will be seen from the game itself.

The continuation 4 B-B4 P-N5 5 0-0 PxN is called the Muzio Gambit. White sacrifices a piece in return for a very strong attack along the KB-file. Therefore, since 4 B-B4 gives him time to consolidate, Black does not answer 4 ... P-N5 but 4 ... B-N2 instead, the so-called Philidor-Hanstein, after which the flank attack with the White KRP (5 P-KR4) is rendered worthless by Black's reply 5 ... P-KR3.

| 4 ... | P-N5 |

Since Black cannot maintain his Pawn on his KN4, he pushes it to his KN5, attacking the White Knight.

Let us see what would happen if Black tried to maintain his Pawn on his KN4. (a) If 4 ... P-KR3 5 PxP and Black cannot retake without losing his Rook. (b) The move 4 ... P-KB3 is a weakening move which can be met in various ways. Considering the attacking possibilities along the diagonals Q1-KR5-K8, the most convincing is 5 NxP PxN 6 Q-R5ch K-K2 7 QxNPch K-K1 (7 ... N-B3? 8 P-K5) 8 Q-R5ch K-K2 9 Q-K5ch, followed by 10 QxR. In this variation, note how White manipulates his Queen until he is able to take the Black Rook without Black's being able to begin a counterattack by playing ... Q-K2.

5 N-N5

This leads to the Allgaier Gambit. White attacks Black's KBP and threatens to attack it doubly by 6 B-B4. There is only one disadvantage: White's Knight has no retreat, and White will be forced to sacrifice it if Black attacks it.

5 N-K5 leads to the Kieseritsky Gambit, which is less risky than the Allgaier Gambit. White can also play 5 B-B4 PxN 6 QxP, which is not very promising.

| 5 ... | P-KR3 |

Black attacks the Knight immediately, so as not to allow White's threatened assault to develop.

6 NxP

This sacrifice is in harmony with the over-all strategy of the King's Gambit, for, by bringing out the Black King, White makes the KB-file still more useful to himself. From a theoretical point of view, it is difficult to judge whether the attacking possibilities are worth a whole piece. But, from a practical point of view, the sacrifice *is* justified, because the defender generally has a more difficult role to play than the aggressor.

6 ...   **KxN**

Black has now won a whole piece, but his King is most vulnerable to attack!

7 N-B3

7 N-B3 brings a new piece into the field, a piece which White will need to conduct the attack. In positions such as these, where the aggressor has sacrificed a piece for the attack, he must get his remaining pieces into play as soon as possible. The cooperation of every White piece is needed now in order to succeed.

In this position, 7 QxP is inferior because it furthers Black's development after 7 ... N-KB3 8 QxBP B-Q3, and Black has the attack. White must avoid moves which allow Black to develop with a tempo, that is, forcing White to move his Queen. 7 QxP would be a very good move if White could attack with the Queen alone, but he cannot.

In former times, 7 B-B4ch used to be played, but after 7 ... P-Q4 8 BxPch K-N2, Black has, at the cost of one Pawn, strengthened his position, especially since after 7 ... P-Q4, his KNP is protected by his QB. Moreover, the possibility of Black's playing ... N-KB3 and attacking the White Bishop on its Q5 affords further opportunity to Black to consolidate his position.

Of the possible moves, 7 N-B3 seems to offer the best development to White and the least opportunity to Black of consolidating his position at White's expense.

7 ...	P-Q4

Black offers a Pawn in order to gain a tempo for the defense. That is, he plays 7 ... P-Q4 in order to protect his Pawn on KN5 and enable his QB to develop.

A preferable move would be the aggressive 7 ... P-B6, since after 8 PxP B-K2, White cannot defend his KRP, which means that Black gets counterchances.

8 P-Q4

White opens lines for his own development, threatens to open the KB-file by BxP, and prevents Black from playing 8 ... P-Q5.

8 ...	N-KB3

Black develops his KN to its natural square, protects the QP, and exerts pressure on the center.

8 ... PxP would lose a tempo for Black, and winning White's KP is not very important for him. It does no harm to White's position and, on the contrary, opens the QB4-KB7 diagonal for White.

9 BxP

White now opens the KB-file. Since Black's King is on this open file, there should soon be a violent attack.

9 ...	P-B3?

Black played this move because he vaguely felt the necessity of strengthening his center Pawn. But this move loses a tempo in a position where Black can least afford to lose tempi, because each move counts. Black should have developed a piece here. Either 9 ... B-K3 or 9 ... B-N5 would have been stronger. In either case, White would follow the same strategy as he uses in this game: that is, B-K2, followed by 0-0, to open a direct attack against the Black King.

Let us examine this position a bit more closely, just to show (a) what a tempo means in an open position like this; (b) how strong White's attack really is.

(a) 9 ... B-K3 10 Q-Q3? N-B3 11 0-0-0 PxP 12 NxP NxN 13 QxN Q-Q4 and Black has refuted White's attack. White can do better: 10 B-K2 N-B3 11 0-0 K-N2 12 P-K5 N-K5 13 BxNP NxN 14 PxN Q-Q2 and Black can hold his own; or 12 PxP! (better than 12 P-K5) 12 ... KNxP 13 NxN QxN 14 P-B4! QxPch 15 QxQ NxQ 16 B-K5ch and White does not seem to be badly off.

(b) 9 ... B-N5 10 B-K2 BxNch 11 PxB N-B3 (to defend the important square K4) 12 0-0 K-N2 (White threatened 13 P-K5) 13 P-B4! (to carry through P-Q5, thus gaining control over K5) 13 ... NxKP 14 PxP N-B6 (after 14 ... QxRP 15 PxN P-N6 16 B-K5ch K-N3 17 B-R5ch wins. The same after 14 ... QxQP 15 P-B4 followed by 16 P-Q5) 15 PxN!! (overwhelming) NxQ 16 B-K5ch K-N3 17 B-Q3ch K-R4 18 PxP! B-K3 (18 ... BxP 19 R-B5ch and mate in two)

19 PxR(Q) QxQ 20 QRxN R-KB1 21 RxR QxR 22 R-KB1 Q-K2 23 R-B6 and White must win.

10 B-K2

Planning to bring his KR to bear on the open KB-file through castling.

10 ...   **B-N5**

By pinning the White Knight, Black hopes to take pressure from the center and by exchanging his Bishop for the White Knight hopes to reduce the number of pieces on the board. Black reasons that if he can exchange piece for piece, he will end up with an advantage, since he is a Knight to the good. White, of course, has better development to compensate for his lost Knight. But he must act fast, or Black will make his superior numbers felt.

11 0-0

Now White has attained his strategic goal—the complete domination of the KB-file. Castling brings the White Rook into a direct line with the Black King. This holds within it an element of danger for Black, even though his Knight comes between his King and the White Rook. White now has two direct threats: 12 P-K5 and 12 B-K5.

11 ...   **K-K1**

Realizing the dangerous position of his King, Black moves it to a relatively safer file, but thereby loses one more tempo. He would have done better to play 11 ... BxN first, since 12 B-K5 doesn't mean much after 12 ... QN-Q2.

12 P-K5

In order to win the Black KNP after the Black Knight moves and in order to bring more pieces into play.

12 ...   **BxN**

Black now exchanges to reduce the number of pieces and the danger of attack. But such moves contribute nothing to Black's defense or development. Since White is not forced to retake the Black Bishop, 12 ... N-K5 would have been better, although also useless in the long run.

13 PxN

13 ...   **B-N5**

Black, who is playing by general principles instead of being guided by the requirements of the specific position, is delighted to have saved his Two Bishops, but his Two Bishops have no bearing on the position at hand.

If Black had played 13 ... BxNP, 14 R-N1 would have led to about the same type of game. But 14 BxNP would have been stronger in that case and might have led to an overwhelming attack after 14 ... BxR 15 BxB QxB 16 Q-K2ch and mate in a few moves.

14 BxNP

By opening more lines and bringing out more pieces, White eliminates the last obstacles to his attack. The threat is 15 B-R5ch K-B1 16 Q-B1, followed by 17 BxRPch.

14 ...   N-Q2

After 14 ... BxB 15 QxB Q-Q2, White wins by 16 P-B7ch followed by: (a) 16 ... K-B1 17 BxPch RxB 18 Q-N8ch; or (b) 16 ... K-K2 17 Q-N8 RxQ 18 PxR(Q); or (c) 16 ... K-Q1 17 Q-N8ch, etc.; or (d) 16 ... QxP 17 Q-B8ch K-K2 18 QxR or 18 QR-K1ch.

15 B-R5ch

White now takes advantage of the wide-open lines. These lines are at White's disposal but not at Black's. This is because White has developed his pieces, whereas Black has not. Open lines favor the side which has the attack.

15 ...   K-B1
16 Q-N4

Threatening mate. Black cannot play 16 ... R-KN1 on account of 17 BxPch.

16 ...   NxP

The KB-file is now wide-open.

17 Q-N6

Again threatening mate.

17 ...   B-K3

Or 17 ... Q-K2 18 B-K5.

18 B-Q6ch

Here 18 B-K5 B-K2 19 RxNch BxR 20 R-KB1 also leads to a win. But the text is prettier.

18 ...   Resigns

For 18 ... BxB 19 RxNch K-K2 20 Q-N7ch and mate on the next move.

Game 25

The theory of the Giuoco Piano

Breaking up the center with a freeing move

Pawn sacrifices for greater development

Importance of making active rather than indifferent moves

The sham sacrifice

Play against the King in the center of the open board

R + P's vs. R + P's ending

Losing a tempo in the end game

When a player has superior mobility, he must make use of it fairly soon or it may vanish, leaving him with nothing to show for it. Often, the best use which can be made of mobility is to drive the opposing pieces into less favorable positions, thus creating problems for the opponent.

How should one proceed against a King in the center of an open board when one has only Rooks and minor pieces at one's disposal? Of prime importance in such circumstances is the realization that the advantage of having attacking possibilities against a hostile King with such pieces is of a rather volatile character. It can suddenly disappear. Ironically, as soon as the Rook and minor pieces are exchanged and the King in the center of the board no longer has to fear an attack, it then suddenly stands better than the opponent's King, which is safely guarded on his 1st rank. In such cases, a disadvantage can easily become an advantage and vice versa.

In the game, Black does find the most energetic moves against the White King in the center of the open board. Finally, he wins a Pawn, but even then the winning of the game is not an easy task. Black has to maneuver very carefully and make use of all kinds of finesses, such as *Zugzwang*, losing a move, and keeping the enemy King from coming too close to his Pawns, in order to reach his final victory.

Giuoco Piano

Amateur	Master
1 P-K4	P-K4
2 N-KB3	N-QB3
3 B-B4	

Stationed at its QB4, this Bishop helps control the center, exercises pressure along two important diagonals, and is trained on Black's KB2. Yet 3 B-N5 has even greater latent possibilities, because it exerts greater pressure on the center by its restraining effect on the Black QN, which will be pinned as soon as the Black QP moves (see Game 12).

3 ...	B-B4

The Giuoco Piano or Italian Opening, one of the oldest in the history of chess. This opening is characterized by a rapid development of the pieces.

Stationed at its QB4, the Black Bishop also exercises pressure along two important diagonals, helps to control the center, and is trained on White's KB2. Yet 3 ... N-B3 is perhaps stronger, because, in addition to exerting pressure on the center squares, it attacks White's KP and forces White to take measures to protect that Pawn.

4 P-B3

White prepares to occupy the center by 5 P-Q4. If he can control the center, he can paralyze the actions of his opponent to a considerable extent.

If White should play 4 P-Q4 immediately, he would lose a Pawn, since his Q4 would be protected by two pieces (KN and Q), whereas Black attacks the same square with three pieces

(QN, KB, KP). In order to occupy a square, one must control it with at least as many pieces or Pawns as does one's opponent.

As a matter of fact, 4 P-Q4 PxP 5 0-0 is a famous variation of the Giuoco Piano known as the Max Lange attack, in which White sacrifices a Pawn for a strong attack.

4 ...	N-B3

Attacking White's KP, 4 ... N-B3 is directed against White's aim of obtaining complete control of the center. If instead Black had played the passive 4 ... P-Q3, White could then obtain complete control of the center as follows: 5 P-Q4 PxP (5 ... B-N3 6 PxP wins a Pawn) 6 PxP with complete control of the center.

5 P-Q4

White completes his bid for control of the center. By attacking the Black Bishop and thus compelling his opponent to take action, he gains a tempo.

5 ...	PxP

Forced. If instead Black retreated (5 ... B-N3), White would increase his domination of the center by 6 PxP and if 6 ... KNxP 7 Q-Q5, threatening both 8 QxBP mate and 8 QxN, thus winning the Knight.

In openings where both sides are attempting to occupy the center with Pawns, it is very important to determine whether the Pawns can remain and the tension be maintained, or whether

293

the Pawns must be exchanged to prevent the opponent from gaining overwhelming control. This is one of the most important problems in the theory of individual chess openings. The meaning of this comment will become clearer after Black's 8th move.

6 PxP　　　　　　　　　　　　　　**B-N5ch**

By giving check, Black forces White to take action, thus gaining time in his attempt to destroy White's center, as we shall presently see. Black must work against White's plan to build up an ideal center if he is to survive.

Suppose Black had played 6 ... B-N3. White now has a solid center, which he can use as follows: 7 P-Q5.

> (a) 7 ... N-QR4? 8 B-Q3 with the threat 9 P-QN4.
> (b) 7 ... N-QN1 8 P-K5.
>> (1) 8 ... N-N1? 9 0-0 P-Q3 10 R-K1 PxP 11 NxP N-K2 12 NxP KxN 13 P-Q6 dis ch.
>> (2) 8 ... N-N5 9 0-0 P-Q3 10 P-K6 PxP 11 PxP P-B3 (preparing ... P-Q4) 12 N-N5, threatening both 13 QxN and 13 N-B7.

7 B-Q2

White could have played 7 N-B3, to which Black answers 7 ... KNxP, after which the White center is destroyed, White's strategic plans are countered, and White will have to follow tactical aims instead. This is the Möller variation, which is very complicated and not definitely favorable to one side or the other.

7 ...　　　　　　　　　　　　　　**BxBch**

Today, players make this move automatically. But in the history of chess, plausible alternates had to be analyzed and evaluated. Therefore, 7 ... NxKP, which contributes to destroying White's center, also had to be looked into. The game would then continue: 8 BxB NxB 9 BxPch KxB 10 Q-N3ch P-Q4 11 N-K5ch K-B1 12 QxNch Q-K2 and White has recaptured his Pawn with a slight

294

advantage. But in this case, too, the White center does not play any role.

8 QNxB   **P-Q4**

This is the move that breaks up White's center. White must exchange Pawns (see comment after Black's 5th move), and so, of a once powerful center, only an isolated Pawn remains. This does not mean, however, that White has the worst of it. His QP is isolated, it is true, but, on the other hand, his pieces have full activity, and on many occasions it has been shown that White's chances are not to be underrated.

8 ... P-Q4 not only breaks up White's center; it also opens Black's center so that his pieces have room to develop. For him, it is a freeing move.

9 PxP

For 9 P-K5 PxB 10 PxN QxBP is quite satisfactory for Black.

9 ...   **KNxP**

10 Q-N3

The most active move. It confronts Black with a problem and is therefore stronger than 10 0-0.

10 ...   **0-0**

Surprisingly enough, this is not the sacrifice of a piece, but the sacrifice of a Pawn, as will be seen in a moment. Usually 10 ... QN-K2 11 0-0 0-0 is played here, and White has a slight edge.

295

If Black should play 10 ... N-R4? in order to cut down the attack by exchange, 11 Q-R4ch P-B3 12 B-Q3, and Black's QN is not well placed, especially in view of the threat P-QN4.

11 BxN

If White had castled at this point, Black would have played 11 ... N-R4, and, after having exchanged his Knight for the White Bishop, he would have had a very promising game. In that case, the weakness of White's isolated QP would not have been compensated for by the greater activity of the White pieces.

Whenever the White Queen is on its QN3, the White Bishop on its QB4, and the Black Knight on its QB3, Black may always try to play ... N-QR4 in order to exchange the Bishop for the Knight and cut down White's attack. White must often guard against this possibility (compare Games 7, 10 and 18).

11 ...   N-R4!

This is the key move of Black's little combination. After the White Queen moves, Black captures the Bishop and has a fine game, because of the pressure he exerts against White's isolated Pawn without any compensation on the part of White.

12 BxPch

Practically forced. 12 Q-N5 P-QB3 does not improve matters. With any other Queen move, Black answers 12 ... QxB with a very good position.

12 ...   RxB
13 Q-B3   R-K2ch!

This move is instructive in various ways.

An indifferent move such as 13 ... N-B3 allows White to castle and leaves Black a Pawn down with no compensation.

13 ... R-K2ch is good first because it forces White to act and second because it forces him to act to his detriment. As will be seen in the game, the entire Black strategy is based on the un-

296

favorable position of the White King, which, being only temporary in nature, had to be exploited immediately.

14 N-K5

If 14 K-Q1 or K-B1, White keeps his Pawn but gets into difficulties which are not temporary in nature: e.g., if 14 K-Q1, the White King is exposed; if 14 K-B1, the KR is out of the game.

14 ...   **N-B3**

Threatening ... NxP. Now White loses his Pawn but gets all the play.

White wishes to castle. If he castles, what can Black do, and where will that leave White?

After 15 0-0 NxP 16 KR-K1, Black has no advantage after 15 0-0 QxP?, and White can even win by 16 NxN QxQ 17 NxRch. White, however, chooses another line, which is also satisfactory.

15 QN-B3   **NxP**

A *sham sacrifice*. Black regains his piece immediately.

16 QxN?

Much better is the in-between move 16 Q-B4ch. 17 ... B-K3? 18 QxN loses a piece for Black, and 16 ... K-R1 17 0-0-0 would

297

not be much better for Black, so he is forced to reply 16 ... N-K3, and White certainly does not have the worst of it.

| 16 ... | QxQ |
| 17 NxQ | RxNch |

Now the King must lose his castling privilege, which is not so serious, in general, after Queens are exchanged and even less so in the end game. Most remarkable in this game is the fact that, with Queens exchanged and many of the major pieces removed, the White King still has many difficulties in the middle of the board.

18 K-Q2

Of course, it is of major importance to connect the Rooks, and for the moment it cannot be seen that the King risks too much on the Q-file. No better is 18 K-B1. With best play after the text, White could have drawn.

| 18 ... | P-B4 |

This is the logical continuation. Black must somehow take advantage of the open position of the activated White King, who could otherwise be powerful in the end game. A less incisive move, such as 18 ... B-Q2, would allow White to get his Rooks into play.

19 N-B2

White avoids 19 N-B3, because it enables Black to win a tempo and thereby bring the second Rook into the game as follows: 19 ... R-Q4ch 20 K-B3 B-N5 and if White does not wish to permit Black to double his Pawns by ... BxN, he must move his Knight, and Black then has the opportunity to play ... QR-Q1, threatening ... R-Q6ch, with all kinds of prospects.

| 19 ... | B-K3 |

To exert some pressure on White's QRP.

20 N-K3

White reasons as follows: 20 N-K3 looks like the best move, because the Knight is so well placed and exercises control over so many central squares.

But this is more apparent than real.

If, in this position, White had played 20 KR-K1, it would have reduced Black's positional advantage to microscopic proportions. After 20 ... RxR 21 NxR, Black still has a slight advantage, because he has a Pawn majority on the Q-side and a Good Bishop. But, in view of the reduced material, it is quite doubtful that this would have led to a win.

| 20 ... | R-KB1 |

The strength of this move becomes apparent from the following continuation: 21 P-B3? losing a piece after 21 ... R-Q1ch 22 K-K2 B-B5ch 23 K-B2 R-Q7ch 24 K-K1 R-K7ch, winning the Knight.

21 KR-KB1

Forced. Black has played in such a way that both White Rooks are tied down to the defense of Pawns. Naturally, this is not the most efficient way to use one's Rooks.

| 21 ... | B-Q2 |

Threatening to win a Pawn by 22 ... B-N4, forcing the Rook to move.

22 P-B3

22 N-B4? loses a Pawn in a most remarkable way: 22 ... R-N4 and the KNP cannot be defended unless White prefers to lose his KBP; 23 P-KN3 B-R6 again forcing the KR to move. If 23 N-K3 B-N4.

| 22 ... | B-N4 |
| 23 KR-K1 | |

He must defend his Knight because of the threat ... R-Q1ch, losing the Knight.

23 ...	R-Q1ch
24 K-B2	B-Q6ch
25 K-B3	B-N3

The Bishop retreats, threatening to win a piece by ... R-Q6ch.

26 N-N4

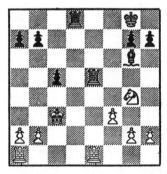

If 26 QR-Q1, either 26 ... RxR 27 RxR RxNch or 26 ... RxNch at once.

Black must now play very carefully or White will obtain equality.

(a) If 26 ... RxR 27 RxR R-Q6ch, leading to a continuation like that of the game.

(b) If 26 ... R/4-Q4 27 N-K5 and Black does not have many chances left. For instance, 27 ... R-Q7 28 NxB PxN 29 R-K8ch, leading to equality.

| 26 ... | R-Q6ch |

Black continues with a check in order to retain the initiative.

27 K-B4	RxR
28 RxR	R-Q7

The maneuvers have finally resulted in Black's getting control of the 7th rank, a most important rank, especially in the ending, because a Rook on that rank threatens the Pawns horizontally, and in this direction they have no power to defend themselves.

29 R-K7

White adopts the same strategy, but one move later. A tempo is important.

29 ...	RxQNP
30 KxP	P-N3ch

Again gaining a tempo—the Pawn gets out of the attack by the Rook with a check.

31 K-B6	RxRP

Black has finally won a Pawn, but, in view of the rather active position of both of White's pieces, there are still some difficulties to surmount.

32 N-K5	K-B1
33 NxBch	

The alternative here would be 33 R-N7 B-K1ch 34 K-Q6 P-QN4, and it doesn't seem likely that White could stop Black's passed Pawns in the long run.

33 ...	PxN
34 R-N7	P-KN4

To prevent the blocking of the King by P-N4-N5.

35 K-Q6	K-N1
36 K-K6	K-R2
37 K-B7	

Threatening 38 K-B8, winning a Pawn. Therefore, Black feels obliged to simplify. But, as a matter of fact, the situation is favorable for simplification, since the White King is far from his home base and, in particular, is not able to protect his K-side Pawns.

As far as the exchange of the last piece (in this case a Rook) is concerned, so that a pure Pawn ending may be reached, it is a question of judging what the Pawn ending will give, which is not too difficult, special cases excepted. In Pawn endings, the plus Pawn decides in more than 90 per cent of the cases. However, if simplification means exchanging one or more Pawns for others, it is difficult to give general rules. In Rook endings, the stronger side should exchange Pawns if he is sure to improve his situation in so doing. In case of doubt, he should not exchange.

37 ...	RxP
38 RxP	R-KB7
39 R-N7	

Not 39 R-R3 on account of 39 . . . P-N5.

39 ...	RxBPch
40 K-K6	R-B3ch

Typical in Rook endings; the Rook protects his most vulnerable Pawn and keeps the enemy from a certain area of the chessboard.

41 K-K5	P-N5
42 R-R7	

A kind of reciprocal *Zugzwang*. If either player moves, he weakens his position. Black must protect his QNP and his KNP/N2. White must maintain the pressure on these Pawns.

If Black now plays 42 ... K-R3 in order to continue later with ... P-N3 to relieve the pressure after he has removed his Rook, White then plays 43 R-N7 and Black's *Zugzwang* is complete: (a) 43 ... K-N3 44 K-K4!; (b) 43 ... R moves on his 3rd rank 44 K-B4; (c) 43 ... R moves on KB-file 44 RxPch.

That is why Black first plays:

42 ...   K-N3!

and only after

43 R-N7

continues by

43 ...   K-R3!

We note that Black could reach this position only by going from R2 to R3 in two moves, that is, via N3. Now White's *Zugzwang* is complete. White must relieve the pressure: (a) 44 R-N8 K-N4; (b) R moves on 7th rank R-B7; (c) 44 K-K4 P-N3. This is the key and explains the difference between 43 ... K-N3 and 43 ... K-R3.

44 K-K4

If 44 R-R7 R-B7 45 R-R6 RxP 46 RxPch K-N4; if 44 R-N8 K-N4 45 R-N7 P-N3.

44 ...	P-N3
45 K-K5	K-N4

Black has come a little farther, and this enables him to give up his QNP for White's RP.

46 K-K4	R-B7

This simplification is the quickest way to win.

47 RxP	R-K7ch

A very important tactical finesse—first drive the King away. The farther the White King is from the Pawns, the better it will be for Black.

48 K-Q3	RxP

In general, this ending is won, but Black has to play exactly, and from what follows we see that Black always prevents the White King from coming too near. As long as Black keeps the White King away from his Pawns, the game must be won.

49 K-K3	R-R7
50 R-N1	K-R5
51 R-R1ch	K-N6

In such positions, the King must get in front of his Pawns.

52 R-N1ch	K-R6

After 52 ... R-N7 53 R-KR1, Black has to make another move with his Rook in order to enable the King to advance and support the Knight Pawns.

53 R-R1ch	**R-R7**
54 R-R1	**P-N6**
55 R-R8	**R-KB7**
56 R-R8ch	**K-N7**
Resigns	

A possible continuation to show how Black wins very easily: 57 R-KN8 R-B3 58 R-N7 R-K3ch 59 K-B4 K-B7 60 R-QR7 P-N7 61 R-R2ch R-K7, etc.

Index

References are to pages (*ex.:* 125), to pages and moves (*ex.:* 35, W10; 149, B7), occasionally to pages and games (*ex.:* 217, G19), and to introductory pages and sections (*ex.:* xxviii, §37).

308

Damiano Defense, 9, G2

Defender, attack on, 46, B5

Desperado, 165, B15

Developed piece, moving twice a, 32, W6; 83, W9–10; 84, W12; 126, W12; 232, W9; 234, W13; 248, B8

Development
breaking rules of, 229–30; 232, W8–9; 248, B8
necessity for, after sacrificing, 284, W7; 286, B9
sacrificing for, 102; 103, W4; 104, W5
superiority of, 77; 84, B10, W17; 116, B7; 148, B6; 151, B12

Diagonals, 3, WB1, B2; 5, B4; 6, B5; 12, B2, W3; 58, B7

Differences between master and amateur, ix, §§2–3; xii, §7; xiv–xv, §§11–13; 232, W8–9

Discarded lines, 8; 11, B2

Discovered check shuttle attack, 74, B25

Double check, force of, 36, B13; 38, B21; 120, W20

Double isolated Pawns, 46, W7; 164, W14, 165, W16–19; 169, W28; 197, B9; 200, W13, B14

Doubled Pawn, when not a weakness, 99, W13; 197, B9

En passant, xxxiii, W9

Equality, xxii, §23

"Exchange," the, 25, B17; 235, W15; 275, W17

Exchange, motives for
to acquire mobility, 266, W17
to attain superior position, 33, B6
to avoid loss of tempo, 125–26, W11; 178, W10

to bring piece to better square, 25, B17
to eliminate opponent's active piece, 182, B19
to eliminate opponent's threats, 199, W12
to eliminate strong Knight, 252, W18
to exchange Good Bishop for Bad Bishop, 262–63, W9
to exchange undeveloped for developed piece, 46, B6
to exchange a well-posted for a poorly posted piece, 225, W13
to make lines available, 119, W15; 124–25, W8
to make square available, 38, B22
material advantage, when one has, 97, B9; 155, W32
to mutilate opponent's Pawn structure, 35, B10; 46, B6; 200, B13, W14
to obtain more freedom of action, 124, W7
of piece that has no more work, 245, W6
to reduce attacking power, 48, W10; 66, B6–7; 108, W11; 154, B23; 211, B17; 274, B13; 288, B12
to reduce lead in development, 206, B7
to reduce number of pieces, 89, B29; 288, B12
to remove opponent's well-posted piece, 119, W15
to retain initiative, 264, B12
to strip piece of defense, 35, B10
to win material, 19, B5

Exchange, when not to
to maintain big advantage, 112, W24
to retain attacking power, 48, W10; 276, W20
when one's piece is better situated, 125, W8; 160, W6
when one's Queen is more active, 88, W21

A CATALOG OF SELECTED DOVER

BOOKS IN ALL FIELDS OF INTEREST

CONCERNING THE SPIRITUAL IN ART, Wassily Kandinsky. Pioneering work by father of abstract art. Thoughts on color theory, nature of art. Analysis of earlier masters. 12 illustrations. 80pp. of text. 5⅜ x 8½. 23411-8 Pa. $3.95

ANIMALS: 1,419 Copyright-Free Illustrations of Mammals, Birds, Fish, Insects, etc., Jim Harter (ed.). Clear wood engravings present, in extremely lifelike poses, over 1,000 species of animals. One of the most extensive pictorial sourcebooks of its kind. Captions. Index. 284pp. 9 x 12. 23766-4 Pa. $12.95

CELTIC ART: The Methods of Construction, George Bain. Simple geometric techniques for making Celtic interlacements, spirals, Kells-type initials, animals, humans, etc. Over 500 illustrations. 160pp. 9 x 12. (USO) 22923-8 Pa. $9.95

AN ATLAS OF ANATOMY FOR ARTISTS, Fritz Schider. Most thorough reference work on art anatomy in the world. Hundreds of illustrations, including selections from works by Vesalius, Leonardo, Goya, Ingres, Michelangelo, others. 593 illustrations. 192pp. 7⅛ x 10¼. 20241-0 Pa. $9 95

CELTIC HAND STROKE-BY-STROKE (Irish Half-Uncial from "The Book of Kells"): An Arthur Baker Calligraphy Manual, Arthur Baker. Complete guide to creating each letter of the alphabet in distinctive Celtic manner. Covers hand position, strokes, pens, inks, paper, more. Illustrated. 48pp. 8¼ x 11. 24336-2 Pa. $3.95

EASY ORIGAMI, John Montroll. Charming collection of 32 projects (hat, cup, pelican, piano, swan, many more) specially designed for the novice origami hobbyist. Clearly illustrated easy-to-follow instructions insure that even beginning papercrafters will achieve successful results. 48pp. 8¼ x 11. 27298-2 Pa. $2.95

THE COMPLETE BOOK OF BIRDHOUSE CONSTRUCTION FOR WOODWORKERS, Scott D. Campbell. Detailed instructions, illustrations, tables. Also data on bird habitat and instinct patterns. Bibliography. 3 tables. 63 illustrations in 15 figures. 48pp. 5¼ x 8½. 24407-5 Pa. $2.50

BLOOMINGDALE'S ILLUSTRATED 1886 CATALOG: Fashions, Dry Goods and Housewares, Bloomingdale Brothers. Famed merchants' extremely rare catalog depicting about 1,700 products: clothing, housewares, firearms, dry goods, jewelry, more. Invaluable for dating, identifying vintage items. Also, copyright-free graphics for artists, designers. Co-published with Henry Ford Museum & Greenfield Village. 160pp. 8¼ x 11. 25780-0 Pa. $9.95

HISTORIC COSTUME IN PICTURES, Braun & Schneider. Over 1,450 costumed figures in clearly detailed engravings—from dawn of civilization to end of 19th century. Captions. Many folk costumes. 256pp. 8⅜ x 11¾. 23150-X Pa. $12.95

CATALOG OF DOVER BOOKS

STICKLEY CRAFTSMAN FURNITURE CATALOGS, Gustav Stickley and L. & J. G. Stickley. Beautiful, functional furniture in two authentic catalogs from 1910. 594 illustrations, including 277 photos, show settles, rockers, armchairs, reclining chairs, bookcases, desks, tables. 183pp. 6½ x 9¼.   23838-5 Pa. $9.95

AMERICAN LOCOMOTIVES IN HISTORIC PHOTOGRAPHS: 1858 to 1949, Ron Ziel (ed.). A rare collection of 126 meticulously detailed official photographs, called "builder portraits," of American locomotives that majestically chronicle the rise of steam locomotive power in America. Introduction. Detailed captions. xi + 129pp. 9 x 12.   27393-8 Pa. $12.95

AMERICA'S LIGHTHOUSES: An Illustrated History, Francis Ross Holland, Jr. Delightfully written, profusely illustrated fact-filled survey of over 200 American lighthouses since 1716. History, anecdotes, technological advances, more. 240pp. 8 x 10¾.
                                                                     25576-X Pa. $12.95

TOWARDS A NEW ARCHITECTURE, Le Corbusier. Pioneering manifesto by founder of "International School." Technical and aesthetic theories, views of industry, economics, relation of form to function, "mass-production split" and much more. Profusely illustrated. 320pp. 6⅛ x 9¼. (USO)   25023-7 Pa. $9.95

HOW THE OTHER HALF LIVES, Jacob Riis. Famous journalistic record, exposing poverty and degradation of New York slums around 1900, by major social reformer. 100 striking and influential photographs. 233pp. 10 x 7⅞.
                                                                      22012-5 Pa. $10.95

FRUIT KEY AND TWIG KEY TO TREES AND SHRUBS, William M. Harlow. One of the handiest and most widely used identification aids. Fruit key covers 120 deciduous and evergreen species; twig key 160 deciduous species. Easily used. Over 300 photographs. 126pp. 5⅜ x 8½.   20511-8 Pa. $3.95

COMMON BIRD SONGS, Dr. Donald J. Borror. Songs of 60 most common U.S. birds: robins, sparrows, cardinals, bluejays, finches, more—arranged in order of increasing complexity. Up to 9 variations of songs of each species.
                                                          Cassette and manual 99911-4 $8.95

ORCHIDS AS HOUSE PLANTS, Rebecca Tyson Northen. Grow cattleyas and many other kinds of orchids—in a window, in a case, or under artificial light. 63 illustrations. 148pp. 5⅜ x 8½.   23261-1 Pa. $4.95

MONSTER MAZES, Dave Phillips. Masterful mazes at four levels of difficulty. Avoid deadly perils and evil creatures to find magical treasures. Solutions for all 32 exciting illustrated puzzles. 48pp. 8¼ x 11.   26005-4 Pa. $2.95

MOZART'S DON GIOVANNI (DOVER OPERA LIBRETTO SERIES), Wolfgang Amadeus Mozart. Introduced and translated by Ellen H. Bleiler. Standard Italian libretto, with complete English translation. Convenient and thoroughly portable—an ideal companion for reading along with a recording or the performance itself. Introduction. List of characters. Plot summary. 121pp. 5¼ x 8½.
                                                                       24944-1 Pa. $2.95

TECHNICAL MANUAL AND DICTIONARY OF CLASSICAL BALLET, Gail Grant. Defines, explains, comments on steps, movements, poses and concepts. 15-page pictorial section. Basic book for student, viewer. 127pp. 5⅜ x 8½.
                                                                       21843-0 Pa. $4.95

BRASS INSTRUMENTS: Their History and Development, Anthony Baines. Authoritative, updated survey of the evolution of trumpets, trombones, bugles, cornets, French horns, tubas and other brass wind instruments. Over 140 illustrations and 48 music examples. Corrected and updated by author. New preface. Bibliography. 320pp. 5⅜ x 8½. 27574-4 Pa. $9.95

HOLLYWOOD GLAMOR PORTRAITS, John Kobal (ed.). 145 photos from 1926-49. Harlow, Gable, Bogart, Bacall; 94 stars in all. Full background on photographers, technical aspects. 160pp. 8⅜ x 11¼. 23352-9 Pa. $11.95

MAX AND MORITZ, Wilhelm Busch. Great humor classic in both German and English. Also 10 other works: "Cat and Mouse," "Plisch and Plumm," etc. 216pp. 5⅜ x 8½. 20181-3 Pa. $6.95

THE RAVEN AND OTHER FAVORITE POEMS, Edgar Allan Poe. Over 40 of the author's most memorable poems: "The Bells," "Ulalume," "Israfel," "To Helen," "The Conqueror Worm," "Eldorado," "Annabel Lee," many more. Alphabetic lists of titles and first lines. 64pp. 5³⁄₁₆ x 8¼. 26685-0 Pa. $1.00

PERSONAL MEMOIRS OF U. S. GRANT, Ulysses Simpson Grant. Intelligent, deeply moving firsthand account of Civil War campaigns, considered by many the finest military memoirs ever written. Includes letters, historic photographs, maps and more. 528pp. 6⅛ x 9¼. 28587-1 Pa. $11.95

AMULETS AND SUPERSTITIONS, E. A. Wallis Budge. Comprehensive discourse on origin, powers of amulets in many ancient cultures: Arab, Persian Babylonian, Assyrian, Egyptian, Gnostic, Hebrew, Phoenician, Syriac, etc. Covers cross, swastika, crucifix, seals, rings, stones, etc. 584pp. 5⅜ x 8½. 23573-4 Pa. $12.95

RUSSIAN STORIES/PYCCKNE PACCKA3bl: A Dual-Language Book, edited by Gleb Struve. Twelve tales by such masters as Chekhov, Tolstoy, Dostoevsky, Pushkin, others. Excellent word-for-word English translations on facing pages, plus teaching and study aids, Russian/English vocabulary, biographical/critical introductions, more. 416pp. 5⅜ x 8½. 26244-8 Pa. $8.95

PHILADELPHIA THEN AND NOW: 60 Sites Photographed in the Past and Present, Kenneth Finkel and Susan Oyama. Rare photographs of City Hall, Logan Square, Independence Hall, Betsy Ross House, other landmarks juxtaposed with contemporary views. Captures changing face of historic city. Introduction. Captions. 128pp. 8¼ x 11. 25790-8 Pa. $9.95

AIA ARCHITECTURAL GUIDE TO NASSAU AND SUFFOLK COUNTIES, LONG ISLAND, The American Institute of Architects, Long Island Chapter, and the Society for the Preservation of Long Island Antiquities. Comprehensive, well-researched and generously illustrated volume brings to life over three centuries of Long Island's great architectural heritage. More than 240 photographs with authoritative, extensively detailed captions. 176pp. 8¼ x 11. 26946-9 Pa. $14.95

NORTH AMERICAN INDIAN LIFE: Customs and Traditions of 23 Tribes, Elsie Clews Parsons (ed.). 27 fictionalized essays by noted anthropologists examine religion, customs, government, additional facets of life among the Winnebago, Crow, Zuni, Eskimo, other tribes. 480pp. 6⅛ x 9¼. 27377-6 Pa. $10.95

FRANK LLOYD WRIGHT'S HOLLYHOCK HOUSE, Donald Hoffmann. Lavishly illustrated, carefully documented study of one of Wright's most controversial residential designs. Over 120 photographs, floor plans, elevations, etc. Detailed perceptive text by noted Wright scholar. Index. 128pp. 9¼ x 10¾. 27133-1 Pa. $11.95

THE MALE AND FEMALE FIGURE IN MOTION: 60 Classic Photographic Sequences, Eadweard Muybridge. 60 true-action photographs of men and women walking, running, climbing, bending, turning, etc., reproduced from rare 19th-century masterpiece. vi + 121pp. 9 x 12. 24745-7 Pa. $10.95

1001 QUESTIONS ANSWERED ABOUT THE SEASHORE, N. J. Berrill and Jacquelyn Berrill. Queries answered about dolphins, sea snails, sponges, starfish, fishes, shore birds, many others. Covers appearance, breeding, growth, feeding, much more. 305pp. 5¼ x 8¼. 23366-9 Pa. $8.95

GUIDE TO OWL WATCHING IN NORTH AMERICA, Donald S. Heintzelman. Superb guide offers complete data and descriptions of 19 species: barn owl, screech owl, snowy owl, many more. Expert coverage of owl-watching equipment, conservation, migrations and invasions, etc. Guide to observing sites. 84 illustrations. xiii + 193pp. 5⅜ x 8½. 27344-X Pa. $8.95

MEDICINAL AND OTHER USES OF NORTH AMERICAN PLANTS: A Historical Survey with Special Reference to the Eastern Indian Tribes, Charlotte Erichsen-Brown. Chronological historical citations document 500 years of usage of plants, trees, shrubs native to eastern Canada, northeastern U.S. Also complete identifying information. 343 illustrations. 544pp. 6½ x 9¼. 25951-X Pa. $12.95

STORYBOOK MAZES, Dave Phillips. 23 stories and mazes on two-page spreads: Wizard of Oz, Treasure Island, Robin Hood, etc. Solutions. 64pp. 8¼ x 11. 23628-5 Pa. $2.95

NEGRO FOLK MUSIC, U.S.A., Harold Courlander. Noted folklorist's scholarly yet readable analysis of rich and varied musical tradition. Includes authentic versions of over 40 folk songs. Valuable bibliography and discography. xi + 324pp. 5⅜ x 8½. 27350-4 Pa. $7.95

MOVIE-STAR PORTRAITS OF THE FORTIES, John Kobal (ed.). 163 glamor, studio photos of 106 stars of the 1940s: Rita Hayworth, Ava Gardner, Marlon Brando, Clark Gable, many more. 176pp. 8⅜ x 11¼. 23546-7 Pa. $12.95

BENCHLEY LOST AND FOUND, Robert Benchley. Finest humor from early 30s, about pet peeves, child psychologists, post office and others. Mostly unavailable elsewhere. 73 illustrations by Peter Arno and others. 183pp. 5⅜ x 8½. 22410-4 Pa. $6.95

YEKL and THE IMPORTED BRIDEGROOM AND OTHER STORIES OF YIDDISH NEW YORK, Abraham Cahan. Film Hester Street based on Yekl (1896). Novel, other stories among first about Jewish immigrants on N.Y.'s East Side. 240pp. 5⅜ x 8½. 22427-9 Pa. $6.95

SELECTED POEMS, Walt Whitman. Generous sampling from *Leaves of Grass*. Twenty-four poems include "I Hear America Singing," "Song of the Open Road," "I Sing the Body Electric," "When Lilacs Last in the Dooryard Bloom'd," "O Captain! My Captain!"—all reprinted from an authoritative edition. Lists of titles and first lines. 128pp. 5³⁄₁₆ x 8¼. 26878-0 Pa. $1.00

THE BEST TALES OF HOFFMANN, E. T. A. Hoffmann. 10 of Hoffmann's most important stories: "Nutcracker and the King of Mice," "The Golden Flowerpot," etc. 458pp. 5⅜ x 8½. 21793-0 Pa. $9.95

FROM FETISH TO GOD IN ANCIENT EGYPT, E. A. Wallis Budge. Rich detailed survey of Egyptian conception of "God" and gods, magic, cult of animals, Osiris, more. Also, superb English translations of hymns and legends. 240 illustrations. 545pp. 5⅜ x 8½. 25803-3 Pa. $11.95

FRENCH STORIES/CONTES FRANÇAIS: A Dual-Language Book, Wallace Fowlie. Ten stories by French masters, Voltaire to Camus: "Micromegas" by Voltaire; "The Atheist's Mass" by Balzac; "Minuet" by de Maupassant; "The Guest" by Camus, six more. Excellent English translations on facing pages. Also French-English vocabulary list, exercises, more. 352pp. 5⅜ x 8½. 26443-2 Pa. $8.95

CHICAGO AT THE TURN OF THE CENTURY IN PHOTOGRAPHS: 122 Historic Views from the Collections of the Chicago Historical Society, Larry A. Viskochil. Rare large-format prints offer detailed views of City Hall, State Street, the Loop, Hull House, Union Station, many other landmarks, circa 1904-1913. Introduction. Captions. Maps. 144pp. 9⅜ x 12¼. 24656-6 Pa. $12.95

OLD BROOKLYN IN EARLY PHOTOGRAPHS, 1865-1929, William Lee Younger. Luna Park, Gravesend race track, construction of Grand Army Plaza, moving of Hotel Brighton, etc. 157 previously unpublished photographs. 165pp. 8⅞ x 11¾. 23587-4 Pa. $13.95

THE MYTHS OF THE NORTH AMERICAN INDIANS, Lewis Spence. Rich anthology of the myths and legends of the Algonquins, Iroquois, Pawnees and Sioux, prefaced by an extensive historical and ethnological commentary. 36 illustrations. 480pp. 5⅜ x 8½. 25967-6 Pa. $8.95

AN ENCYCLOPEDIA OF BATTLES: Accounts of Over 1,560 Battles from 1479 B.C. to the Present, David Eggenberger. Essential details of every major battle in recorded history from the first battle of Megiddo in 1479 B.C. to Grenada in 1984. List of Battle Maps. New Appendix covering the years 1967-1984. Index. 99 illustrations. 544pp. 6½ x 9¼. 24913-1 Pa. $14.95

SAILING ALONE AROUND THE WORLD, Captain Joshua Slocum. First man to sail around the world, alone, in small boat. One of great feats of seamanship told in delightful manner. 67 illustrations. 294pp. 5⅜ x 8½. 20326-3 Pa. $5.95

ANARCHISM AND OTHER ESSAYS, Emma Goldman. Powerful, penetrating, prophetic essays on direct action, role of minorities, prison reform, puritan hypocrisy, violence, etc. 271pp. 5⅜ x 8½. 22484-8 Pa. $6.95

MYTHS OF THE HINDUS AND BUDDHISTS, Ananda K. Coomaraswamy and Sister Nivedita. Great stories of the epics; deeds of Krishna, Shiva, taken from puranas, Vedas, folk tales; etc. 32 illustrations. 400pp. 5⅜ x 8½. 21759-0 Pa. $10.95

BEYOND PSYCHOLOGY, Otto Rank. Fear of death, desire of immortality, nature of sexuality, social organization, creativity, according to Rankian system. 291pp. 5⅜ x 8½. 20485-5 Pa. $8.95

A THEOLOGICO-POLITICAL TREATISE, Benedict Spinoza. Also contains unfinished Political Treatise. Great classic on religious liberty, theory of government on common consent. R. Elwes translation. Total of 421pp. 5⅜ x 8½. 20249-6 Pa. $9.95

MY BONDAGE AND MY FREEDOM, Frederick Douglass. Born a slave, Douglass became outspoken force in antislavery movement. The best of Douglass' autobiographies. Graphic description of slave life. 464pp. 5⅜ x 8½. 22457-0 Pa. $8.95

FOLLOWING THE EQUATOR: A Journey Around the World, Mark Twain. Fascinating humorous account of 1897 voyage to Hawaii, Australia, India, New Zealand, etc. Ironic, bemused reports on peoples, customs, climate, flora and fauna, politics, much more. 197 illustrations. 720pp. 5⅜ x 8½. 26113-1 Pa. $15.95

THE PEOPLE CALLED SHAKERS, Edward D. Andrews. Definitive study of Shakers: origins, beliefs, practices, dances, social organization, furniture and crafts, etc. 33 illustrations. 351pp. 5⅜ x 8½. 21081-2 Pa. $8.95

THE MYTHS OF GREECE AND ROME, H. A. Guerber. A classic of mythology, generously illustrated, long prized for its simple, graphic, accurate retelling of the principal myths of Greece and Rome, and for its commentary on their origins and significance. With 64 illustrations by Michelangelo, Raphael, Titian, Rubens, Canova, Bernini and others. 480pp. 5⅜ x 8½. 27584-1 Pa. $9.95

PSYCHOLOGY OF MUSIC, Carl E. Seashore. Classic work discusses music as a medium from psychological viewpoint. Clear treatment of physical acoustics, auditory apparatus, sound perception, development of musical skills, nature of musical feeling, host of other topics. 88 figures. 408pp. 5⅜ x 8½. 21851-1 Pa. $10.95

THE PHILOSOPHY OF HISTORY, Georg W. Hegel. Great classic of Western thought develops concept that history is not chance but rational process, the evolution of freedom. 457pp. 5⅜ x 8½. 20112-0 Pa. $9.95

THE BOOK OF TEA, Kakuzo Okakura. Minor classic of the Orient: entertaining, charming explanation, interpretation of traditional Japanese culture in terms of tea ceremony. 94pp. 5⅜ x 8½. 20070-1 Pa. $3.95

LIFE IN ANCIENT EGYPT, Adolf Erman. Fullest, most thorough, detailed older account with much not in more recent books, domestic life, religion, magic, medicine, commerce, much more. Many illustrations reproduce tomb paintings, carvings, hieroglyphs, etc. 597pp. 5⅜ x 8½. 22632-8 Pa. $11.95

SUNDIALS, Their Theory and Construction, Albert Waugh. Far and away the best, most thorough coverage of ideas, mathematics concerned, types, construction, adjusting anywhere. Simple, nontechnical treatment allows even children to build several of these dials. Over 100 illustrations. 230pp. 5⅜ x 8½. 22947-5 Pa. $7.95

DYNAMICS OF FLUIDS IN POROUS MEDIA, Jacob Bear. For advanced students of ground water hydrology, soil mechanics and physics, drainage and irrigation engineering, and more. 335 illustrations. Exercises, with answers. 784pp. 6⅛ x 9¼. 65675-6 Pa. $19.95

SONGS OF EXPERIENCE: Facsimile Reproduction with 26 Plates in Full Color, William Blake. 26 full-color plates from a rare 1826 edition. Includes "The Tyger," "London," "Holy Thursday," and other poems. Printed text of poems. 48pp. 5¼ x 7. 24636-1 Pa. $4.95

OLD-TIME VIGNETTES IN FULL COLOR, Carol Belanger Grafton (ed.). Over 390 charming, often sentimental illustrations, selected from archives of Victorian graphics—pretty women posing, children playing, food, flowers, kittens and puppies, smiling cherubs, birds and butterflies, much more. All copyright-free. 48pp. 9¼ x 12¼. 27269-9 Pa. $5.95

PERSPECTIVE FOR ARTISTS, Rex Vicat Cole. Depth, perspective of sky and sea, shadows, much more, not usually covered. 391 diagrams, 81 reproductions of drawings and paintings. 279pp. 5⅜ x 8½. 22487-2 Pa. $6.95

DRAWING THE LIVING FIGURE, Joseph Sheppard. Innovative approach to artistic anatomy focuses on specifics of surface anatomy, rather than muscles and bones. Over 170 drawings of live models in front, back and side views, and in widely varying poses. Accompanying diagrams. 177 illustrations. Introduction. Index. 144pp. 8⅜ x11¼. 26723-7 Pa. $8.95

GOTHIC AND OLD ENGLISH ALPHABETS: 100 Complete Fonts, Dan X. Solo. Add power, elegance to posters, signs, other graphics with 100 stunning copyright-free alphabets: Blackstone, Dolbey, Germania, 97 more–including many lower-case, numerals, punctuation marks. 104pp. 8⅛ x 11. 24695-7 Pa. $8.95

HOW TO DO BEADWORK, Mary White. Fundamental book on craft from simple projects to five-bead chains and woven works. 106 illustrations. 142pp. 5⅜ x 8. 20697-1 Pa. $4.95

THE BOOK OF WOOD CARVING, Charles Marshall Sayers. Finest book for beginners discusses fundamentals and offers 34 designs. "Absolutely first rate . . . well thought out and well executed."–E. J. Tangerman. 118pp. 7¾ x 10⅝. 23654-4 Pa. $6.95

ILLUSTRATED CATALOG OF CIVIL WAR MILITARY GOODS: Union Army Weapons, Insignia, Uniform Accessories, and Other Equipment, Schuyler, Hartley, and Graham. Rare, profusely illustrated 1846 catalog includes Union Army uniform and dress regulations, arms and ammunition, coats, insignia, flags, swords, rifles, etc. 226 illustrations. 160pp. 9 x 12. 24939-5 Pa. $10.95

WOMEN'S FASHIONS OF THE EARLY 1900s: An Unabridged Republication of "New York Fashions, 1909," National Cloak & Suit Co. Rare catalog of mail-order fashions documents women's and children's clothing styles shortly after the turn of the century. Captions offer full descriptions, prices. Invaluable resource for fashion, costume historians. Approximately 725 illustrations. 128pp. 8⅜ x 11¼. 27276-1 Pa. $11.95

THE 1912 AND 1915 GUSTAV STICKLEY FURNITURE CATALOGS, Gustav Stickley. With over 200 detailed illustrations and descriptions, these two catalogs are essential reading and reference materials and identification guides for Stickley furniture. Captions cite materials, dimensions and prices. 112pp. 6½ x 9¼. 26676-1 Pa. $9.95

EARLY AMERICAN LOCOMOTIVES, John H. White, Jr. Finest locomotive engravings from early 19th century: historical (1804–74), main-line (after 1870), special, foreign, etc. 147 plates. 142pp. 11⅜ x 8¼. 22772-3 Pa. $10.95

THE TALL SHIPS OF TODAY IN PHOTOGRAPHS, Frank O. Braynard. Lavishly illustrated tribute to nearly 100 majestic contemporary sailing vessels: Amerigo Vespucci, Clearwater, Constitution, Eagle, Mayflower, Sea Cloud, Victory, many more. Authoritative captions provide statistics, background on each ship. 190 black-and-white photographs and illustrations. Introduction. 128pp. 8⅞ x 11¾. 27163-3 Pa. $13.95

EARLY NINETEENTH-CENTURY CRAFTS AND TRADES, Peter Stockham (ed.). Extremely rare 1807 volume describes to youngsters the crafts and trades of the day: brickmaker, weaver, dressmaker, bookbinder, ropemaker, saddler, many more. Quaint prose, charming illustrations for each craft. 20 black-and-white line illustrations. 192pp. 4⅝ x 6. 27293-1 Pa. $4.95

VICTORIAN FASHIONS AND COSTUMES FROM HARPER'S BAZAR, 1867–1898, Stella Blum (ed.). Day costumes, evening wear, sports clothes, shoes, hats, other accessories in over 1,000 detailed engravings. 320pp. 9⅜ x 12¼. 22990-4 Pa. $14.95

GUSTAV STICKLEY, THE CRAFTSMAN, Mary Ann Smith. Superb study surveys broad scope of Stickley's achievement, especially in architecture. Design philosophy, rise and fall of the Craftsman empire, descriptions and floor plans for many Craftsman houses, more. 86 black-and-white halftones. 31 line illustrations. Introduction 208pp. 6½ x 9¼. 27210-9 Pa. $9.95

THE LONG ISLAND RAIL ROAD IN EARLY PHOTOGRAPHS, Ron Ziel. Over 220 rare photos, informative text document origin (1844) and development of rail service on Long Island. Vintage views of early trains, locomotives, stations, passengers, crews, much more. Captions. 8⅞ x 11¾. 26301-0 Pa. $13.95

THE BOOK OF OLD SHIPS: From Egyptian Galleys to Clipper Ships, Henry B. Culver. Superb, authoritative history of sailing vessels, with 80 magnificent line illustrations. Galley, bark, caravel, longship, whaler, many more. Detailed, informative text on each vessel by noted naval historian. Introduction. 256pp. 5⅜ x 8½. 27332-6 Pa. $7.95

TEN BOOKS ON ARCHITECTURE, Vitruvius. The most important book ever written on architecture. Early Roman aesthetics, technology, classical orders, site selection, all other aspects. Morgan translation. 331pp. 5⅜ x 8½. 20645-9 Pa. $8.95

THE HUMAN FIGURE IN MOTION, Eadweard Muybridge. More than 4,500 stopped-action photos, in action series, showing undraped men, women, children jumping, lying down, throwing, sitting, wrestling, carrying, etc. 390pp. 7⅞ x 10⅝. 20204-6 Clothbd. $25.95

TREES OF THE EASTERN AND CENTRAL UNITED STATES AND CANADA, William M. Harlow. Best one-volume guide to 140 trees. Full descriptions, woodlore, range, etc. Over 600 illustrations. Handy size. 288pp. 4½ x 6⅜. 20395-6 Pa. $5.95

SONGS OF WESTERN BIRDS, Dr. Donald J. Borror. Complete song and call repertoire of 60 western species, including flycatchers, juncoes, cactus wrens, many more–includes fully illustrated booklet. Cassette and manual 99913-0 $8.95

GROWING AND USING HERBS AND SPICES, Milo Miloradovich. Versatile handbook provides all the information needed for cultivation and use of all the herbs and spices available in North America. 4 illustrations. Index. Glossary. 236pp. 5⅜ x 8½. 25058-X Pa. $6.95

BIG BOOK OF MAZES AND LABYRINTHS, Walter Shepherd. 50 mazes and labyrinths in all–classical, solid, ripple, and more–in one great volume. Perfect inexpensive puzzler for clever youngsters. Full solutions. 112pp. 8⅛ x 11. 22951-3 Pa. $4.95

PIANO TUNING, J. Cree Fischer. Clearest, best book for beginner, amateur. Simple repairs, raising dropped notes, tuning by easy method of flattened fifths. No previous skills needed. 4 illustrations. 201pp. 5⅜ x 8½. 23267-0 Pa. $6.95

A SOURCE BOOK IN THEATRICAL HISTORY, A. M. Nagler. Contemporary observers on acting, directing, make-up, costuming, stage props, machinery, scene design, from Ancient Greece to Chekhov. 611pp. 5⅜ x 8½. 20515-0 Pa. $12.95

THE COMPLETE NONSENSE OF EDWARD LEAR, Edward Lear. All nonsense limericks, zany alphabets, Owl and Pussycat, songs, nonsense botany, etc., illustrated by Lear. Total of 320pp. 5⅜ x 8½. (USO) 20167-8 Pa. $6.95

VICTORIAN PARLOUR POETRY: An Annotated Anthology, Michael R. Turner. 117 gems by Longfellow, Tennyson, Browning, many lesser-known poets. "The Village Blacksmith," "Curfew Must Not Ring Tonight," "Only a Baby Small," dozens more, often difficult to find elsewhere. Index of poets, titles, first lines. xxiii + 325pp. 5⅜ x 8¼. 27044-0 Pa. $8.95

DUBLINERS, James Joyce. Fifteen stories offer vivid, tightly focused observations of the lives of Dublin's poorer classes. At least one, "The Dead," is considered a masterpiece. Reprinted complete and unabridged from standard edition. 160pp. 5³⁄₁₆ x 8¼. 26870-5 Pa. $1.00

THE HAUNTED MONASTERY and THE CHINESE MAZE MURDERS, Robert van Gulik. Two full novels by van Gulik, set in 7th-century China, continue adventures of Judge Dee and his companions. An evil Taoist monastery, seemingly supernatural events; overgrown topiary maze hides strange crimes. 27 illustrations. 328pp. 5⅜ x 8½. 23502-5 Pa. $8.95

THE BOOK OF THE SACRED MAGIC OF ABRAMELIN THE MAGE, translated by S. MacGregor Mathers. Medieval manuscript of ceremonial magic. Basic document in Aleister Crowley, Golden Dawn groups. 268pp. 5⅜ x 8½. 23211-5 Pa. $8.95

NEW RUSSIAN-ENGLISH AND ENGLISH-RUSSIAN DICTIONARY, M. A. O'Brien. This is a remarkably handy Russian dictionary, containing a surprising amount of information, including over 70,000 entries. 366pp. 4½ x 6⅛. 20208-9 Pa. $9.95

HISTORIC HOMES OF THE AMERICAN PRESIDENTS, Second, Revised Edition, Irvin Haas. A traveler's guide to American Presidential homes, most open to the public, depicting and describing homes occupied by every American President from George Washington to George Bush. With visiting hours, admission charges, travel routes. 175 photographs. Index. 160pp. 8¼ x 11. 26751-2 Pa. $11.95

NEW YORK IN THE FORTIES, Andreas Feininger. 162 brilliant photographs by the well-known photographer, formerly with *Life* magazine. Commuters, shoppers, Times Square at night, much else from city at its peak. Captions by John von Hartz. 181pp. 9¼ x 10¾. 23585-8 Pa. $12.95

INDIAN SIGN LANGUAGE, William Tomkins. Over 525 signs developed by Sioux and other tribes. Written instructions and diagrams. Also 290 pictographs. 111pp. 6⅛ x 9¼. 22029-X Pa. $3.95

ANATOMY: A Complete Guide for Artists, Joseph Sheppard. A master of figure drawing shows artists how to render human anatomy convincingly. Over 460 illustrations. 224pp. 8⅜ x 11¼. 27279-6 Pa. $10.95

MEDIEVAL CALLIGRAPHY: Its History and Technique, Marc Drogin. Spirited history, comprehensive instruction manual covers 13 styles (ca. 4th century thru 15th). Excellent photographs; directions for duplicating medieval techniques with modern tools. 224pp. 8⅜ x 11¼. 26142-5 Pa. $11.95

DRIED FLOWERS: How to Prepare Them, Sarah Whitlock and Martha Rankin. Complete instructions on how to use silica gel, meal and borax, perlite aggregate, sand and borax, glycerine and water to create attractive permanent flower arrangements. 12 illustrations. 32pp. 5⅜ x 8½. 21802-3 Pa. $1.00

EASY-TO-MAKE BIRD FEEDERS FOR WOODWORKERS, Scott D. Campbell. Detailed, simple-to-use guide for designing, constructing, caring for and using feeders. Text, illustrations for 12 classic and contemporary designs. 96pp. 5⅜ x 8½. 25847-5 Pa. $2.95

SCOTTISH WONDER TALES FROM MYTH AND LEGEND, Donald A. Mackenzie. 16 lively tales tell of giants rumbling down mountainsides, of a magic wand that turns stone pillars into warriors, of gods and goddesses, evil hags, powerful forces and more. 240pp. 5⅜ x 8½. 29677-6 Pa. $6.95

THE HISTORY OF UNDERCLOTHES, C. Willett Cunnington and Phyllis Cunnington. Fascinating, well-documented survey covering six centuries of English undergarments, enhanced with over 100 illustrations: 12th-century laced-up bodice, footed long drawers (1795), 19th-century bustles, 19th-century corsets for men, Victorian "bust improvers," much more. 272pp. 5⅝ x 8¼. 27124-2 Pa. $9.95

ARTS AND CRAFTS FURNITURE: The Complete Brooks Catalog of 1912, Brooks Manufacturing Co. Photos and detailed descriptions of more than 150 now very collectible furniture designs from the Arts and Crafts movement depict davenports, settees, buffets, desks, tables, chairs, bedsteads, dressers and more, all built of solid, quarter-sawed oak. Invaluable for students and enthusiasts of antiques, Americana and the decorative arts. 80pp. 6½ x 9¼. 27471-3 Pa. $7.95

HOW WE INVENTED THE AIRPLANE: An Illustrated History, Orville Wright. Fascinating firsthand account covers early experiments, construction of planes and motors, first flights, much more. Introduction and commentary by Fred C. Kelly. 76 photographs. 96pp. 8¼ x 11. 25662-6 Pa. $8.95

THE ARTS OF THE SAILOR: Knotting, Splicing and Ropework, Hervey Garrett Smith. Indispensable shipboard reference covers tools, basic knots and useful hitches; handsewing and canvas work, more. Over 100 illustrations. Delightful reading for sea lovers. 256pp. 5⅜ x 8½. 26440-8 Pa. $7.95

FRANK LLOYD WRIGHT'S FALLINGWATER: The House and Its History, Second, Revised Edition, Donald Hoffmann. A total revision–both in text and illustrations–of the standard document on Fallingwater, the boldest, most personal architectural statement of Wright's mature years, updated with valuable new material from the recently opened Frank Lloyd Wright Archives. "Fascinating"–*The New York Times*. 116 illustrations. 128pp. 9¼ x 10¾. 27430-6 Pa. $11.95

CATALOG OF DOVER BOOKS

AUTOBIOGRAPHY: The Story of My Experiments with Truth, Mohandas K. Gandhi. Boyhood, legal studies, purification, the growth of the Satyagraha (nonviolent protest) movement. Critical, inspiring work of the man responsible for the freedom of India. 480pp. 5⅜ x 8½. (USO) 24593-4 Pa. $8.95

CELTIC MYTHS AND LEGENDS, T. W. Rolleston. Masterful retelling of Irish and Welsh stories and tales. Cuchulain, King Arthur, Deirdre, the Grail, many more. First paperback edition. 58 full-page illustrations. 512pp. 5⅜ x 8½. 26507-2 Pa. $9.95

THE PRINCIPLES OF PSYCHOLOGY, William James. Famous long course complete, unabridged. Stream of thought, time perception, memory, experimental methods; great work decades ahead of its time. 94 figures. 1,391pp. 5⅜ x 8½. 2-vol. set.
Vol. I: 20381-6 Pa. $12.95
Vol. II: 20382-4 Pa. $12.95

THE WORLD AS WILL AND REPRESENTATION, Arthur Schopenhauer. Definitive English translation of Schopenhauer's life work, correcting more than 1,000 errors, omissions in earlier translations. Translated by E. F. J. Payne. Total of 1,269pp. 5⅜ x 8½. 2-vol. set.
Vol. 1: 21761-2 Pa. $11.95
Vol. 2: 21762-0 Pa. $11.95

MAGIC AND MYSTERY IN TIBET, Madame Alexandra David-Neel. Experiences among lamas, magicians, sages, sorcerers, Bonpa wizards. A true psychic discovery. 32 illustrations. 321pp. 5⅜ x 8½. (USO) 22682-4 Pa. $8.95

THE EGYPTIAN BOOK OF THE DEAD, E. A. Wallis Budge. Complete reproduction of Ani's papyrus, finest ever found. Full hieroglyphic text, interlinear transliteration, word-for-word translation, smooth translation. 533pp. 6½ x 9¼. 21866-X Pa. $10.95

MATHEMATICS FOR THE NONMATHEMATICIAN, Morris Kline. Detailed, college-level treatment of mathematics in cultural and historical context, with numerous exercises. Recommended Reading Lists. Tables. Numerous figures. 641pp. 5⅜ x 8½. 24823-2 Pa. $11.95

THEORY OF WING SECTIONS: Including a Summary of Airfoil Data, Ira H. Abbott and A. E. von Doenhoff. Concise compilation of subsonic aerodynamic characteristics of NACA wing sections, plus description of theory. 350pp. of tables. 693pp. 5⅜ x 8½. 60586-8 Pa. $14.95

THE RIME OF THE ANCIENT MARINER, Gustave Doré, S. T. Coleridge. Doré's finest work; 34 plates capture moods, subtleties of poem. Flawless full-size reproductions printed on facing pages with authoritative text of poem. "Beautiful. Simply beautiful."—*Publisher's Weekly.* 77pp. 9¼ x 12. 22305-1 Pa. $6.95

NORTH AMERICAN INDIAN DESIGNS FOR ARTISTS AND CRAFTSPEOPLE, Eva Wilson. Over 360 authentic copyright-free designs adapted from Navajo blankets, Hopi pottery, Sioux buffalo hides, more. Geometrics, symbolic figures, plant and animal motifs, etc. 128pp. 8⅜ x 11. (EUK) 25341-4 Pa. $8.95

SCULPTURE: Principles and Practice, Louis Slobodkin. Step-by-step approach to clay, plaster, metals, stone; classical and modern. 253 drawings, photos. 255pp. 8⅛ x 11. 22960-2 Pa. $10.95

PHOTOGRAPHIC SKETCHBOOK OF THE CIVIL WAR, Alexander Gardner. 100 photos taken on field during the Civil War. Famous shots of Manassas Harper's Ferry, Lincoln, Richmond, slave pens, etc. 244pp. 10⅝ x 8¼.　22731-6 Pa. $9.95

FIVE ACRES AND INDEPENDENCE, Maurice G. Kains. Great back-to-the-land classic explains basics of self-sufficient farming. The one book to get. 95 illustrations. 397pp. 5⅜ x 8½.　20974-1 Pa. $7.95

SONGS OF EASTERN BIRDS, Dr. Donald J. Borror. Songs and calls of 60 species most common to eastern U.S.: warblers, woodpeckers, flycatchers, thrushes, larks, many more in high-quality recording.　Cassette and manual 99912-2 $8.95

A MODERN HERBAL, Margaret Grieve. Much the fullest, most exact, most useful compilation of herbal material. Gigantic alphabetical encyclopedia, from aconite to zedoary, gives botanical information, medical properties, folklore, economic uses, much else. Indispensable to serious reader. 161 illustrations. 888pp. 6½ x 9¼. 2-vol. set. (USO)　Vol. I: 22798-7 Pa. $9.95
Vol. II: 22799-5 Pa. $9.95

HIDDEN TREASURE MAZE BOOK, Dave Phillips. Solve 34 challenging mazes accompanied by heroic tales of adventure. Evil dragons, people-eating plants, blood-thirsty giants, many more dangerous adversaries lurk at every twist and turn. 34 mazes, stories, solutions. 48pp. 8¼ x 11.　24566-7 Pa. $2.95

LETTERS OF W. A. MOZART, Wolfgang A. Mozart. Remarkable letters show bawdy wit, humor, imagination, musical insights, contemporary musical world; includes some letters from Leopold Mozart. 276pp. 5⅜ x 8½.　22859-2 Pa. $7.95

BASIC PRINCIPLES OF CLASSICAL BALLET, Agrippina Vaganova. Great Russian theoretician, teacher explains methods for teaching classical ballet. 118 illus-trations. 175pp. 5⅜ x 8½.　22036-2 Pa. $5.95

THE JUMPING FROG, Mark Twain. Revenge edition. The original story of The Celebrated Jumping Frog of Calaveras County, a hapless French translation, and Twain's hilarious "retranslation" from the French. 12 illustrations. 66pp. 5⅜ x 8½.
22686-7 Pa. $3.95

BEST REMEMBERED POEMS, Martin Gardner (ed.). The 126 poems in this superb collection of 19th- and 20th-century British and American verse range from Shelley's "To a Skylark" to the impassioned "Renascence" of Edna St. Vincent Millay and to Edward Lear's whimsical "The Owl and the Pussycat." 224pp. 5⅜ x 8½.
27165-X Pa. $4.95

COMPLETE SONNETS, William Shakespeare. Over 150 exquisite poems deal with love, friendship, the tyranny of time, beauty's evanescence, death and other themes in language of remarkable power, precision and beauty. Glossary of archaic terms. 80pp. 5³⁄₁₆ x 8¼.　26686-9 Pa. $1.00

BODIES IN A BOOKSHOP, R. T. Campbell. Challenging mystery of blackmail and murder with ingenious plot and superbly drawn characters. In the best tradition of British suspense fiction. 192pp. 5⅜ x 8½.　24720-1 Pa. $6.95

THE WIT AND HUMOR OF OSCAR WILDE, Alvin Redman (ed.). More than 1,000 ripostes, paradoxes, wisecracks: Work is the curse of the drinking classes; I can resist everything except temptation; etc. 258pp. 5⅜ x 8½. 20602-5 Pa. $5.95

SHAKESPEARE LEXICON AND QUOTATION DICTIONARY, Alexander Schmidt. Full definitions, locations, shades of meaning in every word in plays and poems. More than 50,000 exact quotations. 1,485pp. 6½ x 9¼. 2-vol. set.
Vol. 1: 22726-X Pa. $16.95
Vol. 2: 22727-8 Pa. $16.95

SELECTED POEMS, Emily Dickinson. Over 100 best-known, best-loved poems by one of America's foremost poets, reprinted from authoritative early editions. No comparable edition at this price. Index of first lines. 64pp. $5\frac{3}{16}$ x 8¼.
26466-1 Pa. $1.00

CELEBRATED CASES OF JUDGE DEE (DEE GOONG AN), translated by Robert van Gulik. Authentic 18th-century Chinese detective novel; Dee and associates solve three interlocked cases. Led to van Gulik's own stories with same characters. Extensive introduction. 9 illustrations. 237pp. 5⅜ x 8½. 23337-5 Pa. $6.95

THE MALLEUS MALEFICARUM OF KRAMER AND SPRENGER, translated by Montague Summers. Full text of most important witchhunter's "bible," used by both Catholics and Protestants. 278pp. 6⅝ x 10. 22802-9 Pa. $12.95

SPANISH STORIES/CUENTOS ESPAÑOLES: A Dual-Language Book, Angel Flores (ed.). Unique format offers 13 great stories in Spanish by Cervantes, Borges, others. Faithful English translations on facing pages. 352pp. 5⅜ x 8½.
25399-6 Pa. $8.95

THE CHICAGO WORLD'S FAIR OF 1893: A Photographic Record, Stanley Appelbaum (ed.). 128 rare photos show 200 buildings, Beaux-Arts architecture, Midway, original Ferris Wheel, Edison's kinetoscope, more. Architectural emphasis; full text. 116pp. 8¼ x 11. 23990-X Pa. $9.95

OLD QUEENS, N.Y., IN EARLY PHOTOGRAPHS, Vincent F. Seyfried and William Asadorian. Over 160 rare photographs of Maspeth, Jamaica, Jackson Heights, and other areas. Vintage views of DeWitt Clinton mansion, 1939 World's Fair and more. Captions. 192pp. 8⅞ x 11. 26358-4 Pa. $12.95

CAPTURED BY THE INDIANS: 15 Firsthand Accounts, 1750-1870, Frederick Drimmer. Astounding true historical accounts of grisly torture, bloody conflicts, relentless pursuits, miraculous escapes and more, by people who lived to tell the tale. 384pp. 5⅜ x 8½. 24901-8 Pa. $8.95

THE WORLD'S GREAT SPEECHES, Lewis Copeland and Lawrence W. Lamm (eds.). Vast collection of 278 speeches of Greeks to 1970. Powerful and effective models; unique look at history. 842pp. 5⅜ x 8½. 20468-5 Pa. $14.95

THE BOOK OF THE SWORD, Sir Richard F. Burton. Great Victorian scholar/adventurer's eloquent, erudite history of the "queen of weapons"–from prehistory to early Roman Empire. Evolution and development of early swords, variations (sabre, broadsword, cutlass, scimitar, etc.), much more. 336pp. 6⅛ x 9¼.
25434-8 Pa. $9.95

CATALOG OF DOVER BOOKS

THE INFLUENCE OF SEA POWER UPON HISTORY, 1660–1783, A. T. Mahan. Influential classic of naval history and tactics still used as text in war colleges. First paperback edition. 4 maps. 24 battle plans. 640pp. 5⅜ x 8½. 25509-3 Pa. $12.95

THE STORY OF THE TITANIC AS TOLD BY ITS SURVIVORS, Jack Winocour (ed.). What it was really like. Panic, despair, shocking inefficiency, and a little heroism. More thrilling than any fictional account. 26 illustrations. 320pp. 5⅜ x 8½. 20610-6 Pa. $8.95

FAIRY AND FOLK TALES OF THE IRISH PEASANTRY, William Butler Yeats (ed.). Treasury of 64 tales from the twilight world of Celtic myth and legend: "The Soul Cages," "The Kildare Pooka," "King O'Toole and his Goose," many more. Introduction and Notes by W. B. Yeats. 352pp. 5⅜ x 8½. 26941-8 Pa. $8.95

BUDDHIST MAHAYANA TEXTS, E. B. Cowell and Others (eds.). Superb, accurate translations of basic documents in Mahayana Buddhism, highly important in history of religions. The Buddha-karita of Asvaghosha, Larger Sukhavativyuha, more. 448pp. 5⅜ x 8½. 25552-2 Pa. $9.95

ONE TWO THREE . . . INFINITY: Facts and Speculations of Science, George Gamow. Great physicist's fascinating, readable overview of contemporary science: number theory, relativity, fourth dimension, entropy, genes, atomic structure, much more. 128 illustrations. Index. 352pp. 5⅜ x 8½. 25664-2 Pa. $8.95

ENGINEERING IN HISTORY, Richard Shelton Kirby, et al. Broad, nontechnical survey of history's major technological advances: birth of Greek science, industrial revolution, electricity and applied science, 20th-century automation, much more. 181 illustrations. ". . . excellent . . ."–*Isis.* Bibliography. vii + 530pp. 5⅜ x 8¼. 26412-2 Pa. $14.95

DALÍ ON MODERN ART: The Cuckolds of Antiquated Modern Art, Salvador Dalí. Influential painter skewers modern art and its practitioners. Outrageous evaluations of Picasso, Cézanne, Turner, more. 15 renderings of paintings discussed. 44 calligraphic decorations by Dalí. 96pp. 5⅜ x 8½. (USO) 29220-7 Pa. $4.95

ANTIQUE PLAYING CARDS: A Pictorial History, Henry René D'Allemagne. Over 900 elaborate, decorative images from rare playing cards (14th–20th centuries): Bacchus, death, dancing dogs, hunting scenes, royal coats of arms, players cheating, much more. 96pp. 9¼ x 12¼. 29265-7 Pa. $11.95

MAKING FURNITURE MASTERPIECES: 30 Projects with Measured Drawings, Franklin H. Gottshall. Step-by-step instructions, illustrations for constructing handsome, useful pieces, among them a Sheraton desk, Chippendale chair, Spanish desk, Queen Anne table and a William and Mary dressing mirror. 224pp. 8⅛ x 11¼. 29338-6 Pa. $13.95

THE FOSSIL BOOK: A Record of Prehistoric Life, Patricia V. Rich et al. Profusely illustrated definitive guide covers everything from single-celled organisms and dinosaurs to birds and mammals and the interplay between climate and man. Over 1,500 illustrations. 760pp. 7½ x 10⅛. 29371-8 Pa. $29.95

Prices subject to change without notice.

Available at your book dealer or write for free catalog to Dept. GI, Dover Publications, Inc., 31 East 2nd St., Mineola, N.Y. 11501. Dover publishes more than 500 books each year on science, elementary and advanced mathematics, biology, music, art, literary history, social sciences and other areas.